A. OBADIA

Applied Linguistics and

GENERAL EDITOR: C.

D0429864

français
on
FA
Si de   française
BU   UNIVERSITY
V5A 1S6   , B.C.

André   ADIA
P   tion
                   çaise
BURNA   RSITY
V5A 1

Applied Linguistics and Language Study

GENERAL EDITOR: C. N. CANDLIN

Error Analysis

Perspectives on Second Language Acquisition

Edited by
JACK C. RICHARDS

LONGMAN

Longman
1724-1974

Longman Group Limited, London

*Associated companies, branches and
representatives throughout the world*

© Longman Group Limited 1974

First published 1974
Third impression †1977

ISBN 0 582 55044 0

Filmset by Keyspools Ltd, Golborne,
Lancs.

**Printed in Singapore by
Singapore Offset Printing (Pte) Ltd.**

Acknowledgements

We are grateful to the following for permission to reproduce copyright material:

The publishers of *English Language Teaching* and *Language Learning* for two of the author's own papers, *International Review of Applied Linguistics in Language Teaching* for 'The Significance of Learners' Errors' by S. P. Corder from *IRAL*, Vol. V/4 1967, 'Idiosyncratic Dialects and Error Analysis' by S. P. Corder from *IRAL*, Vol. IX/2, May 1971, 'Approximative Systems of Foreign Language Learners' by W. Nemser, from *IRAL*, Vol. IX/2, May 1971, 'Language Acquisition in A Second Language Environment' by R. Ravem from *IRAL*, Vol. VI/2, 1968, and 'Interlanguage' by L. Selinker from *IRAL*, Vol. X/3, 1972.

EDITOR'S NOTE

I am especially grateful to Roar Ravem for contributing a previously unpublished paper, and to those colleagues who agreed to write papers for this volume – Heidi Dulay and Marina Burt, Gloria Sampson and M. P. Jain.

J.R.

The Contributors

Marina K. Burt
Far West Regional Laboratory,
Berkeley, California

S. P. Corder
University of Edinburgh

Heidi C. Dulay
Bilingual Children's Television,
Oakland, California

M. P. Jain
Indian Institute of Technology,
New Delhi

William Nemser
Center for Applied Linguistics,
Washington, D.C.

Roar Ravem
University College for Teachers,
Norway

Jack C. Richards
Regional English Language Centre,
Singapore

Gloria P. Sampson
University of Alberta,
Edmonton

Larry Selinker
University of Washington,
Seattle

Preface

One of the more important shifts in Applied Linguistic interest in recent years has been from the view of the teacher as the controller of language learning towards a more learner-centered view which stresses the learner's powers of hypothesis formation as he moves towards that bilingual competence sufficient for his communicative needs. One major result of this shift of attention has been an increasing concern in the monitoring and analysis of learner's language. This is an important concern both for language teacher and linguist. From the standpoint of practical teaching we have become more aware of the long-term value of Error Analysis as a chief means of both assessing the pupil's learning in general and of the degree of match between his learning 'syllabus' and the teacher's teaching one. Linguistically, the concepts of 'interlanguage' and 'approximative system' present challenging areas of descriptive enquiry. They raise issues of the validity of the competence/performance distinction and suggest useful analogies more widely to the links that may be made between the language learner's language and 'continuum' languages in general, particularly Creoles. Error Analysis has thus important Applied Linguistic justification in that data from the classroom can both serve as input to theoretical discussion and, after evaluation, feed back to the design of remedial curricula.

There is considerable value, therefore, in Dr Richards bringing together in one volume a set of readings spanning these related fields. His important introductions and commentaries serve to make the interconnections apparent. He has begun from the teacher concerned with practicalities of error evaluation, levels of error gravity and deviation, and the links that can be drawn between these and performance assessment. From these and further problems of explanation posed by the determination of error source he has looked for descriptive evidence both to clarify these issues and to suggest to the language teacher the wider connections that can be made between the classroom and fundamental psycholinguistic questions of relationships between L1 acquisition and L2 learning.

Three objectives have been proposed for Error Analysis, and all are treated in this volume. Firstly, that far from there being a fundamental opposition between Contrastive Analysis and Error Analysis, the latter serves as an important source of corroboration to contrastive linguistic analyses in their claims for predictability of error. Indeed such corroboration is vital if we are to move beyond taxonomy to explanatory and predictive power. Secondly, that the study of learner error should permit the formulation of rules for learners' interlingual systems, thus providing incidentally for the teacher confirmation of what remains to be learned. Thirdly, charting a learner's language development through error study has psycholinguistic importance in that it submits transfer theory to critical observation and provides data on the nature and significance of the obstacles that lie in the path towards discovery of the target language rules.

Although the theme of individualization in teaching and learning lies behind many of the contributions, it would be misleading to imagine that they present one uniform view; we are hardly at the point where such uniformity is imaginable. In a rapidly changing and emerging field of research this collection serves as a framework for the posing of questions, not as a body of doctrine. There are many questions to investigate:

(i) If charting the language development of the learner demands a longitudinal testing programme, how can the variable modifications in the learner's language system be controlled so as to permit the identification of the units of transitory interlanguages? Handling the problems of instability and fossilization presents both descriptive and pedagogic difficulty.

(ii) The theory of interlingual autonomy poses the question of whether interlanguages are to be regarded as 'deviant' or systems in their own right. If the latter, the term 'error' may need to be discarded, since apart from performance failure, nothing could be regarded as 'wrong'.

(iii) The problem of descriptive model for error analysis becomes important if one accepts the suggestion that similarities and differences of surface structure may be more relevant to error analysis than examining deep structure relations. Furthermore, how well equipped are we to treat communicative or functional error in addition to errors in language form?

(iv) The need to distinguish between the description of what is incorrect and the processes that were involved in the production of the error highlights the absence in error analysis of an optimal means for linking error identification in linguistic terms with diagnosis in psycholinguistic terms.

Christopher N. Candlin, 1973
General Editor

Contents

PART ONE

Introductory

These two papers serve as an introduction to this book. The first paper offers an overview of the field of error analysis and is intended to help the reader integrate the other papers in the collection into an overall perspective; it also links current interest in *learner English* to earlier research on second language learning. Why study the learner's language? Interest in the language learning process, whether it be for first language acquisition or for second language learning, is comparatively recent, and has interest both for general linguistic theory and for language teaching practice. In the field of general linguistic theory, language learning is surely a testing ground for theories of language. If language is systematically structured in particular ways, we should expect to see evidence of this in observing how the child or adult copes with the cognitive and rule governed aspects of language as he becomes a member of a linguistic community. Study of the child-learner's errors does indeed throw light on the types of cognitive and linguistic processes that appear to be part of the language learning process (Menyuk, 1971). In second language learning, as Corder observes, the learner's errors are indicative both of the state of the learner's knowledge, and of the ways in which a second language is learned. Corder makes an important distinction between *mistakes* or performance errors, and true errors, or markers of the learner's transitional competence. Sentences containing errors would be characterized by systematic deviancy. While the learner's correct sentences do not necessarily give evidence of the rules the learner is using or of the hypotheses he is testing, his errors suggest the strategies he employs to work out the rules of the new language and the rules he has developed at given stages of his language development. Corder suggests that the hypotheses the learner tests will be 'Are the systems of the new language the same or different from those of the language I know? And if different, what is their nature?' An alternative view of the

1

role of interference is suggested elsewhere in this volume by Dulay and Burt.

Corder's paper raises a question crucial to an understanding of language teaching. What is the relationship between what we teach and what is learned? Such a question can only be answered by studying what happens after we have prepared and taught our instructional syllabus. Corder suggests that the learner himself employs or establishes his own syllabus for learning and this may be a more effective syllabus than one prepared from *ad hoc* speculation. The nature of this syllabus and some of the ways in which it may be characterized are described in the paper by Richards and Sampson, which isolates seven factors as characterizing and influencing the learner's language use: language transfer, intralingual interference, the effects of the sociolinguistic situation, the modality of exposure to the target language and the modality of production, the age of the learner, the instability of the learner's linguistic system, and the effects of the inherent difficulty of the particular item being learned.

1

The Study of Learner English

JACK C RICHARDS AND
GLORIA P SAMPSON

This paper was written for this volume.

1 Introduction

Theories of second language acquisition traditionally have been
the offspring of general linguistic theory, sometimes supplemented
by insights from psychology. While current linguistic theories are
more insightful than previous ones, there has not been a corresponding increase in the descriptive or explanatory powers of
theories of second language acquisition. The utility of generative
linguistic theories in second language research is not especially
obvious at the present time. This apparent lack of a linguistic
paradigm for second language research, however, may be a pro-
pitious occurrence. Lacking an obviously relevant linguistic theory,
researchers in second language learning may be compelled to
develop new theories relevant to the particular domain under
investigation. Such theories might be specific to second language
acquisition. At the same time the data gathered could perhaps
provide corrective feedback to general linguistic theory and to
language teaching practice. While lack of a linguistic research
paradigm is frustrating for the researcher, it may yet lead to interesting and original findings.

2 The Study of Learners' Approximative Systems

New directions of research in second language acquisition are a
product of the history of research to date as a brief review reveals.
Because synchronic linguistic theory was preparadigmatic in the
late nineteenth century, so too were early observations about
second language learning. Boaz pointed out the apparent fluctua-
tions in learners' (linguists') perceptions of sounds in new languages
(Boaz, 1889). He suggested that learners perceived sounds in new

3

languages in terms of their native language or other languages to which they had earlier been exposed. With the emergence of the notion of language as a system however, the question of second language acquisition could be viewed as the juxtaposition of two systems.

Juxtaposition of language systems could lead to a new super-system which combined features of both systems (Fries and Pike, 1949), or to intersystemic interference (Weinreich, 1953). The notion of interference between two systems struck linguists and teachers as especially interesting, since it appeared to account for the problems of second language learning, particularly of adults. The writings of Lado (1957), for example, tended to emphasize points of contrast between two language systems. Contrastive analysis subsequently arose as a field of research. To be sure, contrast between systems was understood not to be the only factor involved in second language learning.

Subsequent attempts to rectify what was seen as an overly theoretical approach to language learning evolved into what some linguists refer to as error analysis. The major defect of contrastive analysis was deemed to be the attention paid to the analysis of two grammars. Some linguists proposed closer study of the performance of actual learners. Corder (1967), for instance, suggested that linguists study the process of language acquisition and the various strategies learners may use. Strevens (1969) hypothesized that errors should not be viewed as problems to be overcome, but rather as normal and inevitable features indicating the strategies that learners use. He conjectured that if a regular pattern of errors could be observed in the performance of all learners in a given situation, and if a learner were seen to progress through this pattern, his errors could be taken as evidence not of failure but of success and achievement in learning. But the pioneering studies of learner errors were still done within a framework which stressed interference between languages inas-much as they stressed errors *per se*. For example, Nemser (1971) in his early work aimed at 'the collection and evaluation of relevant interference data.' Brière (1968) attempted to 'test empirically the amount of interference that would ensue from competing phono-logical categories.' Errors which did not fit systematically into the native language or target language system were, for the most part, ignored. Both Brière and Nemser, however, noted that some replacements occurred which were not in either the learner's native language or the (artificial) target language.

Recently it has been suggested that errors alone are of little interest; rather the entire linguistic system of the second language learner should be investigated. Hence current research tends to focus on the learner himself as generator of the grammar of his sentences in the new language. This emphasis is reflected in a growing terminology for a field of research which deals with the learner's attempts to internalize the grammar of the language he is learning. This terminology includes *error analysis, idiosyncratic dialects, interlanguage, approximative systems, transitional competence, l'état de dialecte.* (Corder, 1967, 1971a, 1971b; Selinker, 1972; Nemser, this volume; Richards, 1971). The learner's partial success, reflected in the construction of rules which do not necessarily reflect those of the mother tongue or target language, is seen as representing the construction of evolving systems of grammatical and phonological rules. The small amount of research and speculation about learners' approximative systems (term borrowed from Nemser, this volume) suggests that seven factors may influence and characterize these second language learner systems. These factors are discussed below.

3 Language Transfer

The first factor is language transfer. Sentences in the target language may exhibit interference from the mother tongue. This of course was considered to be the major, but not the only, source of difficulty by linguists doing contrastive analysis. Interference analysis tends to be from the deviant sentence back to the mother tongue. Contrastive analysis works the other way, predicting errors by comparing the linguistic systems of the mother tongue and the target language. The history and theoretical origins of contrastive analysis in behaviourist psychology are reviewed by Dulay and Burt (1972). George (1971) found that one-third of the deviant sentences from second language learners could be attributed to language transfer, a figure similar to that given by Lance (1969) and Brudhiprabha (1972). It would however be almost impossible to assess the precise contribution of systemic language interference at this time. As subsequent discussion will indicate, a number of factors interact in determining the learner's approximative language system. Until the role of some of these other factors is more clearly understood, it is not possible to evaluate the amount of systemic interference due to language transfer alone.

4 Intralingual Interference

The second factor, termed intralingual interference by Richards (1970), refers to items produced by the learner which reflect not the structure of the mother tongue, but generalizations based on partial exposure to the target language. In an analysis of English errors produced by speakers of a multitude of unrelated languages representing several language families, Richards noted subcategories of error types which seem to be common to speakers of diverse languages as they develop hypotheses about the structure of English. Like first language learners, the second language learner tries to derive the rules behind the data to which he has been exposed, and may develop hypotheses that correspond neither to the mother tongue nor target language. In an experiment on learning Russian word order, Torrey (1966) found that subjects sometimes adopted a consistent word order different from either Russian or English. Richards (1971a) found systematic intralingual errors to involve overgeneralization, ignorance of rule restrictions, incomplete application of rules, and semantic errors. These have been quantified for Thai learners of English by Brudhiprabha (1972). These studies suggest that many intralingual errors represent the learning difficulty of what are often low level rules in the target language, such as differences between the verb inflection in *I walk, she walks.* It may be inferred that once basic rules such as those concerning subject-object relationships, predication, negation, etc. are acquired, a considerable amount of difficulty in second language learning is related to selectional restrictions and to surface structure and contextual rules of the language. Both language transfer and intralingual errors confirm the traditional notion of transfer of training; that is, previous learning may influence later learning.

5 Sociolinguistic Situation

A third factor is the sociolinguistic situation. Different settings for language use result in different degrees and types of language learning. These may be distinguished in terms of the effects of the socio-cultural setting on the learner's language and in terms of the relationship holding between the learner and the target language community and the respective linguistic markers of these relations and identities. Included here are thus the effects of the learner's particular motivations for learning the second language as well as the effects of the socio-cultural setting.

The distinction of compound/co-ordinate bilingualism (Wein-reich, 1953; Ervin and Osgood, 1954; Lambert, 1961) rests upon an assumption that different settings for language learning may moti-vate different processes of language learning. For example, two languages may be learned in the same socio-cultural setting or in two different settings. If the languages are learned in the same setting, the learner may develop a given type of semantic structure. Imagine the case of a child raised bilingually in the home. English *bread* and French *pain* might be identified with a single concept (compound bilingualism). On the other hand, if *bread* were learned in the home setting and *pain* later in another setting, the two lexemes might be stored separately (co-ordinate bilingualism). Although it has been criticized as too simple a model to explain real linguistic differences (Macnamara, 1971), it is still found useful for sociolinguistic analysis (Pride, 1971). More generally however the focus on the relationship between the opportunities for learning and the learner's developing system is a useful one, since it leads to such distinctions as to whether the learning opportunities are limited to those pro-vided by the school course (English as a foreign language) or are mainly outside of the school program (English as a second language) and to a consideration of the effects of these differences on the learner's language (Richards, this volume).

Consideration of the sociolinguistic situation also leads to inclusion of the general motivational variables which influence language learning. Psychologists have related the types of language learning achieved to the role of the language in relation to the learner's needs and perceptions. The 'instrumental' type of motiva-tion is described as that motivating a learner to study a language for largely utilitarian purposes, and not as a means for integration with members of another cultural linguistic group. It is said to be appro-priate for short term goals but inappropriate for the laborious task of acquiring a language for which an 'integrative' motivation is necessary. In focusing on the type of relationship holding between the learner and the target language community it would be appro-priate to consider non-standard dialects (Labov, 1971), pidgins and creoles (Hymes, 1971) and immigrant language learning (Richards, this volume) as illustration of the influence of social processes on the transmission and use of language.

In both first and second language acquisition particular forms and patterns of language learning may be attributable to social variables. Whether the learner produces *When are you coming? When you come?, When you's coming?*, may depend on the social situation, the learner's values and attitudes, or some other social factor in the learning context. The phenomenon of simplification in some language contact situations, represented by the absence of the copula, reduction of morphological and inflectional systems, and grammatical simplification, may likewise be socially motivated (Ferguson, 1971). When the need is for communication of simple information with the help of non-linguistic clues, vocabulary items and word order may be the most crucial elements to be acquired, as the experience of tourists in foreign countries and the linguistic folklore exemplified in comic-book caricatures (Me Tarzan, you Jane) testify.

The influence of the mother tongue on the learner's language may also vary according to the sociolinguistic situation. Mackey (1962) notes that in describing interference one must account for variation according to the medium, style, or register in which the speaker is operating. For example, the medium may be spoken or written, the register may be formal or informal, and the speaker may play any one of a number of varied social roles. Sampson (1971) suggests that varying situations evoke different kinds of errors in varying quantities when children are trying to use the target language.

6 Modality

The learner's language may vary according to a fourth factor, the modality of exposure to the target language and the modality of production. Production and perception may involve the acquisition of two partially overlapping systems. Vildomec observes that interference between the bilingual's languages is generally on the productive rather than receptive side. People often report instances of intrusion of elements of their mother tongue in speech production, but rarely in their understanding of another language (Vildomec, 1963). Nemser's research suggests that two different systems may be internalized in the target language depending on the modality. He found that in the productive modality, phonological replacements differed depending on whether the learner was imitating utterances he heard or producing speech spontaneously (Nemser, 1971a). In fact in first language acquisition Lieberman (1970) has proposed that some phonological features exist because their 'acoustic correlates "match" a particular neural acoustic detector. Other features exist because it is easy to produce a particular articulatory manoeuvre with the human vocal apparatus; the features "match" an articulatory constraint. Still other features may represent an optimization along both these dimensions; the features may have articulatory correlates that are "easy" to produce and result in acoustic correlates that are readily perceptible.' It is not therefore unrealistic to assume that second language learners acquire some distinctions on the basis of auditory cues, some on the basis of articulatory cues, and others on the basis of a combination of these cues. An example of learning on the basis of auditory cues would be the discrimination between initial /f/ and /θ/ on the one hand and /v/ and /ð/ in English on the basis of formant transitions. A case where visible articulatory movements would be the basis for discrimination would be the contrast between bilabial and velar stops in English. The standard second-language prescription to first aurally discriminate and only secondly to produce a given contrast in a target language may not be an optimal procedure for all classes of sounds. George describes learning difficulties derived from audiolingual introduction to *is, has,* in unstressed positions, which may be realized as·/z/, leading to identification as a single lexical item and to such sentences as *She is a book, Her name has Sita.* Written presentation of the forms may avoid this confusion (George, 1971). Spelling pronunciations, and confusions of written and spoken styles, would be other examples of modality affecting the learner's approximative system.

7 Age

The fifth factor which may affect the approximative system of the second language learner is his age. Some aspects of the child's learning capacities change as he grows older and these may affect language learning. The child's memory span increases with age. He acquires a greater number of abstract concepts, and he uses these to interpret his experience. Lenneberg (1967) notes a period of primary language acquisition, postulated to be biologically determined, beginning when the child starts to walk and continuing until puberty. Some of the characteristics of child language have been attributed to the particular nature of his memory and processing strategies in childhood. Brown and Bellugi (1964) relate aspects of children's language to limitations on the length of utterances imposed by the child's inability to plan ahead more than a few words. Hence in some ways adults are better prepared for language learning than children. Adults have better memories, a larger store of abstract concepts that can be used in learning, and a greater ability to form new concepts. Children however are better imitators of speech sounds. Ervin-Tripp (1970) suggests that adult mother tongue development is primarily in terms of vocabulary. The adult's strategies of language learning may be more vocabulary oriented than syntactic. Acquisition of syntax poses a task for the adult which is no longer easy (Ervin-Tripp, 1970). The language acquisition device (or processes) by means of which he was able to rapidly induce the rules of his mother tongue in childhood is perhaps not readily activated. Selinker suggests that this device is activated in only 5% of adults (those who achieve native speaker competence in the new language). Most language learners (those who fail to achieve native speaker competence) activate a different though still genetically determined structure (Selinker, this volume).

No categorical statement about the relationship of language learning to age can be made. As Braine (1971) remarks, the question is not so much whether children are biologically predisposed to acquire language, but rather a question of how child language learning resembles or differs from adult language learning, and this leads to an examination of the different language learning situations which typify child and adult language learning. Macnamara (1971) and Kennedy (1973) hence see differences in results according to age as reflecting mainly motivational and situational differences. The need to understand and speak are much more crucial problems for young children than for many adults learning a new language.

Research into second language learning and bilingualism has not gone very far towards explaining how the rules for the generation of sentences in two or more languages by the same speaker are related, a question which becomes more crucial when the age factor is added. Swain (1971), working with children from 2.1 to 4.10 who had been exposed to two languages from birth suggests that for the learner of this age, the differentiation of two or more linguistic codes is not a significantly different problem from that faced by the monolingual child who acquires control of several different varieties (formal-informal, intimate-serious) of one language. A model that suggested separate sets of rules for each code would be inefficient in terms of memory storage. 'More efficient would be a common core of rules with those specific to a particular code tagged as such through a process of differentiation' (Swain, 1971, 6). Looking at the simultaneous acquisition of yes/no questions, she found that linguistic rules which were common to both languages were first to be acquired by bilingual children. Rules which were language specific and/or more complex, were acquired later. Ravem (1968) provides data on differentiation from the speech of a 6-year-old child, who followed the English rule for some items, the Norwegian pattern for others, and elsewhere developed an intermediate position of his own. In learning the rules of the English negative system he produced sentences like those produced by children learning English as a mother tongue (*I not like that*) although the Norwegian type would be with the negative element after the verb (*I like that not*). In learning the question system he began with an inversion pattern, as in Norwegian (*Like you ice-cream?*). This study suggests that the child's language learning device, working with data from two languages, deals with them at times independently and at times as a single code. Research done by Kessler (in press) on Italian-English bilingual children aged 6 to 8 provides evidence that structures shared by the two languages are acquired at approximately the same rate and in the same sequence. For structural variants between the two languages, the linguistically more complex ones are acquired later. This patterning of sequential acquisitions supports Swain's (1971) theory that a bilingual's two languages are not encoded separately. Kessler concludes that shared rules are actually the same rule, allowing for language-specific lexical insertions. Children who are going through natural developmental stages in the acquisition of their native language could thus be expected to use processes in second language acquisition similar to those they utilize in mother tongue acquisition. Mother tongue acquisition is a long process which may last until age 10 or later (Chomsky, 1969).

8 Successions of Approximative Systems

The sixth factor concerns the lack of stability of the learner's approximative system. Such systems are usually unstable in given individuals, since there is invariably continuing improvement in learning the target language. Because the circumstances for individual language learning are never identical, the acquisition of new lexical, phonological and syntactic items varies from one individual to another. Novel items or structures in the learner's dialect do not occur regularly. It is rare for a learner to use a replacement (error) or overuse a given structure 100 % of the time. Yet the general direction which the learner's system takes may be predictable (Whinnom,

12   JACK C. RICHARDS AND GLORIA P. SAMPSON

1971). Since most studies of second language learners systems have dealt with the learner's production rather than his comprehension of language, the question also arises as to whether the grammar by which the learner understands speech is the same as that by which he produces speech, since as we saw above, modality may influence the type of system developed. Assuming the learner hears and understands standard English but produces a significant number of deviant sentences, the distinction between his receptive competence (the rules he understands) and his productive competence (the rules he uses) may be useful (Troike, 1969). The learner may often produce for example, *I has a book* but understand when he hears it *I have a book*. Which rule is present in his grammar? As in first language acquisition, in the development of a second language rule system many elements are observed to go through a stage where they are sometimes used and sometimes omitted. A grammar for such features might contain the rule but specify that it was optional. Thus if rules for items or structures unique to learners' approximative systems are to be written they will need to be embodied in a format reflecting their probability of occurrence, if this can be ascertained. Possibly a format like that proposed by Labov to handle the sociolinguistic variable will be useful. Labov et al. (1968) suggest that a specific quantity be associated with each variable rule to denote the proportion of cases in which the rule applies. This would be part of the rule structure itself.

It is to be expected too that the rules characterizing the approximative system may cover data (replacements) which have no source in either native or target language. For example, evidence from earlier studies (Brière, 1968; Nemser, 1971; Nababan, 1971) indicates that many phonological replacements found in the speech of second language learners are unique to the approximative system. The existence of such novel data is strong support for the autonomy of approximative systems as distinct from native and target systems. This claim of autonomy for approximative systems does not, however, preclude their dependence upon either native or target systems.

9 Universal Hierarchy of Difficulty

Unlike the factors characteristic of approximative systems so far, the seventh factor has received little attention in the literature of second language acquisition. This factor is concerned with the inherent difficulty for man of certain phonological, syntactic or semantic items and structures. Some forms may be inherently difficult to learn no matter what the background of the learner. For example, it is well known that the English pairs /v/—/ð/ and /f/—/θ/ are very hard to distinguish, not only for non-native speakers but for native speakers as well (Delattre, Liberman and Cooper, 1962). Therefore if a hierarchy of difficulty is postulated for learners of a given language background, it must include not only interlanguage difficulties but also take into account a possible universal hierarchy of difficulty.

The concept of difficulty may be presumed to affect the learner's organization of what he perceives (for which the term learning strategy may be useful) and the organization of what he produces (for which the term communication strategy may be used). Focusing on learning strategies directs attention to the cues which the learner uses to identify elements in the new language. Where cognates, derivatives and loan words exist for example, these may make the identification of certain elements in the new language easier, likewise where the target language follows a structure in the mother tongue. Prediction of difficulty in terms of interlingual difference (the motivation for contrastive analysis) presumes however that it is feasible to compare categories across languages, a comparison which in practice may not be possible. What is syntax in one language may be vocabulary in another. As Torrey (1971) comments, 'many aspects of language learning are very difficult to analyse into specific responses, and even where it is possible the responses are various and at different levels (one item may belong to two levels in one language and four in another) . . . degrees of learning would have to be examined in terms of specific instances rather than with the general category of responses.' What the learner finds difficult will also depend on the degree and nature of what he has acquired of the second language. His knowledge of the target language will form part of the data by which he infers the meaning of new elements. Carton suggests that 'cues such as specific pluralizing markers applicable only to nouns, tense markers applicable only to verbs and word order constraints of a given language will fall into this category' (Carton, 1971). Tucker et al. (1969) found that native speakers of French are able to determine the gender of nouns with either real or invented examples, without awareness of the processes they use, by their knowledge of the distinctive characteristics of the endings of French words. English speakers however exposed randomly to French have great difficulty with gender and require special training to recognize such features. Their errors indicate their search for regularities in the French gender system.

Difficulty in language learning has been defined by psycholinguists in terms of such factors as sentence length, processing time required, derivational complexity, types of embedding, number of transformations, and semantic complexity. Experimental evidence has not however confirmed a direct relationship between ease of comprehension of an utterance by an adult listener and the number of rules used by the linguist in describing the utterance. Ease of comprehension seems to be defined by the type of rule involved (Fodor and Garrett, 1966). Russian work on the factors affecting the order of development of grammatical categories suggests that the difficulty of the concepts expressed by the category rather than formal grammatical complexity influences order of acquisition. Categories of more concrete reference develop before those expressing more abstract or relational ideas. The conditional in Russian develops relatively late, though its structure is quite simple (Braine, 1971).

The learner's comprehension and efforts at comprehension may now be compared with his production. His output may likewise be organized in terms of what he finds easiest to say, which is not necessarily identifiable with what he knows. Learners may avoid a word or structure they find difficult to say. This may force choice of a particular tense instead of the required one (*I'm going to telephone you tonight* instead of *I'll telephone you tonight*). Facility and economy of effort may explain why first learned words and structures tend to be overused and may resist replacement by later taught items. This is often the case with such contrasts as simple present / present continuous. Once the present continuous is introduced (or the simple present) it is often used more frequently than necessary. Likewise an early learned question form may replace all other question forms in the learner's speech, despite constant exposure to other types of questions. Words with broad semantic extension may become overused in preference to more specific vocabulary learned later. Nickel refers to this as the factor of chronology. 'We all know that patterns learned first have priority over patterns learned at a later date because of the convenient simplicity of these first basic structures. This kind of intrastructural interference will take place even against an interstructural contrastive background. Thus Norwegian learners of German will very often use word order of the main clause type in subordinate clauses even though conditions in their mother tongue are similar to those in the German target language, because the main clause word order has been deeply engrained in the brains of the learners' (Nickel, 1971).

10 Significance of Learner Systems

In short, the seven factors discussed above suggest that the approximative systems of language learners are much richer in linguistic, pedagogic and social significance than heretofore suspected. No linguistic paradigm at present encompasses them all but this is to be expected, for they are the results of social, psychological and linguistic interactions. Future research on the systems of language learners will take into account perhaps the interaction of all of these factors (as well as others yet to be discovered). While approximative systems of language learners may be studied as entities worthy of attention in and of themselves, the results of such study should also provide feedback to language teaching practice and to general linguistic theory.

Further detailed longitudinal studies of the sort carried out by Ravem (1968, 1970), and comparisons of longitudinal development in both the mother tongue and the target language, might suggest the degree to which the learner's hypotheses about the grammatical rules of the mother tongue and other tongue are related, and at what stage systematic introduction to particular elements of the target language is likely to be of greatest benefit. Description and analysis of learning modalities and strategies will help with the development of teaching procedures that make optimal use of the learner's way of learning. Close observation of natural second language learning, together with studies of the learning of languages in formal classroom settings could provide a major part of the input for pedagogical grammars.

At the level of pragmatic classroom experience, error analysis will continue to provide one means by which the teacher assesses learning and teaching and determines priorities for future effort. This is not to suggest that we expect syllabus design to orientate itself exclusively around 'error based' progression or gradation, since, as we have seen, the number of variables likely to affect the learner's performance is too great to be summarized in any one formula or approach. Planned achievement levels at given stages in a language course however should include expectation of particular varieties of language use. Close study of learner English will provide the sort of data on which realistic predictions about learning and teaching can be based. Instead of expecting learners to pass directly to native speaker competence in the new language, more realistic goals may be set for particular learning situations, based on generalizations derived from observation of how others have performed under similar circumstances. Teacher training manuals should familiarize future teachers with the varieties of language which learners may be expected, and indeed encouraged, to produce at given stages of learning. These will not correspond directly with the well-formed sentences in the course book, drill or dialogue.

Study of learners' learning systems also has interest for linguistic theory. The results of error analysis studies cited above indicate that theories of contrastive analysis cannot explain why numerous replacements for the target sounds occurred. As Nababan (1971) points out, discussing the replacements for English /θ/ made by Javanese and Indonesian speakers, it is not clear why people with the same linguistic background should make variant substitutions of /s/, /t/, and /f/. He states that 'this is the more interesting as /f/ is not found in Javanese, and in Indonesian it not only has a light functional load but is found in some words in free variation with /p/ and not with /t/ or /s/.' He comments that 'the /f/ substitution seems to be more commonly made by younger learners.'

If these language problems are viewed in the context of approximative systems, it appears that several factors are at work here. First, the age factor is relevant. As we saw above, it is probable that strategies of language acquisition differ in adults and children. Some information about language difficulties of children might be gleaned from the many educational studies done on oral language readiness as a prerequisite to reading ability. Second, phoneticians have shown that in sound discrimination, the second- and third-formant transitions from a fricative into the vowel are important cues in identifying place of articulation (Delattre, et al., 1962). Rudegair (1970), working with first-grade native speakers of English, found that his subjects made significantly more errors on the contrasts /f/ versus /θ/ and /v/ versus /ð/ in the context of a front vowel as opposed to a back vowel. The longer transition length to the back vowel seems to provide a better cue for the correct discrimination of the fricative. Varying vowel environments for English /s/, on the other hand, seem to be irrelevant because its noise portion provides strong cues in terms of frequency, intensity, and duration. Thus the transition information is not needed. These data make it clear that looking at the speech stream, perceptual or productive, as a series of independent, discrete units cannot provide a useful model for second language acquisition (or first language acquisition for that matter). It has often been assumed that the overlapping of sounds in the speech stream was due simply to the mechanical or neuromuscular limitation of the human sound processing apparatus; MacNeilage (1968) argues that this is simply not the case. Bondarko (1969) and Kozhevnikov and Chistovich (1965) believe that the phonetic correlates of the distinctive features of phonemes are various. In different situations different phonetic characteristics can assume significance for the realization of one phoneme. Further, the same phonetic features can have a different significance depending on the nature of the neighboring sounds. For these researchers there is no question that the syllable, not the phoneme, is the minimal unit of pronunciation.

Prompted by these findings Tarone (1972) suggests the syllable as a prime in the production modality of second language learning. Treon (1970) presents evidence that the largest perceptual influence unit, at least for consonant perception and identification, is even larger than the syllable and at least of the size CVCVC (where C is a consonant and V is a vowel). On the basis of a preliminary study Lehiste (1971) proposes the word as a prime in production. She notes, interestingly, that 'unless some further evidence is provided by later stages of the study, it must be concluded that the *morphemic* structure of a word does not have any influence on its temporal organization in English' (italics added).

A basically atomistic systematic phonemic theory such as that described in Chomsky and Halle's *The Sound Pattern of English* (1968) cannot explain the data mentioned above. A modification of the Chomsky-Halle approach which took into account the position of the phoneme in the syllable or word would be the first step in the right direction if second language acquisition is to be described accurately (see Sampson, 1971). But even greater concern with the position and interaction of sound 'segments' within the word is necessary, as well as greater attention to the phonetic substratum. Use of insights from the presently neglected Firthian prosodic analysis could prove productive (see, for example, Firth's study on 'The Structure of the Chinese Monosyllable in a Hunanese Dialect (Changsha)', 1957).

In summary, viewing the approximative systems of language learners not as pathologies to be eradicated but as necessary stages in the gradual acquisition of the target system may result in a deeper understanding of language in general and a more humane approach to language teaching.

2

The Significance of Learners' Errors

S P CORDER

Reprinted from IRAL, Vol. V/4, 1967, published by Julius Groos Verlag, Heidelberg.

When one studies the standard works on the teaching of modern languages it comes as a surprise to find how cursorily the authors deal with the question of learners' errors and their correction. It almost seems as if they are dismissed as a matter of no particular importance, as possible annoying, distracting, but inevitable by-products of the process of learning a language about which the teacher should make as little fuss as possible. It is of course true that the application of linguistic and psychological theory to the study of language learning added a new dimension to the discussion of errors; people now believed they had a principled means for account-ing for these errors, namely that they were the result of interference in the learning of a second language from the habits of the first language. The major contribution of the linguist to language teaching was seen as an intensive contrastive study of the systems of the second language and the mother tongue of the learner; out of this would come an inventory of the areas of difficulty which the learner would encounter and the value of this inventory would be to direct the teacher's attention to these areas so that he might devote special care and emphasis in his teaching to the overcoming, or even avoid-ing, of these predicted difficulties. Teachers have not always been very impressed by this contribution from the linguist for the reason that their practical experience has usually already shown them where these difficulties lie and they have not felt that the contribution of the linguist has provided them with any significantly new informa-tion. They noted for example that many of the errors with which they were familiar were not predicted by the linguist anyway. The teacher has been on the whole, therefore, more concerned with *how* to deal with these areas of difficulty than with the simple identifica-

19

tion of them, and here has reasonably felt that the linguist has had little to say to him.

In the field of methodology there have been two schools of thought in respect of learners' errors. Firstly the school which maintains that if we were to achieve a perfect teaching method the errors would never be committed in the first place, and therefore the occurrence of errors is merely a sign of the present inadequacy of our teaching techniques. The philosophy of the second school is that we live in an imperfect world and consequently errors will always occur in spite of our best efforts. Our ingenuity should be concentrated on techniques for dealing with errors after they have occurred.

Both these points of view are compatible with the same theoretical standpoint about language and language learning, psychologically behaviourist and linguistically taxonomic. Their application to language teaching is known as the audiolingual or fundamental skills method.

Both linguistics and psychology are in a state at the present time of what Chomsky has called 'flux and agitation' (Chomsky, 1966). What seemed to be well established doctrine a few years ago is now the subject of extensive debate. The consequence of this for language teaching is likely to be far reaching and we are perhaps only now beginning to feel its effects. One effect has been perhaps to shift the emphasis away from a preoccupation with *teaching* towards a study of *learning*. In the first instance this has shown itself as a renewed attack upon the problem of the acquisition of the mother tongue. This has inevitably led to a consideration of the question whether there are any parallels between the processes of acquiring the mother tongue and the learning of a second language. The usefulness of the distinction between acquisition and learning has been emphasised by Lambert (1966) and the possibility that the latter may benefit from a study of the former has been suggested by Carroll (1966).

The differences between the two are obvious but not for that reason easy to explain: that the learning of the mother tongue is inevitable, whereas, alas, we all know that there is no such inevitability about the learning of a second language; that the learning of the mother tongue is part of the whole maturational process of the child, whilst learning a second language normally begins only after the maturational process is largely complete; that the infant starts with no overt language behaviour, while in the case of the second language learner such behaviour, of course, exists; that the motivation (if we can properly use the term in the context) for learning a first language is quite different from that for learning a second language.

On examination it becomes clear that these obvious differences imply nothing about the *processes* that take place in the learning of first and second language. Indeed the most widespread hypothesis about how languages are learned, which I have called behaviourist, is assumed to apply in both circumstances. These hypotheses are well enough known not to require detailing here, and so are the objections to them. If then these hypotheses about language learning are being questioned and new hypotheses being set up to account for the process of child language acquisition, it would seem reasonable to see how far they might also apply to the learning of a second language.

Within this new context the study of errors takes on a new importance and will I believe contribute to a verification or rejection of the new hypothesis.

This hypothesis states that a human infant is born with an innate predisposition to acquire language; that he must be exposed to language for the acquisition process to start; that he possesses an internal mechanism of unknown nature which enables him from the limited data available to him to construct a grammar of a particular language. How he does this is largely unknown and is the field of intensive study at the present time by linguists and psychologists. Miller (1964) has pointed out that if we wished to create an automaton to replicate a child's performance, the order in which it tested various aspects of the grammar could only be decided after careful analysis of the successive stages of language acquisition by human children. The first steps therefore in such a study are seen to be a longitudinal description of a child's language throughout the course of its development. From such a description it is eventually hoped to develop a picture of the procedures adopted by the child to acquire language (McNeill, 1966).

The application of this hypothesis to second language learning is not new and is essentially that proposed fifty years ago by H. E. Palmer (1922). Palmer maintained that we were all endowed by nature with the capacity for assimilating language and that this capacity remained available to us in a latent state after the acquisition of a primary language. The adult was seen as capable as the child of acquiring a foreign language. Recent work (Lenneberg, 1967) suggests that the child who fails for any reason i.e. deafness, to acquire a primary language before the age of 12 thereafter rapidly loses the capacity to acquire language behaviour at all. This finding does not of course carry with it the implication that the language learning capacity of those who have successfully learned a primary language also atrophies in the same way. It still remains to be shown that the process of learning a second language is of a fundamentally different nature from the process of primary acquisition.

If we postulate the same mechanism, then we may also postulate that the procedures or strategies adopted by the learner of the second language are fundamentally the same. The principal feature that then differentiates the two operations is the presence or absence of motivation. If the acquisition of the first language is a fulfilment of the predisposition to develop language behaviour, then the learning of the second language involves the replacement of the predisposition of the infant by some other force. What this consists of is in the context of this paper irrelevant.

Let us say therefore that, *given motivation,* it is inevitable that a human being will learn a second language if he is exposed to the language data. Study of language aptitude does in some measure support such a view since motivation and intelligence appear to be the two principal factors which correlate significantly with achievement in a second language.

I propose therefore as a working hypothesis that some at least of the *strategies* adopted by the learner of a second language are substantially the same as those by which a first language is acquired. Such a proposal does not imply that the course or *sequence* of learning is the same in both cases.

We can now return to the consideration of errors made by learners. When a two-year-old child produces an utterance such as 'This mummy chair' we do not normally call this deviant, ill-formed, faulty, incorrect or whatever. We do not regard it as an error in any sense at all, but rather as a normal childlike communication which provides evidence of the state of his linguistic development at that moment. Our response to that behaviour has certain of the characteristics of what would be called 'correction' in a classroom situation. Adults have a very strong tendency to repeat and expand the child's utterance in an adult version; something like 'Yes, dear, that's Mummy's chair'.

No one expects a child learning his mother-tongue to produce from the earliest stages only forms which in adult terms are correct or non-deviant. We interpret his 'incorrect' utterances as being evidence that he is in the process of acquiring language and indeed, for those who attempt to describe his knowledge of the language at any point in its development, it is the 'errors' which provide the important evidence. As Brown and Frazer (1964) point out the best evidence that a child possesses construction rules is the occurrence of systematic errors, since, when the child speaks correctly, it is quite possible that he is only repeating something that he has heard. Since we do not know what the total input has been we cannot rule out this possibility. It is by reducing the language to a simpler system than it is that the child reveals his tendency to induce rules.

In the case of the second language learner it might be supposed that we *do* have some knowledge of what the input has been, since this is largely within the control of the teacher. Nevertheless it would be wise to introduce a qualification here about the control of input (which is of course what we call the syllabus). The simple fact of presenting a certain linguistic form to a learner in the classroom does not necessarily qualify it for the status of input, for the reason that input is 'what goes in' not what is *available* for going in, and we may reasonably suppose that it is the learner who controls this input, or more properly his intake. This may well be determined by the characteristics of his language acquisition mechanism and not by those of the syllabus. After all, in the mother-tongue learning situation the data available as input is relatively vast, but it is the child who selects what shall be the input.

Ferguson (1966) has recently made the point that our syllabuses have been based at best upon impressionistic judgements and vaguely conceived theoretical principles where they have had any considered foundations at all. The suggestion that we should take more account of the learner's needs in planning our syllabuses is not new, but has not apparently led to any investigations, perhaps because of the methodological difficulties of determining what the learner's needs might actually be. Carroll (1955) made such a proposal when he suggested it might be worth creating a problem-solving situation for the learner in which he must find, by enquiring either of the teacher or a dictionary appropriate verbal responses for solving the problem. He pointed out that such a hypothesis contained certain features of what was believed to occur in the process of language acquisition by the child.

A similar proposal actually leading to an experiment was made by Mager but not in connection with language teaching (Mager, 1961); it is nevertheless worth quoting his own words:

Whatever sequencing criterion is used it is one which the user calls a 'logical' sequence. But although there are several schemes by which sequencing can be accomplished and, although it is generally agreed that an effective sequence is one which is meaningful to the learner, the information sequence to be assimilated by the learner is traditionally dictated entirely by the instructor. We generally fail to consult the learner in the matter except to ask him to maximize the effectiveness of whatever sequence we have already decided upon.

He points out as the conclusions he draws from his small scale experiment that the next step would be to determine whether the learner-generated sequence, or, as we might call it, his *built-in syllabus,* is in some way more efficient than the instructor-generated sequence. It seems entirely plausible that it would be so. The problem is to determine whether there exists such a built-in syllabus and to describe it. It is in such an investigation that the study of learners' errors would assume the role it already plays in the study of child language acquisition, since, as has been pointed out, the key concept in both cases is that the learner is using a definite system of language at every point in his development, although it is not the adult system in the one case, nor that of the second language in the other. The learner's errors are evidence of this system and are themselves systematic.

The use of the term systematic in this context implies, of course, that there may be errors which are random, or, more properly, the systematic nature of which cannot be readily discerned. The opposition between systematic and non-systematic errors is important. We are all aware that in normal adult speech in our native language we are continually committing errors of one sort or another. These, as we have been so often reminded recently, are due to memory lapses, physical states, such as tiredness and psychological conditions such as strong emotion. These are adventitious artefacts of linguistic performance and do not reflect a defect in our knowledge of our own language. We are normally immediately aware of them when they occur and can correct them with more or less complete assurance. It would be quite unreasonable to expect the learner of a second language not to exhibit such slips of the tongue (or pen), since he is subject to similar external and internal conditions when performing in his first or second language. We must therefore make a distinction between those errors which are the product of such chance circumstances and those which reveal his underlying knowledge of the language to date, or, as we may call it his *transitional competence*. The errors of performance will characteristically be unsystematic and the errors of competence, systematic. As Miller (1966) puts it, 'It would be meaningless to state rules for making mistakes'. It will be useful therefore hereafter to refer to errors of performance as *mistakes,* reserving the term *error* to refer to the systematic errors of the learner from which we are able to reconstruct his knowledge of the language to date, i.e. his *transitional competence*.

Mistakes are of no significance to the process of language learning. However the problem of determining what is a learner's mistake and what a learner's error is one of some difficulty and involves a much more sophisticated study and analysis of errors than is usually accorded them.

A learner's errors, then, provide evidence of the system of the language that he is using (i.e. has learned) at a particular point in the course (and it must be repeated that he is using some system, although it is not yet the right system). They are significant in three different ways. First to the teacher, in that they tell him, if he undertakes a systematic analysis, how far towards the goal the learner has progressed and, consequently, what remains for him to learn. Second, they provide to the researcher evidence of how language is learned or acquired, what strategies or procedures the learner is employing in his discovery of the language. Thirdly (and in a sense this is their most important aspect) they are indispensable to the learner himself, because we can regard the making of errors as a device the learner uses in order to learn. It is a way the learner has of testing his hypotheses about the nature of the language he is learning. The making of errors then is a strategy employed both by children acquiring their mother tongue and by those learning a second language.

Although the following dialogue was recorded during the study of child language acquisition, it bears unmistakable similarities to dialogues which are a daily experience in the second language teaching classroom:

Mother: Did Billy have his egg cut up for him at breakfast?
Child: Yes, I showeds him.
Mother: You what?
Child: I showed him.
Mother: You showed him?

Child: I seed him.
Mother: Ah, you saw him.
Child: Yes, I saw him.

Here the child, within a short exchange, appears to have tested three hypotheses: one relating to the concord of subject and verb in a past tense, another about the meaning of *show* and *see* and a third about the form of the irregular past tense of *see*. It only remains to be pointed out that if the child had answered *I saw him* immediately, we would have no means of knowing whether he had merely repeated a model sentence or had already learned the three rules just mentioned. Only a longitudinal study of the child's development could answer such a question. It is also interesting to observe the techniques used by the mother to 'correct' the child. Only in the case of one error did she provide the correct form herself: *You saw him.* In both the other cases, it was sufficient for her to query the child's utterance in such a form as: *you what?* or *You showed him?* Simple provision of the correct form may not always be the only, or indeed the most effective, form of correction since it bars the way to the learner testing alternative hypotheses. Making a learner try to discover the right form could often be more instructive to both learner and teacher. This is the import of Carroll's proposal already referred to.

We may note here that the utterance of a correct form cannot be taken as proof that the learner has learned the systems which would generate that form in a native speaker, since he may be merely repeating a heard utterance, in which case we should class such behaviour, not as language, but in Spolsky's term (Spolsky, 1966) 'language-like behaviour'. Nor must we overlook the fact that an utterance which is superficially non-deviant is not evidence of a mastery of the language systems which would generate it in a native speaker since such an utterance must be semantically related to the situational context. The learner who produced 'I want to know the English' might have been uttering an unexceptionable sentiment, but it is more likely that he was expressing the wish to know the English language. Only the situational context could show whether his utterance was an error or not.

Although it has been suggested that the strategies of learning a first and second language may be the same, it is nevertheless necessary at this point to posit a distinction between the two. Whilst one may suppose that the first language learner has an unlimited number of hypotheses about the nature of the language he is learning which must be tested (although strong reasons have been put forward for doubting this) we may certainly take it that the task of the second language learner is a simpler one: that the only hypotheses he needs to test are: 'Are the systems of the new language the same or different from those of the language I know?' 'And if different, what is their nature?' Evidence for this is that a large number, but by no means all, of his errors, are related to the systems of his mother tongue. These are ascribed to interference from the habits of the mother tongue, as it is sometimes expressed. In the light of the new hypotheses they are best not regarded as the persistence of old habits, but rather as signs that the learner is investigating the systems of the new language. Saporta (1966) makes this point clear, 'The internal structure of the (language acquisition) device, i.e. the learner, has gone relatively unexplored except to point out that one of its components is the grammar of the learner's native language. It has generally been assumed that the effect of this component has been inhibitory rather than facilitative'. It will be evident that the position taken here is that the learner's possession of his native language is facilitative and that errors are not to be regarded as signs of inhibition, but simply as evidence of his strategies of learning.

We have been reminded recently of Von Humboldt's statement that we cannot really teach language, we can only create conditions in which it will develop spontaneously in the mind in its own way. We shall never improve our ability to create such favourable conditions until we learn more about the way a learner learns and what his built-in syllabus is. When we do know this (and the learner's errors will, if systematically studied, tell us something about this) we may begin to be more critical of our cherished notions. We may be able to allow the learner's innate strategies to dictate our practice and determine our syllabus; we may learn to adapt ourselves to *his* needs rather than impose upon him *our* preconceptions of *how* he ought to learn, *what* he ought to learn and *when* he ought to learn it.

PART TWO

Towards Theories and Models

The papers in this section suggest ways in which learner speech is characterized. Selinker introduces the term *Interlanguage* to suggest the intermediate stages between the native and target language observable in learners' language. Selinker proposes that the data on which theories of second language learning should be based must be the learner's real or attempted communication in the second language. Selinker assumes that there are 'psychological structures' latent in the brain which are activated when one attempts to learn a second language. While not all would see the need to postulate 'different psycholinguistic processes' to explain successful and unsuccessful language learning (cf. Richards and Sampson), since motivation, time available, and numerous other factors may be decisive, the interest in Selinker's paper is his typology of attempted learning, resulting in an interlanguage, that is, a different language system from either the mother tongue or the target language. Selinker refers to language transfer, transfer of training, strategies of learning, strategies of communication, and overgeneralization of target language linguistic material. These or similar concepts are referred to by a number of other contributors to this book (cf. Nemser, Richards, this section). Besides Selinker's useful discussion of these five aspects of interlanguage performance his discussion of the relevant units which characterize second language speech is interesting. He is sceptical of the use of concepts derived from linguistic description of only the target language or native language. Interlingual systems are not necessarily describable in either terms, hence his term *syntactic string* as a suggested interlingual unit of syntax. Likewise *phoneme* is not necessarily the ideal unit for describing the phonological units in the learner's speech (cf. Nemser).

Nemser's terminology is a little different from Selinker's but it is applied to precisely the same phenomenon. He uses the term *approximative system* for *interlanguage*. This term has the advantage of implying the developmental nature of language learning, since the learners' system is continually being modified as new elements are incorporated throughout the learning process. Such developing systems are evident in learner's errors. Nemser notes that the attention to the content rather than the form of utterances by the learner (cf. communication strategy) seen in learners' simplified grammar, may also be characteristic of the teacher's speech (cf. Ferguson, 1971). He gives phonological examples of the intermediate and often independent systems developed by the learner. Such systems have internal coherence and are not simply corrupt versions of the target language or mother tongue and their characteristics change according to the degree of learning. Such systems are illegitimates sociolinguistically—their users do not normally form speech communities (cf. Richards, this section)—though they are not without sociolinguistic significance, as Nemser illustrates.

In the third paper I have tried to suggest how our view of the learner's developing system is determined by the social relationships holding between the learner and the target language community. An attempt is made to relate the linguistic concepts developed elsewhere in this volume (interlanguage, approximative system, overgeneralization, communication strategy, etc.) to an overall view of the different social settings in which the learning of English takes place. The non-linguistic dimensions of language learning illustrated include the effects of the perception of the target language community by the learner, the structure and rigidity of social roles in the community, the economic and social strength of the learners if they form a community, and the roles for which English is used by the learner. An analysis of the learner's developing linguistic system can be complemented by consideration of the social factors which give these features significance. The paper hence makes distinctions between second language and foreign language contexts for the learning of English which have important consequences for our view of the learner's interlanguage or developing system.

3

Interlanguage

LARRY SELINKER

Reprinted from IRAL, Vol. X/3, 1972, published by Julius Groos Verlag, Heidelberg.

1 Introduction

This paper[1] discusses some theoretical preliminaries for researchers concerned with the linguistic aspects of the psychology of second language learning. These theoretical preliminaries are important because without them it is virtually impossible to decide what data are relevant to a psycholinguistic theory of second language learning.

It is also important to distinguish between a teaching perspective and a learning one. As regards the 'teaching' perspective, one might very well write a methodology paper which would relate desired output to known inputs in a principled way, prescribing what has to be done by the teacher in order to help the learner achieve learning. As regards the 'learning' perspective, one might very well write a paper describing the process of attempted learning of a second language, successful or not; teaching, textbooks, and other 'external aids' would constitute one, but only one, important set of relevant variables. In distinguishing between the two perspectives,[2] claims about the internal structures and processes of the learning organism take on a very secondary character in the teaching perspective; such claims may not even be desirable here. But such claims do provide the *raison d'être* for viewing second language learning from the learning perspective. This paper is written from the learning perspective, regardless of one's failure or success in the attempted learning of a second language.

In the learning perspective, what would constitute the psychologically relevant data of second language learning?[3] My own position is that such data would be those behavioral events which would lead to an understanding of the psycholinguistic structures and processes underlying 'attempted meaningful performance' in a

31

second language. The term 'meaningful performance' will be used here to refer to the situation where an 'adult'[4] attempts to express meanings, which he may already have, in a language which he is in the process of learning. Since performance of drills in a second language classroom is, by definition, not meaningful performance, it follows that from a learning perspective, such performance is, in the long run, of minor interest. Also, behavior which occurs in experiments, using nonsense syllables fits into the same category and for the same reason. Thus, data resulting from these latter behavioral situations are of doubtful relevancy to meaningful performance situations, and thus to a theory of second language learning.

It has long seemed to me that one of our greatest difficulties in establishing a psychology of second language learning which is relevant to the way people actually learn second languages, has been our inability to identify unambiguously the phenomena we wish to study. Out of the great conglomeration of second language behavioral events, what criteria and constructs should be used to establish the class of those events which are to count as relevant in theory construction? One set of these behavioral events which has elicited considerable interest is the regular reappearance in second language performance of linguistic phenomena which were thought to be eradicated in the performance of the learner. A correct understanding of this phenomenon leads to the postulation of certain theoretical constructs, many of which have been set up to deal with other problems in the field. But they also help clarify the phenomenon under discussion. These constructs, in turn, give us a framework within which we can begin to isolate the psychologically relevant data of second language learning. The new perspective which an examination of this phenomenon gives us is thus very helpful both in an identification of relevant data and in the formulation of a psycholinguistic theory of second language learning. The main motivation for this paper is the belief that it is particularly in this area that progress can be made at this time.

2 'Interlanguage' and latent structures

Relevant behavioral events in a psychology of second language learning should be made identifiable with the aid of theoretical constructs which assume the major features of the psychological structure of an adult whenever he attempts to understand second language sentences or to produce them. If, in a psychology of second language learning, our goal is explanation of some important aspects of this psychological structure, then it seems to me that we are concerned in large part with how bilinguals make what Weinreich (1953, p. 7) has called 'interlingual identifications'. In his book *Languages in Contact,* Weinreich discusses—though briefly—the practical need for assuming in studies of bilingualism that such identifications as that of a phoneme in two languages, or that of a grammatical relationship in two languages, or that of a semantic feature in two languages, have been made by the individual in question in a language contact situation. Although Weinreich takes up many linguistic and some psychological questions, he leaves completely open questions regarding the *psychological structures* within which he assumes 'interlingual identifications' exist; we assume that there is such a *psychological structure* and that it is *latent* in the brain, activated when one attempts to learn a second language.

The closest thing in the literature to the concept *latent psychological structure* is the concept of *latent language structure* (Lenneberg, 1967, especially pp. 374–379) which, according to Lenneberg, (a) is an already formulated arrangement in the brain, (b) is the biological counterpart to universal grammar, and (c) is transformed by the infant into the *realized structure* of a particular grammar in accordance with certain maturational stages. For the purposes of this paper, I will assume the existence of the latent structure described by Lenneberg, I shall further assume that there exists in the brain an already formulated arrangement which for most people is different from and exists in addition to Lenneberg's latent language structure. It is important to state that with the latent structure described in this paper as compared to Lenneberg's, there is no genetic timetable;[5] there is no direct counterpart to any grammatical concept such as 'universal grammar'; there is no guarantee that the latent structure will be activated at all, there is no guarantee that the latent structure will be 'realized' into the actual structure of any natural language (i.e. there is no guarantee that attempted learning will prove successful), and there is every possibility that an overlapping exists between this latent language acquisition structure and other intellectual structures.

The crucial assumption we are making here is that those adults who 'succeed' in learning a second language so that they achieve native-speaker 'competence' have somehow reactivated the *latent language structure* which Lenneberg describes. This absolute success in a second language affects, as we know from observation, a small percentage of learners—perhaps a mere 5%. It follows from this assumption that this 5% go through very different psycholinguistic processes than do most second language learners and that these successful learners may be safely ignored—in a counterfactual sense[6]—for the purposes of establishing the constructs which point to the psychologically relevant data pertinent to most second language learners. Regarding the study of the latter group of learners (i.e. the vast majority of second language learners who fail to achieve native speaker competence), the notion of 'attempted learning' is independent and logically prior to the notion of 'successful learning'. In this paper we will focus on attempted learning by this group of learners, successful or not, and will assume that they activate a different, though still genetically determined structure (referred to here as the *latent psychological structure*) whenever they attempt to produce a sentence in the second-language, that is, whenever they attempt to express meanings which they may already have, in a language which they are in the process of learning.

This series of assumptions must be made, I think, because the second language learner who actually achieves native speaker competence, cannot possibly have been taught this competence, since linguists are daily—in almost every generative study—discovering new and fundamental facts about particular languages. Successful learners, in order to achieve this native-speaker competence, must have acquired these facts (and most probably important principles of language organization) *without* having explicitly been taught them.[7]

Regarding the ideal second language learner who will *not* 'succeed' (in the absolute sense described above) and who is thus representative of the vast majority of second language learners, we can idealize that from the beginning of his study of a second language, he has his attention focused upon one norm of the language whose sentences he is attempting to produce. With this statement, we have idealized the picture we wish to sketch in the following ways:[8] the generally accepted notion 'target language' (TL), i.e. the second language the learner is attempting to learn, is here restricted to mean that there is only one norm of one dialect within the interlingual focus of attention of the learner. Furthermore, we focus our analytical attention upon *the only observable data to which we can relate theoretical predictions*:[9] the utterances which are produced when the learner attempts to say sentences of a TL. This set of utterances for *most* learners of a second language is not identical to the hypothesized corresponding set of utterances which would have been produced by a native speaker of the TL had he attempted to express the same meaning as the learner. Since we can observe that these two sets of utterances are not identical, then in the making of constructs relevant to a theory of second language learning, one would be completely justified in hypothesizing, perhaps even *compelled* to hypothesize, the existence of a separate linguistic system[10] based on the observable output which results from a learner's attempted production of a TL norm. This linguistic system we will call 'interlanguage' (IL).[11] One of the main points of this paper is the assumption that predictions of behavioral events in a theory of second language learning should be primarily concerned with the linguistic shapes of the utterances produced in ILs. Successful predictions of such behavioral events in meaningful performance situations will add credence to the theoretical constructs related to the latent psychological structure discussed in this paper.

It follows from the above that the only observable data from meaningful performance situations we can establish as relevant to interlingual identifications are: (1) utterances in the learner's native language (NL) produced by the learner; (2) IL utterances produced by the learner; and (3) TL utterances produced by native speakers of that TL. These three sets of utterances or behavioral events are, then, in this framework, the psychologically relevant data of second language learning, and theoretical predictions in a relevant psychology of second language learning will be the surface structure of IL sentences.

By setting up these three sets of utterances within one theoretical framework, and by gathering as data utterances related to specific linguistic structures in each of these three systems (under the *same* experimental conditions, if possible) the investigator in the psychology of second language learning can begin to study the psycholinguistic processes which establish the knowledge which underlies IL behavior. I would like to suggest that there are five central processes (and perhaps some additional minor ones), and that they exist in the latent psychological structure referred to above. I consider the following to be processes *central* to second language learning; first, *language transfer*; second, *transfer of training*; third, *strategies of second language learning*; fourth, *strategies of second language communication*; and fifth, *overgeneralization of TL linguistic material.* Each of the analyst's predictions as to the shape of IL utterances should be associated with one or more of these, or other, processes.

3 Fossilization

Before briefly describing these psycholinguistic processes, another notion I wish to introduce for· the reader's consideration is the concept of *fossilization,* a mechanism which is assumed also to exist in the latent psychological structure described above. Fossilizable linguistic phenomena are linguistic items, rules, and subsystems which speakers of a particular NL will tend to keep in their IL relative to a particular TL, no matter what the age of the learner or amount of explanation and instruction he receives in the TL.[12] I have in mind such fossilizable structures as the well-known 'errors'; French uvular /r/ in their English IL, American English retroflex /r/ in their French IL, English rhythm in the IL relative to Spanish, German *Time-Place* order after the verb in the English IL of German speakers, and so on. I also have in mind less well known 'non-errors' such as Spanish monophthong vowels in the IL of Spanish speakers relative to Hebrew, and Hebrew *Object-Time* surface order after the verb in the IL of Hebrew speakers relative to English. Finally, there are fossilizable structures that are much harder to classify such as some features of the Thai tone system in the IL of Thai speakers relative to English. It is important to note that fossilizable structures tend to remain as potential performance, re-emerging[13] in the productive performance of an IL even when seemingly eradicated. Many of these phenomena reappear in IL performance when the learner's attention is focused upon new and difficult intellectual subject matter or when he is in a state of anxiety or other excitement, and strangely enough, sometimes when he is in a state of extreme relaxation. Note that the claim is made here that, whatever the cause, the well-observed phenomenon of 'backsliding' by second language learners from a TL norm is not, as has been generally believed, either random or towards the speaker's NL, but toward an IL norm.[14]

A crucial fact, perhaps the most crucial fact, which any adequate theory of second language learning will have to explain is this regular reappearance or re-emergence in IL productive performance of linguistic structures which were thought to be eradicated. This behavioral reappearance is what has led me to postulate the reality of fossilization and ILs. It should be made clear that the reappearance of such behavior is not limited to the phonetic level.

For example, some of the subtlest input information that a learner of a second language has to master regards subcategorization notions of verbal complementation. Indian English as an IL with regard to English[15] seems to fossilize the 'that complement' or *V that* construction for all verbs that take sentential complements. Even when the correct form has been learned by the Indian speaker of English, this type of knowledge is the first he seems to lose when his attention is diverted to new intellectual subject matter or when he has not spoken the TL for even a short time. Under conditions such as these, there is a regular reappearance of the 'that complement' in IL performance for all sentential complements.

4 Five Central Processes

It is my contention that the most interesting phenomena in IL performance are those items, rules, and subsystems which are fossilizable in terms of the five processes listed above. If it can be experimentally demonstrated that fossilizable items, rules and subsystems which occur in IL performance are a result of the NL, then we are dealing with the process of *language transfer*; if these fossilizable items, rules, and subsystems are a result of identifiable items in training procedures, then we are dealing with the process known as *transfer of training*; if they are a result of an identifiable approach by the learner to the material to be learned, then we are dealing with *strategies of second language learning*; if they are a result of an identifiable approach by the learner to communication with native speakers of the TL, then we are dealing with *strategies of second language communication*; and finally, if they are a result of a clear overgeneralization of TL rules and semantic features, then we are dealing with the *overgeneralization of TL linguistic material*. I would like to hypothesize that these five processes are processes which are *central* to second language learning, and that each process forces fossilizable material upon surface IL utterances, controlling to a very large extent the surface structures of these utterances.

Combinations of these processes produce what we might term entirely fossilized IL competence. Coulter (1968) presents convincing data to demonstrate not only *language transfer* but also a *strategy of communication* common to many second language learners. This strategy of communication dictates to them, internally as it were, that they know enough of the TL in order to communicate. And they stop learning.[16] Whether they stop learning entirely or go on to learn in a minor way, e.g. adding vocabulary as experience demands (cf. Jain) is, it seems to me, a moot point. If these individuals do not also learn the syntactic information that goes with lexical items, then adding a few new lexical items, say on space travel, is, I would argue, of little consequence. The important thing to note with regard to the evidence presented in Coulter (1968) and Jain (1969) is that not only can entire IL competences be fossilized in individual learners performing in their own interlingual situation,[17] but also in whole groups of individuals, resulting in the emergence of a new dialect (here Indian English), where fossilized IL competences may be the normal situation.

We will now provide examples of these processes. The examples presented in section 3 are almost certainly the result of the process of *language transfer*. A few examples relating to the other processes should suffice for this paper.

4.1 *Overgeneralization of TL rules* is a phenomenon well known to language teachers. Speakers of many languages could produce a sentence of the following kind in their English IL.

(1) What did he intended to say?[18]

where the past tense morpheme *-ed* is extended to an environment in which, to the learner, it could logically apply, but just does not. The Indian speaker of English who produces the collocation *drive a bicycle* in his IL performance, as in (2)

(2) After thinking little I decided to start on the *bicycle* as slowly as I could as it was not possible to *drive* fast.

is most probably overgeneralizing the use of *drive* to all vehicles (Jain, 1969, cf. note 26 here). Most learners of English quickly learn the English rule of contraction which forms things like *the concert's* from *the concert is,* but then these learners may overgeneralize this rule to produce sentences like,

(3) Max is happier than Sam's these days

in their English IL. Though this sentence is hypothetical, it illustrates an earlier point. The learner of English who produces contractions correctly in all environments must have learned the following constraint *without* 'explanation and instruction', since this constraint was discovered only recently; "contraction of auxiliaries . . . cannot occur when a constituent immediately following the auxiliary to be contracted has been deleted," e.g. 'happy' in (3) (Lakoff, in press). Dozens of examples of overgeneralization of TL rules are provided in Richards (1971).

4.2 The *transfer of training* is a process which is quite different from language transfer (see Selinker, 1969) and from overgeneralization of TL rules. It underlies the source of a difficulty which Serbo-Croation speakers at all levels of English proficiency regularly have with the *he/she* distinction, producing in their English IL *he* on almost every occasion wherever *he* or *she* would be called for according to any norm of English. There is no language transfer effect here since, with regard to animateness, the distinction between *he* and *she* is the same in Serbo-Croatian as it is in English.[19] According to a standard contrastive analysis then there should be no trouble. It seems to be the case that the resultant IL form, in the first instance, is due directly to the *transfer of training*; textbooks and teachers in this interlingual situation almost always present drills with *he* and never with *she*. The extent of this fossilization can be seen with respect to the speakers of this IL over the age of 18, who even though they are consciously aware of the distinction and of their recurrent error, in fact, regularly produce *he* for both *he* and *she*, stating that they feel they do not need to make this distinction in order to communicate.[20] In this case, then, the fossilizable error is due originally to a type of *transfer of training* and later to a particular *strategy of second language communication*.

4.3 Concerning the notion 'strategy' little is known in psychology about what constitutes a strategy, and a viable definition of it does not seem possible at present. Even less is known about strategies which learners of a second language use in their attempt to master a TL and express meanings in it. It has been pointed out[21] that learner strategies are probably culture-bound to some extent. For example, in many traditional cultures, chanting is used as a learning device, clearly relating to what is learned in those situations. Crucially, it has been argued[22] that strategies for handling TL linguistic material evolve whenever the learner realizes, either consciously or subconsciously, that he has no linguistic competence with regard to some aspect of the TL. It cannot be doubted that various internal strategies[23] on the part of the second language learner affect to a large extent the surface structure of sentences underlying IL utterances. But exactly what these strategies might be and how they might work is at present pure conjecture. Thus, one can only roughly attribute the source of the examples presented herein to one or another strategy.

One example of a *strategy of second language learning* that is widespread in many interlingual situations is a tendency on the part of learners to reduce the TL to a simpler system. According to Jain (1969) the results of this strategy are manifested at all levels of syntax in the IL of Indian speakers of English. For example, if the learner has adopted the strategy that all verbs are either transitive or intransitive, he may produce IL forms such as

(4) I am feeling thirsty

or   (5) Don't worry, I'm hearing him

and in producing them they seem to have adopted the further strategy that the realization of the category 'aspect' in its progressive form on the surface is always with *ing* marking (for further discussion, see Jain, 1969).

Coulter (1968) reports systematic errors occurring in the English IL performance of two elderly Russian speakers of English, due to another strategy which seems also to be widespread in many interlingual situations; a tendency on the part of second language learners to avoid grammatical formatives such as articles (6), plural forms (7), and past tense forms (8);

(6) It was ∅ nice, nice trailer, ∅ big one. (Coulter, 1968, 22)
(7) I have many hundred *carpenter* my own (ibid, 29)
(8) I *was* in Frankfurt when I *fill* application (ibid, 36).

This tendency could be the result of a *learning strategy* of simplification, but Coulter (1968) attributes it to a *communication strategy* due to the past experience of the speaker which has shown him that if he thinks about grammatical processes while attempting to express in English meanings which he already has, then his speech will be hesitant and disconnected, leading native speakers to be impatient with him. Also, Coulter claims that this *strategy of second language communication* seemed to dictate to these speakers that a form such as the English plural 'was not necessary for the kind of communicating they used' (ibid, p. 30).

Not all of these strategies, it must be pointed out, are conscious. A subconscious *strategy of second language learning* called 'cue-copying' has been experimented with by Crothers and Suppes (1967, 211) on Americans learning Russian morphological concepts.

This 'copy the cue' strategy is most probably due to what they call 'probability matching', where the chance that the learner will select an alternative morphological ending related to the cue noun is not random. Crothers and Suppes do not provide examples of the result of this strategy in meaningful performance situations; an example would be the *r* at the end of words like *California* and *saw* which foreign students of English who have had teachers from the Boston area regularly reproduce in their English IL.

4.4 To conclude this section, it should be pointed out that beyond the five so-called *central* processes, there exist many other processes which account to some degree for the surface forms of IL utterances. One might mention *spelling pronunciations,* c.g. speakers of many languages pronounce final -*er* on English words as [ɛ] plus some form of *r*; *cognate pronunciation,* e.g. English *athlete* pronounced as [atlit] by many Frenchmen whether or not they can produce [θ] in other English words;[24] *holophrase learning* (Jain, 1969), e.g. from half-an-hour the Indian learner of English may produce *one and half-an-hour*; *hypercorrection,* e.g. the Israeli who in attempting to get rid of his uvular fricative for English retroflex [r] produces [w] before front vowels, 'a vocalization too far forward'[25]; and most assuredly others such as long exposure to signs and headlines which according to Jain (1969) affect by themselves the shape of English IL utterances of Indians, or at least reinforce some important processes such as *language transfer.*

5 Problems with this perspective

There are certainly many questions one might wish to ask regarding the perspective presented so far in this paper; I shall attempt to deal with five (5.1–5.5). The reader should bear in mind that we are here calling for the discovery, description and experimental testing of fossilizable items, rules and subsystems in interlanguages and the relating of these to the above mentioned processes—especially to the central ones. What seems to be most promising for study is the observation concerning fossilization. Many IL linguistic structures are *never* really eradicated for most second language learners; manifestations of these structures regularly reappear in IL productive performance, especially under conditions of anxiety, shifting attention, and second language performance on subject matter which is new to the learner. It is this observation which allows us to claim that these psycholinguistic structures, even when seemingly eradicated, are still somehow present in the brain, stored by a fossilization mechanism (primarily through one of these five processes) in an IL. We further hypothesize that interlingual identifications uniting the three linguistic systems (NL, IL, and TL) psychologically, are activated in a latent psychological structure whenever an individual attempts to produce TL sentences.

5.1 The first problem we wish to deal with is: can we always unambiguously identify which of these processes our observable data is to be attributable to? Most probably not. It has been frequently pointed out that this situation is quite common in psychology. In studies on memory, for example, one often does not know whether one is in fact studying 'storage' or 'retrieval'. In our case, we may not know whether a particular constituent IL concatenation is a result of language transfer of transfer of training or, perhaps, of both.[26] But this limitation need not deter us, even if we cannot always sort things out absolutely. By applying the constructs suggested in this paper, I believe that relevant data can be found in the very many second language learning situations around us.

5.2 The second problem is: how can we systematize the notion *fossilization* so that from the basis of theoretical constructs, we can predict which items in which interlingual situations will be fossilized? To illustrate the difficulty of attempting to answer this question, note in the following example the non-reversibility of fossilization effects for no apparent reason. According to a contrastive analysis, Spanish speakers should have no difficulty with the *he/she* distinction in English, nor should English speakers have any difficulty with the corresponding distinction in Spanish. The facts are quite different, however: Spanish speakers do, indeed, regularly have trouble with this distinction, while the reverse does not seem to occur with English learners of Spanish.[27] Unlike the Serbo-Croatian example mentioned above, in this case there is no clear-cut explanation why Spanish speakers have trouble and English speakers do not. In cases such as these, it may turn out that one process, e.g. language transfer or transfer of training, overrides other considerations, but the stating of the governing conditions may prove very difficult indeed.

In principle, one feels forced to agree with Stephanie Harries (personal communication) who claims that until a theory of second language learning can answer questions like: 'How do I recognize fossilizable structures in advance?' or 'Why do some things fossilize and others do not?', all experiments conducted within the framework provided in this paper must be regarded as 'exploratory' in nature. (To put things in more familiar jargon: with regard to *fossilization*, our results are 'descriptive' and not 'explanatory' in nature.) But this task of prediction may prove to be impossible; certainly as Lakoff points out (personal communication) this task, on the face of it, may be even tougher than trying to predict errors in second language performance—a task notably lacking in success.

The major justification one has for writing about the construct 'fossilization' at this stage of knowledge is that descriptive knowledge about ILs which turns out to suggest predictions verifiable in meaningful performance situations, leads to a systematic collection of the relevant data; this task, one which is impossible without this construct, is expected to be relevant to serious theory construction in a psychology of second language learning.

5.3 The third problem to be treated here concerns the apparent difficulty of fitting the following type of question into the idealized domain I have been sketching: how does a second language learning novice become able to produce IL utterances whose surface constituents are correct, i.e. correct with respect to the TL whose norm he is attempting to produce? This question finally brings us face-to-face with the notion of 'success' in absolute terms; productive performance in the TL by the second language learner which is identical to that produced by the native speaker of that TL.[28] We noted this in section 2 so as to exclude from our idealized domain of enquiry those learners of second languages who reactivate[29] the latent language structure that is realized into a native language. In this paper, we are concentrating on attempted learning of a second language, unsuccessful in this absolute sense. Of course, 'success' in second language learning need not be defined so absolutely. The teacher or the learner can be satisfied with the learner's achieving what has been called 'communicative competence' (see for example, Jakobovits, 1970, or Hymes, 1972). But this is not the issue here. As was pointed out in section 1, the emphasis upon what the teacher has to do in order to help the learner achieve successful learning belongs to the 'teaching' perspective, which is not the perspective of this paper. Perhaps the rather curious confusion in the literature of 'learning a second language' with 'teaching a second language' (see note 2) can be explained by the failure to see a psychology of second language learning in terms other than those related to 'success'. For example, typical learning-theory experiments when done in the domain of second language learning would demand knowledge of where the learner will tend to end up, not where we would like him to end up. Experiments of this type would also demand knowledge of where the second language learner begins. We would claim that prerequisite to both these types of knowledge are detailed descriptions of ILs—descriptions not presently available to us. Thus, such experiments at present are premature, with the results bound to prove confusing.

Specifically concerning the problem raised in the first sentence of 5.3, it seems to me that this question, though relevant to the psychology of second language learning, is one that should also not be asked for the present since its asking depends upon our understanding clearly the psychological extent of interlingual identifications. For example, before we discover how surface constituents in an IL get reorganized to identify with the TL, we must have a clear idea of what is in that IL, even if we cannot explain why it is there. In Selinker (1969) I believe I have shown that within a very limited interlingual situation, the basis from which linguistic material must be *reorganized* in order to be 'correct' has been operationally and unambiguously established. But I have there said nothing about the way in which successful learners do in fact reorganize linguistic material from this particular IL. Here we can speculate that as part of a definition of 'learning a second language', 'successful learning' of a second language for most learners, involves, to a large extent, the *reorganization of linguistic material* from an IL to identify with a particular TL.

5.4 The fourth problem is: (a) what are the relevant units of this hypothesized latent psychological structure within which inter-lingual identifications exist and (b) is there any evidence for the existence of these units? If the relevant data of the psychology of second language learning are in fact parallel utterances in three linguistic systems (NL, IL, and TL), then it seems to me reasonable to hypothesize that the only relevant, one might say, 'psychologically real', interlingual unit is one which can be described simultaneously for parallel data in the three systems, and, if possible, for experi-mentally induced data in those systems.

Concerning underlying linguistic structures, we should not be too surprised if it turns out not to matter whose model we need, if an eclectic one will do, or even if such notions as the 'cycle', 'tree pruning', or even 'derivation' prove not to have much relevance. If it is reasonable to assume that the only linguistically-relevant unit of a theory of second language learning is one which is identified interlingually across three linguistic systems (NL, TL, and IL) by means of fossilization and the processes described in section 4, then it follows that no unit of linguistic theory, as these units are currently conceived, could fit this criterion. More generally, we should state that there is no necessary connection between relevant units of linguistic theory and linguistically relevant units of a psychology of second language learning.[30] That this assumption is obviously correct is clear to me; that many linguists will not be convinced is also clear.

For evidence of the relevant unit of surface syntactic structure, applying at one and the same time to these three linguistic systems, I refer the reader to experimental evidence appearing in my paper on language transfer (Selinker, 1969). In those experiments subjects responded orally in their native language to questions presented orally in their NL and attempted to respond in English to parallel questions presented in English. The questions came from an interview designed to elicit manifestations of specific types of surface structures in certain syntactic domains. The only experimental instruction given was for each subject to speak in a 'complete sentence'. Replicated results showed that the interlingual unit of surface syntactic structure transferred from NL to IL (*not* to TL) was a unit roughly equivalent to the traditional direct object or to an adverb of time, an adverb of place, an adverb of degree, and so on. I would claim that this unit, a surface constituent labelled the *syntactic string*, has a behavioral unity both in the experimental situation and in meaningful performance situations,[31] and thus, if the results were replicated in other 'interlingual situations' (i.e. other combinations of NL, TL, and IL), would account for a large class of IL events.

With regard to a 'realizational unit', i.e. a syntactic string tied to a specific semantic notion, replicated results from this same series of experiments show that responses concerning a topic such as 'subjects studied in school', as opposed to other topics such as 'buying and receiving things' and 'seeing movies and parades', affected very drastically the surface concatenation of the above mentioned strings.[32] This semantic effect on surface syntactic order in an interlingual study, if further replicated in other interlingual situations, would provide very powerful evidence for the transfer of the whole realizational unit as well as for its candidacy as the unit of realizational structure in interlingual identification.

Concerning the notion of relevant units on the phonological level, it seems to me that Brière (1968) has demonstrated that for his data there are several relevant units. The relevant units do not always correspond to known linguistic units, but rather would depend on the sounds involved; sometimes the taxonomic phoneme is the unit, but the unit in other cases seems not to be describable in purely linguistic terms. Brière evolved an experimental technique which imitated to a large extent actual methods of teaching advocated by applied structural linguists; listening to TL sounds, attempted imitation, use of phonemic transcription, physiological explanations, and so on. If I may be allowed to reinterpret Brière's data, it seems to me that he has been working, in another interlingual situation, with exactly the three systems we are discussing here, NL, TL, and IL: first, NL utterances which were hypothesized utterances in American English; second, TL utterances which were actual utterances in the 'composite language' Brière set up, each utterance having been produced by a native speaker of French, Arabic, or Vietnamese; third, IL utterances which were actual utterances produced by native speakers of this NL when attempting to produce this particular TL norm. Regarding the sounds /ž/ and /ŋ/ in his TL corpus, the unit identified interlingually across these three systems is the taxonomic phoneme defined distributionally within the syllable as opposed to within the word (Brière, 1968, p. 73). For other sounds the relevant phonological unit is not the taxonomic phoneme, but may be based on phonetic parameters some of which, he says, are probably not known (ibid, pp. 64 and 73).

If these units in the domain of interlingual identifications are not necessarily the same units as those in the native speaker domain, then where do they come from? An interesting bit of speculation about native speaker performance units is provided by Haggard (1967, p. 335) who states that searching for 'the unit' in native speaker speech-perception is a waste of time. Alternative units may be available to native speakers, for example under noise conditions.[33] While other explanations are surely possible for the well-known fact that noise conditions affect performance in a second language, and sometimes drastically, we cannot ignore the possible relevance of Haggard's intriguing suggestion: that alternative language units are available to individuals and that these units are activated under certain conditions. It fits very well with the perspective outlined in this paper to postulate a new type of psycholinguistic unit, available whenever he attempts to produce sentences in a second language. This interlingual unit stretches, we hypothesize, across three linguistic systems: NL, IL, and TL, and becomes available to the idealized second language learner who will not achieve native speaker competence in the TL, whenever he attempts to express meanings, which he may already have, in a TL he is learning, i.e. whenever he attempts to produce a TL norm. These units become available to the learner only after he has switched his psychic set or state from the native speaker domain to the new domain of interlingual identifications. I would like to postulate further that these relevant units of interlingual identifications do not come from anywhere; they are latent in the brain in a latent psychological structure, available to an individual whenever he wishes to attempt to produce the norm of any target language.

5.5 The final difficulty with this perspective which we will treat here is the following : how can we experiment with three linguistic systems, creating the same experimental conditions for each, with one unit which is identified interlingually across these systems? I can only refer the reader once again to my own experiments on language transfer (Selinker, 1969) where manifestations of desired concatenations of particular surface syntactic structures were obtained in what, I believe, was an efficient and valid manner. An oral interview technique was used; the purpose of the interview was to achieve a similar framework in the three systems which served the interviewer as a guide in his attempt to elicit certain types of sentences from the subjects. Upon request, I am prepared to make available a transcript of this interview as well as some thoughts for its improvement. Future experimental work, to be undertaken within this perspective, will go towards investigating the kind and extent of linguistic structures amenable to this particular technique.

6 Summary

The following are some assumptions which are necessary for research into the linguistic aspects of the psychology of second language learning and which have been suggested by the above discussion.

1) In a theory of second language learning, those behavioral

events which are to be counted as relevant data are not immediately obvious.

2) These data have to be organized with the help of certain theoretical constructs.

3) Some theoretical constructs relevant to the way in which 'adults' actually learn second languages are: interlingual identifications, native language (NL), target language (TL), interlanguage (IL), fossilization, syntactic string, taxonomic phoneme, phonetic feature.

4) The psychologically relevant data of second language learning are utterances in TL by native speakers, and in NL and IL by second language learners.

5) Interlingual identifications by second language learners is what unites the three linguistic systems (NL, TL, and IL) psychologically. These learners focus upon one form of the TL.

6) Theoretical predictions in a relevant psychology of second language learning must be the surface structures of IL sentences.

7) Successful second language learning, for most learners, is the reorganization of linguistic material from an IL to identify with a particular TL.

8) There exist five distinct processes which are central to second language learning: language transfer, transfer of training, strategies of second language learning, strategies of second language communication, and overgeneralization of TL linguistic material.

9) Each prediction in (6) should be made, if possible, relative to one of the five processes in (8).

10) There is *no* necessary connection between relevant units of linguistic theory and linguistically relevant units of a psychology of second language learning.

11) The only linguistically relevant unit of a psychology of second language learning is one which is identified interlingually across the three linguistic systems; NL, TL, and IL.

12) The *syntactic string* is the unit of surface structure transfer and part of the unit of realizational transfer.

13) The *taxonomic phoneme* is, in the case of some sounds, the unit of interlingual phonology, while in other cases no purely linguistic unit seems relevant.

14) There exists a *latent psychological structure,* i.e. an already formulated arrangement in the brain, which is activated whenever an adult attempts to produce meanings, which he may have, in a second language which he is learning.

15) Interlingual identifications, the units mentioned in (12) and (13), and the processes listed in (8) exist in this latent psychological structure.

16) *Fossilization,* a mechanism which also exists in this latent psychological structure, underlies surface linguistic material which speakers will tend to keep in their IL productive performance, no matter what the age of the learner or the amount of instruction he receives in the TL.

17) The fossilization mechanism accounts for the phenomenon of the regular reappearance in IL productive performance of linguistic material which was thought to be eradicated.

18) This latent psychological structure, for most learners, is different from and exists in addition to the *latent language structure* described by Lenneberg (1967, pp. 374–379).

19) These two latent structures differ in the following ways: (a) the latent psychological structure has no genetic time-table; (b) it has no direct counterpart to any grammatical concept; (c) it may never be realized into a natural language; and (d) it may overlap with other intellectual structures.

20) The qualification ('for most learners') in (7) and (18) is necessary, since those adults who seem to achieve native speaker 'competence', i.e. those who learn a second language so that their 'performance' is indistinguishable from that of native speakers (perhaps a mere 5% of all learners), have not been taught this performance through 'explanation and instruction' but have somehow reactivated this latent language structure.

21) Since it is assumed that the two structures mentioned in (18) are different and since we know very little about the latent language structure and its activation, then the 5% mentioned in (20) should be ignored in setting up the idealizations which guide us to the psychologically-relevant data of second language learning.

NOTES

1 This paper was begun during the 1968–69 academic year while I was a visitor at the Department of Applied Linguistics, University of Edinburgh. Many students and teachers at Edinburgh and at Washington, through their persistent calls for clarity, have helped me to crystallize the ideas presented in this paper to whatever level of clarity is attained herein. I wish to thank them and I especially wish to thank Ruth Clark, Fred Lakoff, Frederick Newmeyer, and Paul Van Buren. An earlier version of this paper

was read at the Second International Congress of Applied Linguistics, Cambridge University, 1969.

2 It is not unfair to say that almost all of the vast literature attempting to relate psycholinguistics to second language learning, whether produced by linguists or psychologists, is characterized by confusion between 'learning' a second language and 'teaching' a second language. (See Mackey, in Jakobovits, 1970, p. IX.) This confusion applies as well to almost all discussions on the topic one hears. For example one might hear the term 'psychology of second language teaching' and not know whether the speaker is referring to what the teacher should do, what the learner should do, or both. This terminological confusion makes one regularly uncertain as to what is being claimed.

3 The answer to this question is not obvious since it is well known that theoretical considerations help point the way to relevant data. See, for example, Fodor (1968, p. 48), '. . . how we count behaviors and what is available as a description depends in part on what conceptual equipment our theories provide . . .'

4 'Adult' is defined as being over the age of 12. This notion is derived from Lenneberg (1967, e.g. pp. 156, 176) who claims that after the onset of puberty, it is difficult to master the pronunciation of a second language since a 'critical' period in brain maturation has been passed, and '. . . language development tends to "freeze"' (ibid, p. 156).

5 First pointed out by Harold Edwards.

6 See Lawler and Selinker, where the relevance of counterfactuals to a theory of second language learning is taken up.

7 Chomsky (1969, p. 68) expresses a very similar view; '. . . it must be recognized that one does not learn the grammatical structure of a second language through "explanation and instruction" beyond the most elementary rudiments, for the simple reason that no one has enough explicit knowledge about this structure to provide explanation and instruction'.

Chomsky gives as a detailed example a property which is clearly central to grammar, that of nominalization (Chomsky, 1969, pp. 52–60 and 68). I see no point in repeating Chomsky's detailed arguments which clearly show that a successful learner of English as a second language could not have learned to make the judgements Chomsky describes through 'explanation and instruction'.

8 We have also idealized out of consideration differences between individual learners which makes this framework quite incomplete. A theory of second language learning that does not provide a central place for individual differences among learners *cannot* be considered acceptable. See Lawler and Selinker for a discussion of this tricky question in terms of profiles of idealized learners who differ one from the other with respect to types of linguistic rules and types of meaningful performance in a second language.

9 There has been a great deal of misunderstanding of this point. I am not taking an antimentalist position here. Neither am I ruling out on an *a-priori* basis perceptual studies in a second language. However, the reader

should be aware that in addition to the usual problems with determining whether a subject perceives or understands an utterance, the analyst in the interlingual domain cannot rely on intuitive grammatical judgements since he will gain information about another system, the one the learner is struggling with, i.e. the TL. (For a similar methodological problem in another domain, see Labov, 1969, p. 715.) Another, and perhaps the most important, argument against perceptual interlingual studies is that predictions based upon them are not testable in 'meaningful performance situations' (see definition above); a reconstruction of the event upon the part of the learner would have to be made in a perceptual interlingual study. Such difficulties do not exist when predictions are related to the shape of utterances produced as the result of the learner attempting to express in the TL meanings which he may already have.

10 Notions of such separate linguistic systems have been developed independently by Jakobovits (1969) and Nemser (this volume).

11 The notion 'interlanguage' is introduced in Selinker (1969).

12 Gillian Brown has pointed out (personal communication) that we should work here towards a dynamic model where fossilization would be defined relative to various, perhaps arbitrary, chronological age-groups.

13 John Laver has helped me to clarify this point.

14 Several people have pointed out that, in this paragraph, there appears to be a connection solely between fossilization and errors. This connection is not intended since it turns out that 'correct' things can also re-emerge when thought to be eradicated, especially if they are caused by processes other than language transfer.

15 Keith Brown (personal communication) has argued that the sociolinguistic status of the 'languages' or 'dialects' called Indian English, Filipino English, West African English, West African French, and so on, places them in a different category from that of the IL situation which I have been describing. From the sociolinguistic point of view this argument might be justified, but I am concerned in this paper with a psychological perspective and the relevant idealizations seem to me to be identical in all of these cases.

16 To describe this situation, Jain (1969) speaks of *functional competence*. Corder (1967) using the term *transitional competence* focuses on the provisional aspect of developing 'competence' in a second language. Both these notions owe their existence in the first place to Chomsky's (1965) notion of linguistic competence which is to be distinguished from actual linguistic performance.

17 An 'interlingual situation' is defined as a specific combination of NL, TL, and IL.

18 This sentence and sentences like it were in fact produced consistently by a middle-aged Israeli who was *very* fluent in English.

19 I am indebted to Wayles Browne (personal communication) for clarification of this point.

20 Reported by George McCreedy (personal communication).

21 Ian Pearson (personal communication).

22 Elaine Tarone (personal communication).

23 That is, what Corder refers to as the learner's 'built-in syllabus' (Corder, 1967).

24 Example taken from Tom Huckin (personal communication).

25 Example from Briana Stateman (personal communication).

26 The *drive a bicycle* example given in section 4 may, in fact, fit this situation (see Jain, 1969, p. 24).

27 Example from Sol Saporta (personal communication).

28 As was pointed out in note 7, Chomsky (1969, p. 68) also adds the ability to provide native-speaker-like grammaticality judgements.

29 Note that this reactivation may be the only explanation possible for an individual who learns *any* part of a second language well. In this light, Cheryl Goodenough (personal communication) has objected to the qualitative split between the 5% who succeed and the rest of all second language learners. Since in this paper we are not concentrating on success in a second language, as one would in the teaching approach, but on the attempt to isolate the latent psychological structure which determines, for any learner, the system underlying attempted production of a TL norm where the total effect of this output is clearly non-identity to the hypothe-sized norm, then resolution of this issue should not affect the discussion. The importance of isolating this 5% is the speculation that these individuals may not go through an IL.

Reibel (1969) stresses the role of the latent language structure in second language learning by suggesting that it is only when second language learners do the wrong things that they do not 'succeed', i.e. 'we seek to explain differences between adult learners, not in terms of differences in the innate learning abilities, but rather in terms of the way in which they are applied'. Kline (1970) attempts to provide a point of contact between Reibel's views and mine by suggesting that any reorganization of an IL to identify with a TL must use the kinds of capacities and abilities Reibel describes.

A different opposing view to the perspective of this paper has been pre-sented by Sandra Hamlett and Michael Seitz (personal communication) who have argued that, even for the vast majority of second language learners, there is no already formulated arrangement existing in the brain, but that the latent psychological structure alluded to here is developed, partly at least, by strategies which change up to the age of 12 and remain with an individual for the rest of his life. There seems to be at present no critical empirical test for deciding between these two alternatives.

30 It is important to bear in mind that we are here working in the domain of 'interlingual identifications' and thus are in a different counterfactual domain (Lawler and Selinker) than linguists who work in the domain of the 'ideal speaker-listener' (Chomsky, 1965). It seems to me that researchers in the psychology of second language learning are in the analogous position of the language teacher who, Chomsky (1966) admonishes, has the

burden of deciding what in linguistics and psychology is relevant to his needs.

Nevertheless, the linguistic status of ILs has still to be determined. One would like to know, for example, whether such things as transformations occur in IL grammars. Watkin (1970) asks whether the rules of IL are of the same general construction or shape as the rules for the same phenomena in the second language, 'or are they in a "recoded" form?' Watkin's data implies the same type of fossilization related to some similarity among rules of different ILs.

31 The surface domain considered was constituent concatenation after the verb. Sample results showed statistically significant parallel trends for NL (Hebrew) and IL (English) *Object* and *Time* constituents on the one hand and (direct) *Object* and *Adverb* (of degree) on the other. That is, whenever an *Object* constituent and a *Time* constituent occurred after the verb, the statistically dominant surface order was *Object-Time*, and not the reverse, both concerning NL responses, e.g. (9), and IL responses, e.g. (10);

> (9) raiti [et haseret haze] [lifney švuaim]
> 'I saw that movie two weeks ago'.
> (10) I met [Mrs Cosman] [today]

But whenever an *Object* constituent and an *Adverb* constituent occurred after the verb, the statistically dominant surface order was *Adverb-Object*, and not the reverse, both concerning NL responses, e.g. (11) and IL responses, e.g. (12);

> (11) ani ohev [mood] [sratim] 'I like movies very much'
> (12) I like [very much] [movies].

Importantly, these and all other experimental results were controlled informally by observing speakers of all ages over 12, from this interlingual situation, producing IL utterances in meaningful performance situations.

32 That is, when the responses concerned the topic 'subjects studied at school' there occurred an almost absolute trend toward both the NL (Hebrew) order *Place-Object* noun after the verb, e.g. (13), and toward the same IL (English) order of surface constituents, e.g. (14),

> (13) ani roca lilmod [bauniversita] [biologia]
> 'I want to study biology at the university'.
> (14) I will study [in the university] [biology]

But when the responses concerned topics such as the two other topics mentioned in the text, there occurred an almost absolute trend toward both the NL order *Object* noun *Place* after the verb, e.g. (15) and toward the same IL order of surface constituents, e.g. (16);

> (15) kaniti [et hašaon] [baranut]
> 'I bought the watch in the store'
> (16) I bought [my watch] [in Tel Aviv]

For further details, see Selinker (1969) sections 3.41 and 3.42.

33 The fact that Haggard is concerned with alternative units which are inclusive in larger units has no bearing on the issue under discussion in this section.

4

Approximative Systems of Foreign Language Learners*

WILLIAM NEMSER

Reprinted from IRAL, Vol. IX/2, May 1971, published by Julius Groos Verlag, Heidelberg.

1 Approximative systems

The language systems represented in a contact situation can be classified in accordance with their functions as follows:

1. The *target* language is that in which communication is being attempted; in the case of a learner it is the language he is learning, when he uses it.

2. The *source* language is that acting as a source of interference (deviations from the norm of the target language);[1] it is normally the learner's native language.

3. An *approximative* system is the deviant linguistic system actually employed by the learner attempting to utilize the target language. Such approximative systems vary in character in accordance with proficiency level; variation is also introduced by learning experience (including exposure to a target language script system), communication function, personal learning characteristics, etc.

For the sake of brevity, the following symbols will be employed throughout this paper:

* This paper represents the development of ideas formulated with Francis Juhasz while at Columbia University some years ago. John Lotz and William W. Gage of the Center for Applied Linguistics have contributed significantly to these ideas and to their presentation here without, however, incurring responsibility for defects in either. An earlier version was published in: *Studies 1*, The Jugoslav Serbo-Croatian English Contrastive Project, Zagreb, 1969, pp. 3 12.

L_T: Target Language
L_S: Source Language
L_a: An approximative system
$L_{a1 \ldots n}$: Indices referring to systems at successive stages of proficiency.

In identifying a specific type of L_a, the name of the L_S precedes that of the L_T: thus 'German-English' refers to an L_a typical of native speakers of German communicating imperfectly in English.

Our assumption is threefold:

1. Learner speech at a given time is the patterned product of a linguistic system, L_a, distinct from L_S and L_T and internally structured.

2. L_a's at successive stages of learning form an evolving series, $L_{a1 \ldots n}$, the earliest occurring when a learner first attempts to use L_T, the most advanced at the closest approach of L_a to L_T (merger, the achievement of perfect proficiency, is rare for adult learners).

3. In a given contact situation, the L_a's of learners at the same stage of proficiency roughly coincide, with major variations ascribable to differences in learning experience.

The speech of a learner, according to the assumption, is structurally organized, manifesting the order and cohesiveness of a system, although one frequently changing with atypical rapidity and subject to radical reorganization through the massive intrusion of new elements as learning proceeds. As such, learner speech should be studied not only by reference to L_S and L_T but in its own terms as well. From the point of view of the history of L_T, Weinreich was undoubtedly correct in assigning interference in the speech of bilinguals, which he likens to 'sand carried by a stream', to the *parole* of L_T along with other accidental and transient phenomena unincorporated by the community of L_T speakers within their communal language system.[2] However, from the point of view of the contact situation proper, to regard these same features, as the term interference implies, exclusively as intrusive L_S elements interrupting the normal flow of L_T—a kind of hiccough view of language contact —is less rewarding, following the hypothesis, than viewing them first in terms of the learner system to which they pertain.

2 Evidence for the systematic nature of the stages of foreign language acquisition

In presenting evidence for the reality and structural autonomy of these L_a's or approximative systems, it should be pointed out that language students, while of special interest here, represent a minority among L_a users. Moreover *learner systems* are by definition transient, while effective language teaching implies preventing, or postponing as long as possible, the formation of permanent intermediate systems and subsystems (deviant phonological and grammatical structures). Nevertheless, it is clear that evidence for L_a is abundantly present in the patterning of errors in the perception and production of a given target language by learners sharing the same native language. This regularity, in fact, forms a principal basis for the belief that a comparison of L_S and L_T provides information essential to pedagogic strategy. Such characteristics constitute the 'foreign accent' typical of learners as well as of other bilinguals sharing the same mother tongue, i.e. speakers of the same L_S attempting to communicate in a given L_T.

Stable varieties of L_a are found in *immigrant speech,* that is, the speech of long-time users of L_t who, often having attained considerable fluency in this language, have yet obviously reached a plateau in their learning.[3] Attested examples of such speech include the regular rendition by many veteran German-English speakers of the English initial /sw/ cluster as [šv], and of the velarized variant of English /l/ in post-vocalic position as a non-velarized phone (English [swɛl] 'swell'> German-English [švɛl]). Similarly many speakers of Hungarian-English regularly omit the plural marker in enumerative phrases (*three boy*) but overtly indicate contingency in both the apodosis and the protasis of conditional sentences (*If I would have gone I would have seen him*).

Moreover the speech of members of the same immigrant groups communicating in their own native language (here German or Hungarian) often reveals the systematic and widespread intrusion of elements of the dominant language of the area (here English), with the interchange of the roles of L_S and L_T and the creation of new L_a systems (English-German, English-Hungarian).[4]

Another subgroup of stable L_a ideolects is formed by *utility systems,* such specialized 'little' languages of limited semantic function, and requiring limited grammars and lexicons, as the systems often used by taxi-drivers, hotel-reservation clerks, bartenders and other groups with frequent but circumscribed requirements to communicate with foreigners.[5]

The term *learner pidgin* can be applied to systems of a related type often employed by language students who have attained fluency in the target language without mastery of its fundamentals, but have arrived at a stage in instruction where attention has largely shifted from form to content. Not only do teachers often concur in the use of this system, but even participate as users (the following exchanges were observed in a language classroom: Arabic-English speaker: *Same?* [i.e. *Are the two words pronounced in the same way?*], Teacher: *Same.;* Teacher: *Short answer* [i.e. *Use the short answer form.*]. *In conversation very good.*) This variety of L_a is also frequently used by other L_T speakers when communicating with non-natives and, apparently, even sometimes with other native speakers:

> 'Another brandy,' he said, pointing to his glass. The waiter who was in a hurry came over. 'Finished,' he said, speaking with that omission of syntax stupid people employ when talking to drunken people or foreigners. 'No more tonight. Close now.'[6]

Moreover these learner pidgins may be preserved in the language-types customarily designated as pidgins and creoles, historically L_a systems usually incorporating L_S grammatical elements and L_T lexical elements.

An argument for the structural independence of an L_a from the source and target systems is the frequent and systematic occurrence in non-native speech of elements not directly attributable to either L_S or L_T. In the phonology, intermediate phones are common (Hungarian subjects in an experimental study often rendered English /θ/, for example, as [fθ] or [sθ]).[7] Similarly, 'internal' interference resulting from the extension of the productive processes of L_T (such formations as *go-ed* are common in learner speech, as they are in child language), and pattern confusion (observed in a language classroom: Serbo-Croatian-English *What does Pat doing now?*) occurs frequently in the grammar.

More theoretically it can be argued that the demands of communication force the establishment of phonological, grammatical and lexical categories, and that the demands of economy force the imposition of the balance and order of a language system.

Finally, there has been at least one attempt to study an L_a variety directly.[8] Customary descriptive procedures were employed to characterize, in *sui generis* terms, the phonology of a native speaker of Hungarian, at an early stage in her learning of English, attempting to communicate in the latter language. Some fluctuation between categories attested to the transient nature of the organization (for example, two high front vowels, [i] and [i:], were sporadically distinguished, on the basis of length). However such fluctuation is, of course, also typical of categories in the process of change in normal language systems, and the analysis revealed a system exhibiting true internal coherence, with distinctive components from both English and Hungarian recombining to form phonological structures differing from those of either language (a mid-central vowel, for example, was opposed to a low-front vowel, representing a merger of E/ε/ and /æ/, on the basis of rounding). Observation of the same speaker's Hungarian English grammar disclosed an analogous tendency toward autonomous organization.

Moreover, there is some evidence that various evolutionary stages of L_a differ not only in amount but in *type* of interference (using 'interference' to cover both external and internal types). Earlier stages are apparently characterized by the extensive *underdifferentiation* (syncretism) of L_T phonological, grammatical and lexical categories, with the learner extending the distribution and (in the case of the grammar and lexicon) semantic domains of the limited number of formal elements he has acquired. Later stages are characterized by the addition, as interference types, of *reinterpretation* (Serbo-Croatian-English speakers allegedly often aspirate English tense stops in all positions, apparently phonemicizing a feature non-distinctive in English), *hypercorrection* (Spanish-English speakers often substitute [ŋ], which does not have phonemic status in Spanish, for /n/: English /sʌn/ 'sun' > Spanish-English [saŋ])[9] and *analogy (go-ed)*.

In addition to the atypical rapidity with which they often undergo structural changes, L_a's differ from normal languages in that L_a speakers do not usually form speech communities. Adult members of such communities normally model speech on that of other members of the same group; children, viewed as groups of speakers of child language at various stages of evolution, model their speech on both internal standards—the speech behavior of their peers— and external standards—the speech behavior of older children and adults (for such child learners of L_T, of course, there is no L_S);[10] L_a speakers, however, primarily select external standards, the speech of native speakers of L_T. Nevertheless, it is likely that L_a speakers frequently provide reinforcement for the speech behavior of each other (even resulting in the creation, in some instances, of such dialects or languages as the varieties of English used by numerous speakers in India),[11] and it is observable that they frequently communicate with each other more easily than with L_T speakers. Moreover, L_a features are sometimes disseminated among learners under special conditions (as was a trilled r substitute for the French uvular phoneme, reportedly, among one group of English-speaking learners at Middlebury College), are sometimes conventionalized in L_a (English /θ/ is regularly merged with /s/ in the instruction at certain schools in Germany), are sometimes transmitted between generations (the children of native speakers of Yiddish in New York, while native speakers of English appear to frequently adopt certain interference patterns from their parents' speech), and even become conventionalized in L_T (during one era in Hungary, some native speakers of Hungarian snobbishly replaced the Hungarian trilled r with the uvular variety of French to suggest prior knowledge of that language and hence higher social status; cf. also widely posited instances of substratum intrusion).

3 Reasons for studying L_a

1. Direct and systematic examination of learner speech has been largely neglected. Classroom teachers, while aware of general patterns in learner behavior and often taking them into account in their teaching, have rarely attempted comprehensive studies of these regularities within a linguistic framework. Contrastive analysis specialists, on the other hand, often primarily concerned with techniques for establishing inter-systemic correspondences, have been content for the most part to derive empirical support for their formulations from impressionistic observation and intuition. Investigation of L_a data would, therefore, yield as its first result new concrete information on learner behavior of high utility to the classroom teacher in the planning of pedagogic strategy.

2. Such investigation is also a prerequisite for the validation of both the strong and weak claims of the contrastive approach:[12]
   a. The strong claim states that learner behavior is predictable on the basis of a comparison of L_S and L_T. However problems immediately arising include: (i) different analyses: different predictions, (ii) predictions are often ambiguous, and (iii) the various levels of linguistic structure are interdependent, with

the result that predictions of phonic interference, for example, must take into account not only the phonologic systems of L_S and L_T but their morphophonemic, grammatical and lexical levels as well. Serious attempts to validate the theory have not been numerous, with investigations not infrequently presenting *ex post facto* reconstructions as evidence of predictive power. The few serious validation studies raise doubts about the tenability of the strong claim.

b. The weak claim of contrastive analysis is that of *accounting for* learner behavior. Even this limited claim proves difficult to support, however. For example, the frequent interpretation by Hungarian-English speakers of the final cluster of English *dogs* as [ks] can be explained as resulting from one, some, or all of the following factors: a) the non-occurrence in Hungarian of /gz/ in final position, b) orthography and the Hungarian phonemic rule requiring clusters uniform in voicing, c) the total unvoicing by some English speakers of final /z/, usually described as distinctively *lax* in English but voiced in Hungarian, and the uniform voicing rule, and d) Hungarian morphophonemic rules making the voicing of a final stem obstruent dependent on that of initial suffix obstruents other than /v/ /(hāz-bɔn/ /hās-tōl/),[13] with the Hungarian-English speakers, for one of the reasons mentioned above, having selected the English allomorph /s/ to represent the plural.

3. It can be shown that the direct examination of L_a is required as well by the suppositions of the contrastive approach itself. The approach is based on a general view of learning according to which prior learning affects subsequent learning, positively where the new skill coincides with one already mastered, negatively where they are opposed (positive and negative transfer). However, language structures, viewed as compendia of verbal skills, are not comparable in their entireties. Phonological elements sometimes have no counterpart in the opposed system (the clicks of certain Bantu languages cannot be related to English phonemic categories), cultural differences clearly often make this true of lexical elements as well, and grammatical categories, too, are often incommensurate. More significantly, however, application of the theory for purposes of predicting and elucidating learner behavior often depends on what can be called the 'blindingflash' fallacy—the supposition that L_S and L_T come into total contact—so far as overlap permits—from the

outset of learning, with L_S categories fusing with their L_T counterparts throughout the systems. Actually, of course, the learner's exposure to L_T is necessarily gradual. This fact entails a dilemma for contrastive analysis which can only be resolved by reference to L_a. At post-initial stages of language learning, the *prior* learning which conditions *subsequent* learning includes not only the learner's knowledge of L_S but his own recent experience in language acquisition—his knowledge of L_a—as well. He is no longer the pristine speaker of L_S assumed by dialinguistic analysis, but also the user of a more recently acquired system. Thus the precepts of contrastive analysis itself force the inclusion of reference to L_a data in the prediction and elucidation of his subsequent learning behavior.[14]

4. Finally L_a's merit examination in their own right, having interest for general linguistic theory comparable on the one hand to child language and on the other to the language of victims of certain types of speech disorder, as dependent systems forming evaluative gradations toward specific languages but falling outside the normal dialectical and stylistic scope of these languages.

4 Summary and conclusion

Evidence suggests that the speech behavior of language learners may be structurally organized, and that the contact situation should therefore be described not only by reference to the native and target languages of the learner (L_S and L_T), but by reference to a learner system (L_a) as well.

Investigation of such learner systems is crucial to the development of contrastive analysis theory and to its applications to language teaching. However, these systems also merit investigation in their own right through their implications for general linguistic theory.

In its present form, the contrastive approach seeks (a) to predict and account for learner behavior by reference to similarities and differences between L_S and L_T and in terms of these systems, and by this means (b) to indicate a strategy for language pedagogy. However, experimental and informal observation reveal serious limitations in the approach, in part because learner behavior cannot be exhaustively described without reference to L_a.

Theoretical and practical considerations therefore converge to suggest the direct and systematic examination of such learner speech, viewed within the general framework of the current theory. Such investigation would (a) provide attested information, of immediate utility in teaching and course development, on patterns of learning behavior for the principal structures of the target languages, (b) permit further assessment of the current suppositions of contrastive analysis, and (c) make possible a preliminary description of L_a, thus progressing toward a reformulated contrastive approach of greater sophistication.

An ultimate goal might be the reformulation of L_S and L_T descriptions in terms permitting the accurate projection of L_a throughout its successive stages in each contact situation. This goal remains in the distant future, however, and no present alternative exists to empirical investigation.

NOTES

1 Weinreich (1953, p. 1).

2 Weinreich, *op. cit.*, p. 11.

3 Such systems have not been extensively studied. For some comments on Swedish–English, Yiddish–English and several others, see Mencken, 1949, pp. 212–222.

4 See Haugen's monumental study, 1953; see also, for example, Macris, 1955, and Pap, 1949. Mencken, *op. cit.*, pp. 616–697, briefly exemplifies English interference in some twenty-eight languages as used by native speakers resident in the United States.

5 Little information has been collected on these systems. However, for two apparently successful attempts to construct such L_a systems (English–Russian; English–Mandarin) for specific, circumscribed communication requirements, see Rocklyn, 1965; and Garvey and Rocklyn, 1965.

6 Hemingway, 1953, p. 381.

7 Nemser, 1961, pp. 56–84.

8 Nemser and Juhasz, 1964, pp. 163–216.

9 See Marckwardt, 1946.

10 Other than earlier phases of their systems: see 3. 3 below.

11 See, for example, Kelkar, 1957.

12 Representative studies are found in Hammer and Rice, 1965.

13 See Lotz, 1966.

14 See Upshur, 1962.

5

Social Factors, Interlanguage, and Language Learning

JACK C RICHARDS

Reprinted from Language Learning, *Vol. 22, No. 2, 1972.*

An earlier version of this paper was read as a guest lecture at the Modern Language Center, Ontario Institute for Studies in Education, Toronto. For comments on the earlier version and encouragement to prepare a publishable version I am grateful to Larry Selinker, Elaine Tarone and Kim Oller (University of Washington, Seattle), David Lawton (Central Michigan University), and to Professor R. LePage (York University, England). Much that is said here is of course tentative, and I would be grateful for comments, suggestions, or additional data.

1 Introduction

A number of diverse contexts for second language learning are considered in this paper and the following questions asked: Under what conditions is standard English learned? What factors lead to the·development of non-standard varieties of English, such as immigrant English? What accounts for the divergence of local varieties of English such as Nigerian or Indian English from British or American norms? Under what circumstances is more marked language divergence likely to occur, such as is found in Creole settings? More generally the paper focuses on the choice of appropriate models for the analysis of second language data. An area of research is illustrated which encompasses both psycholinguistic and sociolinguistic dimensions. The concept of *Interlanguage* is proposed for the analysis of second language learning and illustration is drawn from the processes affecting language learning in the following contexts: immigrant language learning, indigenous minority varieties of English, pidgin and creole settings, local varieties of English, English as a foreign language.

2 Immigrant varieties of English

Despite the huge numbers of immigrants settled in the English-speaking world in the last century, relatively little is known about the learning of English by immigrants. The linguistic dimensions of immigrant assimilation have tended to arouse interest only in instances of unsuccessful adaptation. Some immigrant groups have developed functionally adequate but socially unaccepted or non-standard varieties of English, and these are the focus of analysis here. In isolating the generation of non-standard varieties of immigrant English we are separating the initial language learning problems confronting all immigrant groups, from those which persist and result in the development of distinctive non-standard varieties of English. Studies of immigrant communities in the initial stages of contact have referred to the emergence of particular dialects of English, such as Swedish English, Norwegian English, and German English, many of which have been transient and short lived (Haugen, 1953). We do not hear any longer of Norwegian English or German English as group phenomenon arousing educational concern. Yet Puerto Rican and Mexican-American English have not had the same history. How may we characterize these varieties of English and under what circumstances do they arise? To answer these questions we will consider both the social and the linguistic dimensions of immigrant English.

2.1 *The Social Dimension*

One of the best accounts of the general factors involved in the preservation of the immigrant's mother tongue, which may be used as a guide to assimilation into the majority language group, is given by Kloss, who emphasizes that the factors involved are so variegated that their interplay cannot be summarized by a single formula (Kloss, 1966). Clearly much is dependent on the pattern and area of settlement. Immigrants not inhabiting a compact area are less likely to develop non-standard dialects than those in a compact area. The fate of an individual immigrant arriving in an English-speaking city will provide data on how the individual acquires English, but this is of less general concern here than the fate of an interacting group of immigrants concentrated in a given place, where the outcome of the contact between the immigrant group and the dominant culture is not so much a result of *individual* solutions, depending on motivation, intelligence, perseverance, aptitude, learning strategies, personality, socialization etc., but a result of the social and economic possibilities made available for the group. Besides numerical strength and distribution, a number of other factors can affect immigrant assimilation. These have to do with educational level, cultural and linguistic similarity to the mainstream culture, color, race and other general factors which may determine the attitudes towards the majority group and vice versa.

The evolution of lasting non-standard varieties of a standard language is a consequence of the perception by the immigrant of the larger society, and a reflection of the degree to which the immigrant groups have been admitted into the mainstream of the dominant culture. Psychologists have been able to distinguish between instrumental motivation, where the dominant or new language is acquired primarily for such utilitarian purposes as getting a job, and integrative motivation, which demonstrates a desire for or the perceived possibility of integration with the dominant group. The former may lead to a functionally adequate but non-standard dialect of English. We can predict for example, the sort of English likely to be acquired by an immigrant who mixes exclusively with his own language group and who opens a food shop catering largely, but not exclusively, to that language group. He will probably learn first to reply to a limited set of questions in English, to manipulate a closed class of polite formulae, the vocabulary of some food items, and perhaps the language of simple financial transaction. Whether he goes on to learn standard English or develops a functionally adequate but non-standard personal dialect of English will depend on the degree of interaction and integration he achieves with the English-maintained societal structures. He may have very little control over the degree of interaction possible. If 100,000 such immigrants in similar situations reach only a minimum penetration of mainstream power structures, begin to perpetuate their semi-servile status, and begin to use English among themselves, the setting for the generation of an immigrant variety of English might be present.

Where the learning of English is not associated with societal penetration and upward mobility, but rather with occupational and economic subservience, we can expect language divergence to be the outcome of contact with standard English. As an illustration of the two extremes it may be useful to refer to the fate of German and Puerto Rican immigrants to America. A recent account of the fate of German immigrants to Texas emphasizes that the German immigrants there are not poverty stricken (Gilbert, 1971). They do not live in ghettoes. They suffer under no handicaps whatsoever. They thus learn English easily and well. Although a certain amount of German interference is present in their English, it results in no obvious social discrimination. The people of German descent are thus well-off and pursue the whole range of occupations open to Americans of purely Anglo background. The Puerto Ricans however arrived in New York at a time when economic patterns were already well established, hence the melting pot which they were invited to join was one which applied to the lower rather than the upper end of the social and economic spectrum (Hoffman, 1968). For those immigrants with limited access to social and economic channels the immigrant mother tongue becomes one marker of second-class citizenship; the other is the dialect of English generated and maintained as a consequence of these very same social limitations.

Immigrant varieties of English are the product of particular settings for language learning. There are said to be two levels of communication in society—the horizontal level, which operates among people of the same status—and the vertical level, which is predominantly downward (Hughes, 1970). In the case of non-standard immigrant English we are presumably dealing with the language of horizontal communication, and the contexts in which it occurs are those where there are few informal or friendship contacts with speakers of standard English and no intellectual or high culture networks in English. It may also become part of the expression of ethnic pride. It is a dialect resulting from low spending power, low social influence, and low political power. It reflects not individual limitations, such as inability to learn language, low intelligence, or poor cultural background, but rather the social limitations imposed on the immigrant community. Favorable reception of the immigrant group leads to temporary generation of an immigrant variety of English. This has been the case for many European immigrant groups in the United States (Fishman et al., 1966). Favorable conditions include fluidity of roles and statuses in the community. Unfavorable social conditions lead to maintenance and perpetuation of the immigrant dialect of English. The economic and social possibilities available for some immigrants do not make the learning of standard English either possible, desirable or even helpful. The non-linguistic dimension of the immigrants' task has been emphasized by Leibowitz. 'The issue is indeed a political one

Whether instruction is in English or the native language makes little difference; rather what is important are the opportunities that are thought available to the ethnic group themselves. . . . Educators have provided the most significant evidence to demonstrate this. Increasingly, they have studied the relationship between a pupil's motivation and performance in school to his perception of the society around him and the opportunities he believes await him there. . . . The crucial factor is not the relationship between the home and school, but between the minority group and the local society. Future reward in the form of acceptable occupational and social status keeps children in school. Thus factors such as whether a community is socially open or closed, caste-like or not, discriminatory or not, has restricted roles or non-restricted roles and statuses for its minority group segment, become as important as curriculum and other factors in the school itself, perhaps more important' (Leibowitz, 1970). The difficulties of some immigrant groups thus result from more than simple questions of language learning but depend on the type and degree of interaction and acceptance available in the community for the immigrant group.

2.2 *The Linguistic Dimension*

Having looked at the social background to immigrant varieties of English we may turn to the linguistic problems associated with the description of their particular form and characteristics. The simplest approach is to begin with the source language (L_S) and the target language (L_T) and to describe instances where the learner's speech differs from the target language as interference. This approach is inadequate, however, and obscures the nature of the processes involved. Nemser proposes a three part approach, adding the learner's approximative system as the intermediate stage between the source and target language. 'An approximative system is the deviant linguistic system actually employed by the learner attempting to utilize the target language. Such approximative systems vary in character in accordance with proficiency level; variation is also introduced by learning experience . . . communication function, personal learning characteristics etc. . . . Our assumption is threefold: (1) Learner speech at a given time is the patterned product of a linguistic system, L_a, distinct from L_S and L_T and internally structured. (2) L_a's at successive stages of learning from an evolving series, $L_{a_1 \ldots n}$, the earliest occurring when a learner first attempts to use L_T, the most advanced at the closest approach of L_a to L_T. . . .

(3) In a given contact situation, the L_a's of learners at the same stage of proficiency roughly coincide, with major variations ascribable to differences in learning experience' (Nemser, 1970, p. 116). Nemser proposes that learner speech should thus be studied in its own terms.

I propose to use Selinker's concept of *Interlanguage* to characterize these approximative systems, and to interpret immigrant varieties of English as interlanguages generated from the social circumstances under which English is acquired in particular settings. Selinker's definition of interlanguage focuses on the psycholinguistic processes presumed to contribute to interlanguage. 'If it can be experimentally demonstrated that fossilizable items, rules and subsystems which occur in interlanguage performance are a result of the native language then we are dealing with the process of *language transfer*; if these fossilizable items, rules and subsystems are a result of identifiable items in training procedures, then we are dealing with *transfer of training*; if they are a result of an identifiable approach by the learner to the material to be learned, then we are dealing with *strategies of second language learning*; if they are a result of an identifiable approach by the learner to communication with native speakers of the target language, then we are dealing with *strategies of communication*; and finally if they are the result of a clear *overgeneralization of target language*, then we are dealing with the *overgeneralization of linguistic materials*' (Selinker, 1971). These concepts are discussed and illustrated in Selinker, 1972 and Richards, 1971a.

In using this model as a framework for the analysis of immigrant varieties of English, we begin with the premise that the acquisition of a new language by an immigrant group is always a developmental creative process. In the case of a non-standard immigrant interlanguage we have to account for the generation of a subsystem of rules which are at the same time linguistic and social in origin. '... Within a large and stable bilingual community like the New York City Puerto Rican community, bilinguals interact and communicate with each other, using both languages far more frequently than they interact and communicate with members of the surrounding monolingual community. In such a community, speakers generate their own bilingual norms of correctness which may differ from the monolingual norms, particularly when there is a lack of reinforcement for these monolingual norms' (Ma and Herasimchuk, 1968).

These norms of immigrant English are illustrated by the speech samples given in *Bilingualism in the Barrio* (Fishman *et al.,* 1968). One subject for example, when asked to say where he did his shopping, replied:

No make any difference, but I like when I go because I don't have too many time for buy and the little time we buy have to go to someplace and I find everything there.

On being asked about trips to Puerto Rico, he gives:

I go there maybe about one and half and I find too many job for me. But I can't work over there if I go alone and I have the family here. I work I think 7 or 8 months in Puerto Rico . . .

The concept of interlanguage as applied to this data would lead to a focusing on it as the learner's 'approximative system', and to the isolation of examples of language transfer, strategies of communication, strategies of learning, transfer of training, and over-generalization. Language transfer is illustrated in the second sentence, which closely follows the structure of Puerto Rican Spanish. In the first example however the syntax used cannot be exclusively attributed to the effect of language transfer, since translating the English back into Spanish does not render the sentence directly into Puerto Rican Spanish. To further characterize the interlingual features of the first sentence, we need to refer to the concepts of communication and learning strategies, and to overgeneralization.

Under communication strategies we may characterize interlingual features derived from the fact that heavy communication demands may be made on the second language, forcing the learner to mould what he has assimilated of the language into a means of saying what he wants to say, or of getting done what he wants to get done. The learner, isolated from close interaction with speakers of the target language, may 'simplify' the syntax of the language in an effort to make the language an instrument of his own intentions. Such strategies affect both first and second language performance in English. A child, not possessing the rule for nominalization in English, gave as a definition for *fence*:

to keep the cow . . . don't go out of the field.[1]

This process is seen in many of the constructions produced by second language learners (Richards, 1971b). Referring to a study by Coulter (Coulter, 1968), Selinker notes: 'Coulter reports systematic errors occurring in the English interlanguage performance of two elderly Russian speakers of English, due to . . . a tendency on the part of second language learners to avoid grammatical formatives such as articles, plural forms, and past tense forms. . . . Coulter attributes it to a communication strategy due to the past experience of the speaker, which has shown him that if he thinks about grammatical processes while attempting to express in English meanings he already has, then his speech will be hesitant and disconnected, leading native speakers to be impatient with him . . . this strategy of second language communication seemed to dictate to these speakers of English that a form such as the English plural was not necessary for the kind of English they used.' (Selinker, 1972.)

Strategies of learning and communication refer to the language contact phenomenon, whereby due to the circumstances of learning and the uses required of English, the learner generates a grammar in which many of the marked-unmarked distinctions of the target language are removed, where inflected forms tend to be replaced by uninflected forms, and where preposition, auxiliary and article usage appears to be simplified. Simplification is one way in which speakers of different languages can make a new language easier to learn and use. Ferguson emphasizes the theoretical importance of such processes, and notes that '. . . many, perhaps all speech communities have registers of a special kind for use with people who are regarded for one reason or another as unable to understand the normal speech of the community (e.g. babies, foreigners, deaf people). These forms of speech are generally felt by their users to be simplified versions of the language, hence easier to understand, and they are regarded as imitation of the way the person addressed uses the language himself. . . . The usual outcome of the use of foreigner talk is that one side or the other acquires an adequate command of the other's language and the foreigner talk is used in talking to, reporting on, or ridiculing people who have not yet acquired adequate command of the language. *If the communication context is appropriate however, this foreigner talk may serve as an incipient pidgin and become a more widely used form of speech*' (Ferguson, 1971) (italics added).

In addition to these processes, overgeneralization is frequently observable in interlingual speech. Overgeneralization of target language rules is seen in the sentence *have to go to someplace* (above) where previous experience of *infinitive + to + adverb* is overgeneralized to an inappropriate context. Overgeneralization as a feature of interlingual speech is extensively illustrated in Richards 1971a and 1971b.

In describing immigrant interlanguage, important questions will arise as to the degree to which norms actually exist, since there is always a cline from minimum to full proficiency in English. Writing of *Cocoliche,* an immigrant interlanguage once spoken extensively by Italian immigrants in Argentina, Whinnom notes that the interlanguage was completely unstable in given individuals, since there was almost invariably continuing improvement in learning the target language, and that acquisition of lexical, phonological and syntactic items must have been subject to chance, so that the speech of any two individuals was never identical. 'Nevertheless, the system as a whole, however ephemeral in given individuals, and however broad a series of spectra it encompassed, was fairly clearly *predictable,* and was continually renewed in recognizable form from year to year and from generation of immigrant to generation of immigrant' (Whinnom, in Hymes, 1971, p. 98). In analysing such interlanguages, language transfer, overgeneralization, strategies of learning and communication, and transfer of training (see below) would appear to account for the basic processes involved, and allow for the analysis of language learning in terms of the social conditions, under which learning and communication takes place.

3 Indigenous-minority Varieties of English

In examining the social and linguistic dimensions of immigrant English, we have seen that the size of the immigrant group and their characteristics on dimensions of status, power, mobility, prestige and wealth, can influence the variety of English acquired. All language learning, whether the child learning his mother tongue, or an adult acquiring a second language, proceeds in terms of approximative systems, but under certain conditions in second language learning this interlingual stage may become the end point in the learning process, taking on a new role in in-group communication and hence in ethnic identity and solidarity. The conditions under which such non-standard interlanguages are the outcome of culture/language contact are present to a greater or lesser extent in a number of related situations. The language, educational and economic problems of many Mexican-Americans in the western and southern United States are well known, as well as the particular problems of certain American and Canadian Indian groups. Ornstein analyses Spanish and Indian language questions, and notes the varying and often clashing social systems which have contributed to mother tongue maintenance in the southwest. Ornstein suggests that an interlingual Hispano-Spanish and probably a Hispano-Anglo-Indian interlanguage exist in certain areas of the southwest. Among the forms of English he includes in his taxonomy are Spanish-Indian English pidgin, Spanish-English border pidgin, other Spanish-English pidgins, occupational English and teenage English (Ornstein, in Perren and Trim, 1971, p. 87).

I should like to isolate for consideration here however the varieties of English which result from contact between standard English (i.e. the English of the dominant economic, social and cultural group) and culturally displaced and economically underprivileged indigenous minorities in a number of countries. Evidently a decision to isolate, say, North-American Indian groups for separate consideration and the classification of Mexican American English as an immigrant variety, depends on whether one wishes to emphasize sociological, historical, or linguistic characteristics. The language performances reported for certain American and Canadian Indian and Eskimo groups, for Australian Aboriginals, and for some rural New Zealand Maoris, suggest sufficient historical, sociological and interlingual similarity to justify their inclusion here. Linguistically and socially, we are dealing with the same phenomenon isolated as operating in the immigrant language setting—the development of an interlanguage generated from the limited opportunities for social and economic advancement often associated with membership of an indigenous minority group. Typical descriptions write of loss of or decreasing fluency in the native language, and an inadequate command of English, and local terminologies have evolved for the particular dialects of English encountered: Cree English, Pine Ridge English, Dormitory English, Aboriginal English, Maori English and so on (Darnell, 1971, Wax *et al.,* 1964, Dubin, 1970, Alford, 1970, Benton, 1964). Regretfully, there are virtually no adequate or even partial descriptions of any of these dialects. The closest I know of to an account of such a dialect is that given by Benton for the English of certain rural New Zealand Maoris (Benton, 1964).

Traditionally the so-called 'broken speech' of many children from these cultural groups was attributed to poor learning backgrounds, such as bad speech patterns in the home, lack of adequate English reading materials, limited general experience together with self-consciousness resulting from poor language control. Cultural deprivation was seen as the key to poor language development. Of course failure in the school means alienation from the school and the early drop-out levels reported for many native children reflect an early awareness by the child of the school's non-acceptance of his culture and its values (Ashton-Warner, 1963). The school's failure, rationalized as the child's failure, generated such concepts as cultural deprivation, restricted language development, and even cognitive deficiency, all of which are symptomatic of analysis that fails to recognize the real ingredients of the child's experience.

Recently, emphasis has been placed on the inter-dependence of social and linguistic variables. Plumer points out that 'the relation between knowing English and the ability to perform in school is clearly much more vital and complex for these groups but the general point of view is the same. If they see themselves locked out of society anyway, then their motivation to learn English will be understandably low, especially if in so doing they risk cutting themselves off from associations they already have, namely their peers and families.' (Plumer, 1970, p. 270.) Wax et al. describe the progressive withdrawal of Sioux Indian children from the white environment represented by the school. They refer to the existence of Pine Ridge English, and point out that few Indian children are fluent in the English of the classroom (Wax et al., 1964). Darnell describes an Indian community in Alberta, Canada, and the interaction between Cree and English. 'Interference of Cree with the learning of English is too simple a model to account for the actual behaviour of speakers. English mistakes cannot be accounted for directly by attributing them to differences between the structures of the two languages. Rather it is necessary to define the linguistic repertoire of Calling Lake in terms of at least four, not merely two languages.' (Darnell, 1971.) She refers to Standard English, Cree English, anglicized Cree and traditional Cree.

Recent work by Philips highlights the role played by conflicting learning styles and behavioral expectancies between the Indian child's home environment and the school, which explain his reluctance to participate in many normal school activities (Philips, 1970). Benton notes the role of the non-standard dialect as an instrument of self and group identification and of social perception. 'While the type of language spoken by children as reflected in their performance on reliable verbal tests, is often a guide to their likely educational performance, it may be only one of several factors which retard both the growth of language ability itself, and general scholastic achievement. Ethnic differences also play an important part. Very often children from a minority or low status ethnic group may feel less able to control their own destiny than children from a dominant group. They may find it more difficult to work with a teacher whose ethnic background and general outlook is different from their own, either because they feel less secure with someone in whom they can find no point of common identity, or simply because they do not know how to communicate with this stranger. Many children consciously relate their mode of English speech to their ethnic identity. One teacher reported that a Maori child had told her ' "Maoris say *Who's your name,* so that's what I say". Maori English is often an important sign of group membership and a source of security for these children' (Benton, 1964, p. 93).

The notion of interlanguage is again basic for a description of these dialects of English, which manifest (a) rules which are linguistic in origin, derivable from the mother tongue and from limited exposure to the target language and (b) rules which are social in origin, derived from what we have broadly referred to as communication and learning strategies. Many of the characteristics of these dialects stem historically from the limited functions required of English in the early stages of contact between the indigenous and colonizing groups. Initial uses of English would have been mainly in non-prestige domains, such as trading, and these dialects are characterized by the same structural and morphological simplification observable in immigrant speech. Examples from Benton's Maori English data are:

'Yesterday we going by walk. I shoot one deer and the other deers running away and I saw another deer up on the hill.'
'All her friends going up to her place.'
'She went down to her Nanny's and see if her mother was there.'

Other examples from Benton illustrate features historically derived from limited exposure to English, fossilized through lack of reinforcement from native speakers. For example, *by walk* (from *by foot*); preposition overgeneralizations such as *on their car, we ate dinner on the table*; features derived from transfer of grammatical features of Maori are also noted: *Who's his name?* and absence of the copula: *They in bed*—though copula omission, as Ferguson suggests, may be related to language simplification in certain types of language contact situations. That the distinguishing features of such a dialect serve as signs of group membership and solidarity is illustrated by the use of *you fellows* among rural Maoris, which is a solidarity and 'mateship' marker, though historically derivable according to Benton, from an attempt to parallel a singular/plural *you* distinction in Maori.

The following samples of aboriginal English from Australia suggest that this dialect is closer to the 'incipient pidgin' end of the cline of bilingualism, reflecting sharper social and economic segregation of Australian Aboriginals than for comparable groups elsewhere. As well as omitting certain structures (verbs, auxiliaries, plural s and the copula), constructions such as the following are observed:

'He bin go bump in you.'
'We bin give you a lot of shell, eh?'
'He big one, eh?'
'Ufla (we) got tee vee.'
'You know ufla (our) dog name?'
'Youfla (you) can have one.'
'Oh look at crocodile-la.'
'Look here-la. Him find this-la.'
'You mook mine-la.'   (Alford, 1970).

In studying the history of Cree English, Pine Ridge English, Dormitory English and so on, it may be possible to use the framework proposed by Fishman for unstable bilingual societies, where language domain separation gradually disappears (Fishman, 1967). In the initial stages of contact between the native community and the colonizing group, domain separation of languages obtains, and English is required in certain limited roles and capacities that are not conducive to the acquisition of a standard form of it (Leachman and Hall, 1955). These are the conditions for the generation of a pidgin or a non-standard form of English characterized by structural and morphological simplification and by communication and learning strategies and interference. As domain separation in language use gradually disappears, English becomes an alternative to the mother tongue, especially in family and friendship domains. The non-standard form of English now has functions related to intimacy, solidarity, spontaneity and informality. The standard language, encountered in the school and through contact with outsiders, has formal functions, thus the characteristics of a diglossic setting may obtain where complementary values L(low) and H(high) come to be realized in different varieties of English. This would appear to apply to some members of the Cree community described by Darnell and is found with some monolingual Maoris, where the frequency of Maori English features increases according to the appropriateness of the domain. Features attributable to interlanguage processes can thus achieve stabilization through identification with ethnic roles.

More detailed studies however are needed of the native communities sharing these cultural, economic, social and linguistic features, to determine the degree to which interlanguage features in non-standard dialects are related to the social, economic and political status of the community.

4 Pidginization and Creolization

We have seen that certain non-standard varieties of English may be viewed as interlanguages derived from particular patterns of social interaction. Hymes suggests that the extremes to which social factors can go in shaping the transmission and use of language is seen in the processes of pidginization and creolization (Hymes, 1971, p. 5). The concept of pidgin and creole languages owes much to Hall's distinction between a pidgin as a *lingua franca* spoken as a second language, and a creole as a first language which has developed out of an original pidgin and expanded its resources and functions through becoming the mother tongue of a speech community (Hall, 1966). Not all linguists, however, see a pidgin as a necessary base for a creole. Mafeni notes that in some cases a pidgin may be a *lingua franca* for some members of the community and a mother tongue for others, which is the case for the English-based pidgin spoken in Nigeria, for Krio in Sierra Leone, and of pidgin English in parts of the Cameroon Republic (Mafeni, 1971).

For our present purposes we will define a pidgin as an interlanguage arising as a medium of communication between speakers of different languages, characterized by grammatical structure and lexical content originating in differing sources, by unintelligibility to speakers of the source languages and by stability. A creole is a similarly derived language spoken as a mother tongue.

English based creoles are found in such areas as the Bahamas, Jamaica, Barbados, Trinidad, the English-speaking Windward and Leeward islands, in Guyana and Belize in South America, and in Sierra Leone and the Cameroons in West Africa (De Camp, 1968, Hymes, 1971). In many settings an internationally acceptable standard variety of English is the official language, but the majority of the population speak an English-based creole for the normal purposes of communication. Stewart suggests that in creole settings one tends to find monolingual creole speakers, monolingual standard speakers, and bilinguals, each of the languages having particular functional distributions in the national communication network and being associated with quite different sets of attitudes about their appropriateness (Stewart, 1962). In describing the Jamaican situation, Craig proposes a model with a creole component, an interlanguage, and the standard local variety of English. He uses the interlanguage concept to describe the area between the creole and the standard which is the end point for the majority of young people in Jamaica (Craig, n.d.). When the population is given educational, economic, and social opportunities the creole thus loses its distinctive features and becomes more like the standard. The future history of the creole hence 'depends on the social status of the creole *vis-à-vis* the standard, and the variability of the language and the culture' (De Camp, 1968). Cave gives details of this interlingual continuum in a creole setting (Guyana), the spectrum of speech varieties he illustrates ranging from that used by the aged East-Indian grandmother on a sugar estate, to that used by the educated middle class urban dweller, to that of the speaker of RP at the university (Cave, 1970).

	Form	Used by
1	/aɪ təold hɪm/	Britons and a small number of persons in higher administrative posts imitating white talk for social reasons
2	/aɪ to:ld hɪm/	Important middle class in administrative positions in government and commerce and also professional men
3	/aɪ to:l ɪm/	Ordinary middle class such as clerks, commercial employees, and teachers who have had secondary education
4	/aɪ tɛl ɪm/	Careful speech of non-clerical employees, shop assistants, hairdressers, who have had primary but no or negligible secondary education
5	/a tɛl ɪm/	Alternative for 4
6	/aɪ tɛl ɪ/	Relaxed form of 4
7	/a tɛl ɪ/	Relaxed form of 5
8	/mɪ tɛl ɪ/	Rural laboring class—tradesmen, servants, carters, etc.—who have had probably a primary

education but are often underschooled, semi-
literate and sometimes illiterate

9 /mɪ tɛl æm/ Older generation of East-Indian laboring class
with no schooling.

Pidgin, creole and post-creole phenomena pose typological
questions and more general questions as to the circumstances under
which languages reduce and expand in structure and lexical resources. What factors account for the intelligibility of the immigrant
interlanguage as opposed to the evolution of a new linguistic code
in the case of a creole? Are the processes of language adaptation and
creative generation seen in pidginization similar to the processes of
interlingual generation in other language learning contexts?

One of the earliest to recognize that non-standard forms of English
and English-based creoles should be related to factors in the social
environment, rather than attributed to individual limitations, such
as low intelligence, sloppiness, laziness, etc., was Reinecke, who
wrote a sociolinguistic history of Hawaiian creole in the 30's, under
the influence of Park's sociological account of dialect and language
change (Reinecke, 1969, Park, 1930). Reinecke emphasizes that most
creoles have in common the fact that they are derived from situations
where an imported laboring and indentured servile class were under
the subjection of European masters. The difference between the
integratively motivated immigrant and the plantation worker is that
'the immigrant comes to a country having the ideal of assimilation
of the various immigrant stocks into a fused new nationality ... the
immigrant is usually of the same race and culture. The plantation
laborer is of a different race and culture from his master. He is
typically held in a servile or semi-servile economic and political
status, and is at any rate, completely dependent upon his master.'
(Reinecke, 1969.)

Reinecke's thesis is that creoles are the result, not merely of
linguistic processes, but of the interplay between language, and
economic, social, educational and political factors, deriving from
what we have called 'communication strategies'. The communication structure of a plantation is an important factor, since the plantation environment furnished neither the opportunity nor environment
to learn standard English. The disproportion between English and
non-English-speaking groups resulted in limited interaction networks with native speakers. The division between creole speakers
and standard speakers was a consequence of the deliberately

maintained servile or semi-servile economic status for the laborers, which afforded them little chance to rise into the middle class.

The degree and nature of contact with the upper language differs in the creole setting from that of the immigrant and indigenous minority examples we have looked at. The immigrant and native interlanguages are characterized by settings where the target language dominates, leading to continued opportunity for the learning of English. Complete social assimilation is theoretically possible whereas in the pidgin setting, English was the language of a resident or transient minority who were socially inaccessible, hence the target language was not considered as a model for learning. Occupational, racial and social stratification, the powerlessness and restricted mobility of the slaves or laborers, meant that there was no solidarity between speakers and addressees, and no suggestion that they were to become a single community. The relative presence of these factors in the other learning contexts we have considered leads to interlingual generation which remains however, intelligible to speakers of English (Mintz, 1971, Grimshaw, 1971).

4.1 *Problems of description*

Our basis for the analysis of immigrant and indigenous inter-languages has been the concept of interlanguage, the learner's approximative system, characterized by transfer, transfer of training, strategies of communication and learning and over-generalization. Related concepts have been made use of by creolists in their work, though we lack a complete illustration of the process of creolization due to a relative lack of first hand data. The process of linguistic adaptation as a product of language contact which is the basis of pidginization and creolization, has however been illustrated from second language learning examples by a number of linguists interested in the explanation of creolization. Samarin illustrates what we have referred to as communication and learning strategies in discussing the grammatical adaptation and reduction seen in creoles, drawing comparative examples from second language learning (Samarin, 1971). Whinnom illustrates how certain essential features of pidgin—simplification, and impoverishment in terms of the source languages—could come about if a German and English schoolboy were forced to use French as a medium of communication in a context where no other models for French were available (Whinnom, 1971). Cassidy looks at contextual needs in the learning situation and the use of linguistic adaptation to meet these needs

(Cassidy, 1971). The needs for grammatical change and lexical borrowing are thus related to the social needs for language. Problems of process description are heightened however by the very nature of most creole settings.

Settings where creoles exist in a clearly defined diglossic relation to a status language would presumably allow for a description of learning according to the separate contexts in which each language operates. Speakers themselves however cannot be so clearly compartmentalized. LePage observes that the term interference may be appropriate to describe certain elements of a foreign language learning setting, where the L1 and L2 represent the languages of two sociologically and psychologically distinct speech communities, such as the learning of English in France (LePage, 1968). In many creole settings, as in the other interlingual cases we have looked at, there is no such clear cut dividing line between L1 and L2. If the child's *native language* is indeed an interlanguage derived from exposure to creole and standard English, problems arise in deciding what is known and what is unknown, since unlike the foreign language setting, increased knowledge of standard English adds to the learner's *native language repertoire,* rather than forming a new independent linguistic code. Linguistic competence in such cases cannot be described by reference to the abstract representation of the corporate rules of the speech community but must be seen as the rules governing individual interaction at a variety of social levels, some of these rules belonging to what linguists call L1 and others to L2. There is, however, no homogenous and clearly defined group speaking only either L1 or L2 (Lawton, 1964). Likewise the distinction between standard and non-standard English cannot be unequivocally correlated with the absence or presence of particular speech forms, since individual speakers vary according to the distance they have moved from one norm to another. The speech communities involved are not independent sociologically, culturally, or linguistically. There is no sharp break in social communication but a series of approximations which are represented by successive interlanguages generated according to the degree of social mobility achieved.

The complex and little understood process of pidginization and the related creole and post-creole interlingual continuum hence suggest a field of research which can both illuminate and be illuminated by the study of second language learning. While the social conditions characteristic of pidgin and creole settings are not those of typical language contact situations, our understanding of inter-language processes will surely be clarified by the expanding field of creole studies, illuminating the factors involved both in the learning of a standard language and the dimensions that need to be accounted for in analysing the development of interlingual varieties of English. Typological description of the different settings involved and detailed study of interlanguage processes in contact situations should enable us to predict in instances where English comes in contact with another language, whether the outcome will be a standard form of English, a non-standard form, or a new English-based language.

5 Local Varieties of English

The interlanguages we have looked at so far reflect differing degrees of social, economic and political penetration of societal structures, these structures being controlled by native speakers of the standard language. Another related phenomenon must be considered in reference to the generation of different dialects of English or of English-based languages—the situation where these societal struc-tures are maintained by non-native speakers of English. This is the phenomenon associated with countries where English is not spoken natively but is widely used as a medium of instruction and of official and informal communication. It is the case of English as a second language in multilingual areas such as Commonwealth Africa, India, Pakistan, Malaysia, the Philippines, Fiji and so on. In areas where English is widely used outside of native-speaking environments, local varieties of English have developed; Filipino English, Educated Nigerian English, Indian English etc. We do not have this phenomenon inside a political area where English is widely spoken natively. Thus we do not have 'French-Canadian English' as an alternative to Canadian English. Deviations between French-Canadians' use of English and Canadian English are always con-sidered idiosyncratic, just as the immigrant varieties of English are said to be characterized by errors or by poor learning of English. But the educated Nigerian's or Indian's use of English, though it differs from British or American English, is regarded as a standard, acceptable way of speaking.

In these countries English serves a variety of formal and informal uses (Allen Jones, 1968, Brosnahan, 1963, Fishman *et al.,* 1966, Hunt, 1966, Laver, 1970, Prator, 1968, Spencer, 1971). It may be used often or rarely, but no one has recourse to English for all his language needs. It is reserved for use with specific individuals in a narrowly restricted and clearly defined range of situations. In many of these countries English is the language of commerce, law, politics, administration, education, and of culture at all levels above the local. It exists alongside a complex of local languages, with English functioning as an important auxiliary and sometimes national language. It is invariably learned after the mother tongue in the somewhat artificial environment of the school, consequently it is not often the language of intimacy. It has few emotional connotations. It is largely an urban phenomenon, knowledge of English being correlated with distance from an urban centre. It has the important role too, in many settings, of being the key to social mobility. In West Africa for example, it is through English that an individual breaks the bonds of West African traditional life and enters into some kind of relationship with the westernized sectors of society (Spencer, 1971).

In such settings the concept of interlanguage can be used to describe the processes by which local varieties of English have emerged in many parts of the world. Kachru suggests that the process of Asianization of English in those areas where English functions as a second language 'supplies a rich data for language contact study in a cross-cultural and multilingual context . . . and raises many typologically interesting theoretical and methodological problems about the new Englishes which have developed from the L1 (mother tongue) varieties of English' (Kachru, 1969). Similar problems of description arise in some settings as exist in creole areas, since in any area where English is a second language we find a range of local varieties of English varying from an upper level 'intellectual' to a lower level 'market' English. At the lower end we may find a pidgin or an English-based creole, hence the Caribbean examples discussed above become special instances of the general trends noted here.

Kachru writes of the cline of bilingualism in India and defines three measuring points—a zero point, a central and an upper (ambilingual) point. He defines the zero point as competence in some very restricted domain such as counting. African examples would be the market woman whose English is limited to *customer buy here; my friend buy from me; look tomatoes; what of oranges; Madam I have good pampaw O!* (Spencer, 1971, p. 37). In the Philippines this is presumably the level of the 'halo-halo' (mix-mix) speech (Llamzon, 1969). There is no 'rule-governed creativity' in English. A minimal knowledge in Indian usage is the register of postmen, travel guides and bearers. The central point, in India, is the register of the law courts, administration, and of a large number of civil servants and teachers who learn English as their major subject of study and who are able to make use of English effectively in those restricted fields where English is used in India. The extent to which English is required in prestige settings as opposed to purely functional settings is important as a standardizing factor in these countries, as it is of course in the other contexts we have considered. English trade pidgins represent the effects of purely utilitarian roles for English, and trade or market English likewise represents limited functions for English, where it is not needed as an instrument to manipulate social behavior or the speaker's prestige. The upper level in Indian usage Kachru defines as the language of those who are able to use English effectively for social control in all those social activities in which English is used in India. In other settings the upper level may be defined by the educated uses of government and government officials, the middle level as that which might be heard in and around the secondary school, and the lower level as out-of-school uses. In West Africa the informal out-of-school language may be a local pidgin. There is of course much variety from one country to another but the overall pattern of a cline of bilingualism with the local standard at the upper level (Standard Filipino, Educated Nigerian etc.) is general. There thus appear to be quite distinct feelings of appropriateness in particular contexts for the different levels of English usage, as there are in creole settings for the appropriate use of creole or English. Ure notes that in Ghana the kind of English that is used as a *lingua franca* in the market places is not likely to be used in the classroom, and likewise no one is likely to use classroom English in the market (Ure, 1968).

Studies of the local varieties of English suggest the insufficiency of the concept of *interference,* and confirm the usefulness of an approach which includes interference alongside such notions as communication strategy, transfer of training, overgeneralization, and strategy of learning. Kirk-Greene, writing of African varieties, suggests the need for study of the social role of language in the second language setting: 'Only by understanding both the structure of the first language and the method by which English is acquired as well as the purposes for which it is used can we account for the deviant forms in bilingual usage.' (Kirk-Greene, 1971, p. 61.) Halliday suggests of the local varieties 'their grammar remains that of standard English, with few important variations; their lexis too differs little from normal usage; but the accent is noticeably and identifiably local' (Halliday, 1968). He is of course writing about the upper end of the cline of bilingualism, but his description needs modification. Kachru makes a useful distinction between *deviations* and *mistakes,* a distinction which reflects an interrelating of socio-cultural and linguistic factors in the analysis of local dialects of English. He thus distinguishes between *mistakes* which are outside of the linguistic code of English, and which are consequently not part of the English code of speakers of educated Indian English, and *deviations* which can be explained in terms of the socio-cultural context in which English functions. A mistake in Indian English would thus be *He can to speaks* for example, but *this all* as opposed to *all this* is part of the English code of educated Indian speakers. In Nigerian English *He go work* is not representative of the level of usage in English language newspapers, but sentences like *All of the equipments arrived,* and terms like *motor park* for *parking lot* represent the local standard (Walsh, 1967). Of Indian English Kachru notes that 'the linguistic implications of such acculturation of Indian English are that the more culture-bound it becomes the more *distance* is created between Indian English and other varieties of English. This is well illustrated by the extended domain of the kinship terms of the natively used varieties of English in Indian English, or by contextually-determined Indianisms which are deviant as they function in those contextual units of India which are absent in British culture . . . the distance between the natively used varieties of English and Indian English cannot be explained only by comparative studies of phonology and grammar. The deviations are an outcome of the Indianization of English which has gradually made Indian English culture-bound in the socio-cultural setting of India. The phonological and grammatical deviations are only a part of this Indianization.' (Kachru, 1965, p. 408.)

All of the central processes of interlanguage can be seen in local varieties of English. While we do lack detailed descriptions of any of these dialects, and do not have rigid criteria by which interlingual features can be identified the following examples are representative. In general the concept of language transfer may be used to character-ize geographically defined varieties of English as a second language, such as differences between the pronunciation of English in different parts of Nigeria or the Philippines, of differences between mother tongue based idioms in Filipino and Indian English. Differences between standard Nigerian and regional Nigerian Englishes are seen in the contrast between Nigerian English and Yoruba, Ibo, or Hausa English. Examples of mother tongue transfer in standard Filipino would be:

'I will pass by for you at 4' (*for* I will call for you).
'How are you today? Fine. How do you do to?'
'Close the light/open the light' (*for* turn off/on the light).
'Go down the bus' (*for* Get off the bus).
'to lie on bed' (*for* to lie in bed)   (Llamzon, 1969).

Examples of this sort of mother tongue/local-variety-of-English relationship can be found in many settings where English is a second language. Many of the grammatical characteristics of local usage however must be seen as the results of overgeneralization or rule simplification and redundancy reduction etc. Examples would be the extension of *isn't it* as a question tag in *Your brother was on holiday isn't it,* and such Indianisms as:

'I am doing it since six months'.
'It is done' (*for* it has been done).
'When I will come' (*for* when I come).
'If I will come' (*for* If I come).
'for doing' (*for* to + verb) (*e.g.* imprisonment for improving his character).

These reflect general tendencies observable in the acquisition of a second language, and I have described them elsewhere in terms of *interlingual interference* (Richards, 1971a), that is, as English-based subsystems, derived not from the mother tongue but from the way English is learned and taught.

Many other characteristics of local varieties of English reflect assimilation of English to the cultural mores of the country. Kachru describes these in terms of transfer, collocation-extension, collocation-innovation, and register-range extension, and gives many examples from the Indian setting. All these factors operate to make English part of the socio-cultural structure of the country, hence it is not surprising that those who would use an overseas standard instead of the local standard are regarded as affected and artificial and subjected to ridicule and criticism.

The evolution of local varieties of English is thus an illustration of the adaptation of an overseas variety of English to meet the requirement that a second language in use as a medium of both formal and informal communication and not native to a country, should be capable of expressing the socio-cultural reality of that country. Some of this reality is expressed through modification of the phonological and grammatical system of standard overseas English and description of this modification in terms of the processes of interlanguage illustrates how a second language reflects the contexts in which it is learned and used. The generation of new lexical and grammatical extensions to either reduce some of the unnecessary complexities of English or to accommodate some areas of the local culture which cannot be covered by existing uses of English, are reflections of this interlingual creativity.

6 English as a Foreign Language

The final context I wish to consider for the study of interlanguage phenomena is the learning of English in countries where English is studied as a foreign language in formal settings (such as the school), and where English is not normally a language of instruction but simply a branch of study. English in Japan, France, Indonesia, Russia and so on, is a purely cultural object of study (though it may serve the country's economic plans) and is not involved in societal functions. What are the differences between the learning of English in these settings and in areas where English is a viable second language? There are basic motivational differences. In a foreign language setting there is always an effort to acquire an overseas standard form of English, and not some local form of English. Hence Japanese, Russians, Germans etc. are bilingual in the popular sense when they cannot be distinguished from native speakers of English by their uses of the language, though no such demands are made in the case of English as a second language, where local varieties are accepted as standards. These motivational differences are reflected in the course books in use in foreign language and second language settings. In foreign language contexts, the English lesson is the occasion to bring a sample of American or British life into the classroom, and the lessons are about life and people in English-speaking countries. In second language contexts the content of the school course is usually local, and learners begin to learn English without necessarily knowing or caring what life is like in England or America.

These different learning goals influence the nature of the learner's interlanguage. In the foreign language setting all differences between the learner's use of English and overseas English are *mistakes* or signs of incomplete learning. There is no room here for the concept of *deviancy,* since the socio-cultural basis for deviancy does not exist in the foreign language setting. The learner is generally not satisfied until he has 'eradicated' traces of his foreign accent, though for practical purposes, this may not be possible due to the limited time available in the school course. Limitations to the acquisition of standard English in the foreign language setting are hence not socially imposed limitations, which we encountered with the analysis of domestic dialects; in the foreign language setting limitations are rather *individual,* reflecting personal differences in motivation, perseverance, aptitude and so on. There are no societal limits to the learner's progress in English. In reality those who do acquire accentless English in a foreign language context probably do so because of unique personal opportunities, rather than because of the school programme.

These motivational factors have been emphasized by Reinecke. The desire to acquire an overseas model of the foreign language rather than a variety which is influenced by the conditions of acquisition was 'followed by the Japanese at the two cultural crises of their history, when in the 6th and 7th centuries A.D. select classes learned to read and speak Chinese in order that they might have access to the cultural riches of China, and again when in the 19th century, the educated classes learned Western languages so that they might compete on equal terms with the Occident. The same phenomenon was seen in the Hellenistic age, when the oriental peoples, that is, certain classes, among them, administrators, gentry, priests, littérateurs, and traders, learned the Greek Koiné or common language. By "learned" we are not to understand that all orientals who set themselves to write and speak Greek came to use the language without an admixture of native Greek elements . . . the point is that there was an effort on the part of the well equipped classes really to learn the foreign speech, to get at its cultural treasures, as well as to use it as a mere instrument of communication with the foreigner. There were limitations in the use of the foreign language, but these were due to individual limitations, not social limitations' (Reinecke, 1969, p. 94).

In analysing the English language performance of students in a foreign language setting all differences between the students' performance and an overseas model may be regarded as transitional or undesirable. While in the second language setting the generation of an interlanguage may become institutionalized at the group level, through socio-cultural adaptation of English to the local setting, and through purely linguistic processes such as overgeneralization and interference, in the foreign language setting these characteristics are not institutionalized at the group level but remain a normal part of the learning process. In a foreign language setting, where the major source of the input for English is the teaching manual and the teacher, the concept of transfer of training may be a basic analytic approach, since many of the errors observable are directly traceable to the manner of presentation of the language features in the school course. Selinker illustrates transfer of training as a feature of the learner's interlanguage, through reference to an observed difficulty in distinguishing between *he/she* by Serbo-Croatian learners, although the same distinction occurs in the mother tongue. Textbooks however invariably present drills with only *he* and it is this aspect of the teaching process which influences the learner's interlanguage performance (Selinker, 1972). Language transfer will also be a basic concept, since many of the techniques used to teach English in a foreign language setting will depend on translation from the mother tongue to English. The concept of interlanguage thus differs according to the setting in which English is being learned. James' description of learners' interlanguage is appropriate to the foreign language context: 'The learner of any L2 has a propensity to construct for himself this interlingua, an act of linguistic creativity so natural that it would be unrealistic to expect learners to circumvent it and proceed directly from his L1 to the native speaker's version of the L2. A further reason for allowing the learner to construct the interlingua is that it is immediately usable by him in the context in which he is learning; his classmates have the L1 in common so will converge in tacit agreement on the form of the interlingua. With this they will be able to communicate while they are learning, while the conventional approach, which proscribes the interlingua as a "corpus of error" either stifles the learner's communication drives altogether, or requires that the linguistically mature student becomes as a little child, practising perfectly well-formed native-speaker's sentences, which are, however, often idealized and usually trivial. Accepting the interlingua, like accepting a child's non-standard speech, avoids the necessity to halt the communication process for the sake of the learning process.' (James, 1970.)

We have seen that the nature of a particular interlanguage will depend on the particular context under consideration, which will define whether the feature is to be considered a *deviancy* or a *mistake*, a marker of transitional or terminal competence, the result of interference, simplification, overgeneralization, collocation extension, collocation innovation, register-range extension, or to strategies of learning and communication.

7 Conclusions

I have tried to suggest here that a number of different contexts for language learning can be studied with a common model of analysis. The notion of approximative system or interlanguage focuses on the learner's systematic handling of the language data to which he has been exposed, and the particular form of the learner's interlanguage will be determined by the conditions under which learning takes place. Standard English will be the outcome of language learning when the learner learns in order to become a member of the community who speak that form of English (e.g. the successful immigrant), or in order to invite perception of the learner as a person of equal status to standard speakers (e.g. the foreign student motivated to learn accentless English). Non-standard English will be the outcome of learning when the learner learns under circumstances which hinder his becoming a member of the community of standard speakers. Self-perpetuating social stratification correlated with color, race and other ethnic indicators, leads to the non-standard dialect taking on a new role of ethnic identity and solidarity. Educational planning which ignores this dimension of non-standard English is unlikely to achieve success. Partial learning, resulting from a lack of integrative interaction with standard speakers is reflected in modifications to the grammar of standard English, and these are best described as aspects of interlingual generation, that is, as either language transfer, transfer of training, communication strategies, learning strategies, or overgeneralization. The extreme case of non-integrative motivation affecting language learning is seen in pidgins and creoles, where the learning process contributes to the separateness of the groups in contact, while maintaining solidarity at the lower level. Non-standard dialects differ from pidgins in that in the former, the target language is closer to the learner. There is no sharp break in social communication but rather a gradual merging. Progress towards standard English in a creole setting reflects changing perception of class and status as a consequence of social mobility. A local variety of English such as Indian English is influenced by the perception of English as a tool for nationhood, and reflects the modification of overseas English as the social and cultural mores of the country are accommodated. In a foreign language setting, while many of the interlingual processes are comparable to those seen in other contexts for language learning, they are always considered as indicators of partial learning. They have no social role to play for the learner. The study of approximative systems in language learning thus leads to a focusing on the central processes of second language acquisition, and to a study of the circumstances which give these processes significance.

NOTE

1 Labov, in Hymes, 1971, p. 455.

PART THREE

Developmental Studies of Second Language Acquisition in Children

These three papers present the results of longitudinal studies of the development of syntax in children learning English as a second language. Dulay and Burt give a useful critical account of the theoretical background to contrastive analysis, and examine second language learning in the light of what recent studies have discovered about the nature of first language acquisition. In these studies, the development of rules necessary for the production of increasingly complex sentence types has been studied longitudinally. In looking at second language development in children, Dulay and Burt propose: (1) The language learner possesses a specific type of innate mental organization which causes him to use a limited class of processing strategies to produce utterances in a language; (2) Language learning proceeds by the learner's exercise of these processing strategies in the form of linguistic rules which he gradually adjusts as he organizes more and more of the particular language he hears; (3) This process is guided in first language acquisition by the particular form of the first language system, and in second language acquisition, by the particular form of the second language system. Dulay and Burt show from recent research, that children's 'approximative systems' in language learning demonstrate these propositions, their errors following the developmental sequence of first language development of the language, rather than being dominated by transfer from the mother tongue. In their attempt to account for both 'errors' of this kind and errors generally attributed to interference from the mother tongue, they propose a theory which resembles that of *approximative system* (cf. Nemser) or *interlanguage* (cf. Selinker) though Dulay and Burt prefer to interpret interference-like errors as overgeneralizations. The important questions would then seem to be: Under precisely what conditions can the equation L2 acquisition = L1 acquisition, be made? Up to what age? In both natural and formal settings for language learning?

93

And at what stage does the notion of interference reappear as a genuine characteristic of the learner's speech, requiring theoretical explanation? Only detailed studies of the sort reviewed and proposed by Dulay and Burt, but with older learners, will answer such questions.

Dulay and Burt's paper is followed by the two studies by Ravem which they discuss in several places. Ravem's two papers represent some of the earliest and best attempts to trace the development of syntax in a second language. Ravem presents valuable and difficult to obtain data which suggests that second language learning is 'a creative process not unlike that of first language acquisition'. Ravem's studies of syntactic development of English in Norwegian children tend to confirm Dulay and Burt's hypothesis that children's approximative systems are influenced by the order of development of the same structures in first language acquisition of the language. Dulay and Burt offer alternative interpretation for some of Ravem's data dealing with *yes/no* questions, where Ravem suggests Norwegian word order was followed in the absence of *do*. Ravem offers a word of caution however concerning the relationship between the order of first language and second language acquisition of English. He sees no absolute reason why the same order should be observed, and it is not certain from first language studies that the order need be the same for monolingual learners of English. The similarities however are striking and add further weight to the L2 acquisition = L1 acquisition hypothesis.

6

You Can't Learn Without Goofing
An Analysis of Children's
Second Language 'Errors'

HEIDI C DULAY AND
MARINA K BURT

This paper was written for this volume.

1 Introduction

Most parents who have lived abroad have marvelled at how easily their children pick up a foreign language, and perhaps have wondered about their child's unusual talent. Many children, without the benefit of formal classroom instruction, learn the language of a new country in the first year they are there. How do they do it?

This question encompasses all the aspects of language structure and all the subprocesses that comprise language acquisition. We will focus here on one modest facet of the general question – the production of syntax in second language acquisition by children, from the viewpoint of 'goofs' children make during the acquisition process.[1,2]

Before we proceed let us make these terms more explicit. By 'second language acquisition' we mean the acquisition of another language after having acquired the basics of the first, whereas 'bilingual acquisition' is the acquisition of two languages simultaneously. The term 'goof'[3] signifies deviation from syntactic structures which native adult speakers consider grammatically correct.[4,5]

We will consider two major hypotheses that differ both in the predictions they make about the types of production goofs in second language learning, and in the processes they posit to account for the goofs. They are:

- 1. the contrastive analysis hypothesis
- 2. the L2 acquisition – L1 acquisition hypothesis

95

Briefly the contrastive analysis (CA) hypothesis states that while the child is learning a second language, he will tend to use his native language structures in his second language speech, and where structures in his first language (L1) and his second language (L2) differ, he will goof. For example, in Spanish, subjects are often dropped, so Spanish children learning English should tend to say *Wants Miss Jones* for *He wants Miss Jones*.

The L2 acquisition = L1 acquisition hypothesis holds that children actively organize the L2 speech they hear and make generalizations about its structure as children learning their first language do. Therefore, the goofs expected in any particular L2 production would be similar to those made by children learning that same language as their first language. For example, *Jose want Miss Jones* would be expected, since first language acquisition studies have shown that children generally omit functors, in this case, the *-s* inflection for third person singular present indicative.

Each hypothesis contains two levels: the level of product and the level of process. The level of product describes the actual goof. For example, the CA hypothesis predicts that Spanish-speaking children will delete subjects, as in *Wants Miss Jones,* while the L2 acquisition = L1 acquisition hypothesis predicts that the children will omit functors, as in *Jose want Miss Jones*. The level of process, which is discussed in this paper in terms of 'theoretical assumptions', accounts for the product—the CA hypothesis offers a transfer theory; the L2 acquisition = L1 acquisition hypothesis offers an active mental organization theory. Throughout this paper, the process-product distinction should be borne in mind.

We will discuss the assumptions (process level) of each hypothesis, describe their consequences in terms of predicted goofs (product), and cite empirical studies from a variety of languages[6] that bear on the issue. No study we know of analyses children's ESL speech with the purpose of testing both the above two hypotheses. They will therefore be presented separately, and then a step toward a theory that would resolve the conflict will be proposed.

2 The Contrastive Analysis Hypothesis

2.1 *Statement of the Hypothesis*

The last two decades of enthusiasm for contrastive analysis in foreign language teaching can be traced to Charles Fries who, in 1945, wrote:

The most effective materials are those that are based upon a scientific description of the language to be learned, carefully compared with a parallel description of the native language of the learner. (p. 9)

In 1957 Robert Lado worked out that suggestion in *Linguistics Across Cultures* which is now a classic in the field. The 'fundamental assumption of the book' is the contrastive analysis hypothesis:

> that individuals tend to transfer the forms and meanings, and the distribution of forms and meanings of their native language and culture to the foreign language and culture, both productively when attempting to speak the language . . . and receptively when attempting to grasp and understand the language . . . as practised by natives. (p. 2) . . . in the comparison between native and foreign language lies the key to ease or difficulty in foreign language learning. (p. 1)

More recently, Charles Ferguson (in Stockwell and Bowen, 1965, p. v), Robert Politzer (1967), and Leon Jakobovits (1970) reiterate the importance of L1 interference in L2 learning.[7]

Since Lado's treatise in 1957, the contrastive analysis hypothesis has swept the field like a tidal wave, although its strong version—that it can *predict* most of the errors a learner will make while learning a second language—is being toned down to the claim that it can *account for* a great number of errors that L2 learners have actually made (Wardaugh, 1970, p. 124). Though its impact on foreign language teaching has been felt by almost all concerned, the contrastive analysis claim still remains a hypothesis. Let us examine it more closely.

2.2 *Theoretical Assumptions*

The CA hypothesis rests on the following assumptions about the process of language learning:[8]

- 1. Language learning is habit formation.
- 2. An old habit (that of using one's first language) hinders or facilitates the formation of a new habit (learning a second language) depending on the differences or similarities, respectively, between the old and the new.

The first assumption derives primarily from the general paradigm of behaviorist psychology.[9] Habit formation may be described in a variety of ways that all rely on the principles of Associationism, that is, frequency, contiguity, intensity, etc., of stimulus and response in the occurrence of the event that becomes a habit.

·   The second assumption, which follows from the first, derives from interference theory in verbal learning and memory research.[10] Interference theory until at least 1959[11] rested on the assumption of the association of context and/or stimulus with response. Learning a new response to the same stimulus and/or in the same context would require 'extinction' of the old association. Otherwise, the old habit would prevail. The prevalence of an old habit in attempting to perform a new task is called 'negative transfer'.

Tulving and Madigan (1970) in reviewing the relevant literature from '350 B.C. to 1969' comment that psychologists are currently experiencing a 'revolution in interference theory' (p. 471) supported mainly by several studies which have seriously questioned the nature of the operation of transfer in paired-associate learning. For example, Slamecka (1968) found that part of a free-recall list does not facilitate the recall of the other part of the list; and Ceraso (1968) reported findings which were different from those predicted by the notion of extinction of specific A-B associations.[12] The explanation of transfer is based on the acceptance of learning as habit formation. Since habit formation is automatization of a response, it is theoretically impossible to get away from the necessity of unlearning as an intermediate step to new response acquisition. Thus, in spite of the findings that contradicted the predictions of the extinction notion, the notion of unlearning has been retained as part of the theory, but has been drastically revised.[13] Tulving and Madigan summarize the revision:

> Rather than referring to the extinction of both specific (stimulus-term and response-term) and general (experimental context and specific response terms) associations, [unlearning] is now envisaged as a kind of suppression of the whole first-list repertoire of responses in the course of second-list learning. During learning of the first list, the subject limits his response selection to those occurring in that list. When he comes to learn the second list containing different responses, new 'criteria of selective arousal' must be established. These criteria require the suppression of the first list repertoire. When the subject is asked, immediately after learning the second list, to recall the first list, the selector mechanism cannot shift back to the criteria

used during first list acquisition because of its 'inertia'. With the passage of time, however, the set to give second-list responses dissipates, resulting in the lifting of the suppression of the first-list responses and consequent observable 'spontaneous recovery'. (p. 471)

At least at the moment, 'suppression' seems to be an undefined construct that is entailed not by any part of the existing theory, but by the recent findings. Tulving and Madigan write that they 'suspect it will be a few years before the new theory will acquire clearly identifiable properties and characteristics. In the meantime, interference phenomena will become fair game for heretics . . .' (p. 471).

Because the notion of unlearning is so central to interference theory, it seems surprising that second language learning theorists have relied so heavily on the theory; especially since the notion of extinction was still central to interference theory at the time of the debut of the contrastive analysis hypothesis via Lado's *Linguistics Across Cultures* (1957). To date, this theory is still used as the theoretical base for the CA hypothesis.[14] This is not an unreasonable development, however, because the new developments in psychological theory are still considered radical.

It seems that L2 learning theorists, despite their stated theoretical base, were aware of the untenability of the extinction notion and subtly substituted for it the notion of *difficulty* in L2 learning. See, for example, Lado's Section '4.2 Similarity and difference as determiners of ease and *difficulty*' (1957, p. 59), and Marchese's 'English Patterns *Difficult* for Native Spanish Speaking Students' (1970).[15] Clearly, no one would want to say that L1 has to be unlearned to learn L2, and once L2 is learned it would have to be unlearned when trying to speak L1, and so on. The predicted problem of first language loss is thus not addressed by CA proponents,[16] but instead, the necessity of intensively drilling those aspects of the L2 that comprise the new habit is emphasized.

S. P. Corder has found another solution to the theoretical problems of the CA hypothesis. He has rejected the habit formation-negative transfer assumptions and instead has accepted the assumption of learner as a generator of generalizations about the target language (the hypothesis underlying L1 acquisition research). But Corder's substitution of one theoretical base for another apparently has not affected his belief in first language interference. According to Corder, the L2 learner need only hypothesize:

Are the systems of the new language the same or different from the language I know? And if different, what is their nature?

'Evidence for this is that a large number, by no means all, of [the learner's] errors are related to the systems of his mother tongue.' (Corder, 1968, p. 168.)

In effect, though CA proponents seldom fail to state a theoretical base for their prediction of interference goofs, the nature of that base seems to make little difference in what they predict about a second language learner's goofs.[17]

2.3 *Evidence*

(a) The Child-Adult Distinction in Language Acquisition

Before we discuss the evidence for the CA hypothesis, it is important to point out that a major issue in the field is the difference between children and adults in language acquisition. This difference has been extensively discussed by Lenneberg (1967) who draws on several areas of research to support the distinction. He reports that symptoms of traumatic aphasia ('direct, structural and local interference with neurophysiological processes of language', p. 153) that occur under age 13 are reversible, whereas those that occur after 13 are not. Non-deaf children of deaf parents who are exposed to a normal language environment at school age learn to speak within a year; deaf persons who regain their hearing after puberty never master a spoken language. Lateralization of brain function around the age of puberty seems to be the physical correlate of these phenomena. After puberty the brain becomes, as it were, less plastic and therefore less able to take on certain kinds of new tasks (See Ch. 4).

Ervin-Tripp (1970) suggests a difference in approaches to L2 learning based on previous processing strategies. This results in grouping together adults who have already learned other languages, and children; as opposed to monolingual adults.

An adult who has changed his linguistic system only in minor ways—by adding new vocabulary, for example—for many years may not have available ready strategies for change. An adult who has already learned other languages, or a child who is constantly in the process of reorganizing his processing system and adding to his storage at all levels will have quite different approaches to new input. . . . The most adaptable, sensitive language learner we can find is a young child. Surely we can expect that his L2 learning will reflect many of the same processes of development as he used to discover his first language. On the other hand, in the case of inexperienced adults we can expect the system to be most adaptable just at the point where it changes most readily in adult life—the lexicon. (p. 316)

J. Macnamara (1971), D. A. Reibel (1971), and before them H. Sweet (1899), O. Jespersen (1904) and H. E. Palmer (1922), remind us that they have seen adults perform as well as children in second language learning. Though a significant difference between children and adults is indicated by Lenneberg's research, Reibel points out that there have been no L2 acquisition studies that compare children and adults. In fact, no longitudinal studies of adult L2 acquisition have been made and child studies are just beginning to emerge.

The CA hypothesis does not address the child-adult distinction. ESL materials for children often include a list of 'difficult' structures (Marchese, 1970) or an 'Interference Sheet' (Michigan Oral Language Series, Children's Guide-Kindergarten, 1971) which are enumerations of English structures that differ from the students' native language, and which the teachers are advised to drill intensively. However, the evidence cited by CA proponents is taken primarily from adult studies, especially those of U. Weinreich and E. Haugen. We discuss these in section **b** below. In **c** we present other types of evidence of adult L2 goofs used by CA proponents and, in addition, we offer findings from recent error analysis research on adult speech. In **d** we offer findings from child L2 acquisition research which also support the CA product prediction that L2 goofs reflect native language structure.

(b) Weinreich and Haugen

The bulk of the supportive evidence cited by CA proponents is taken from Uriel Weinreich's work on *Languages in Contact* (1953) and Einar Haugen's two volume work on *The Norwegian Language in America* (1953). Lado writes:

> A practical confirmation of the validity of our assumption has come from the work of linguists who study the effect of close contact between languages in bilingual situations. Extensive studies have been carried out by Haugen and Weinreich in this area. (1957, p. 1)

Indeed, Weinreich and Haugen document their work with study upon study of the speech of bilinguals. Upon closer examination, however, it becomes clear that the phenomenon of 'interference' Weinreich has documented and that of 'linguistic borrowing' that Haugen has documented are the same; and that this phenomenon is quite different from that of first language interference as conceived by CA proponents and described above. The differences are easily seen when we compare Weinreich and Haugen's definitions of interference, types of empirical evidence, functions of interference, and conditions for interference with those of the CA hypothesis.

Definition of Interference   Weinreich defines interference as follows: '. . . those instances of deviation from the norms of either language which occur in the speech of bilinguals as a result of their *familiarity*[18] with more than one language, i.e. as a result of languages in contact . . .' (p. 1).

Haugen defines linguistic borrowing as '. . . an example of cultural diffusion, the spread of an item of culture from people to people. Borrowing is linguistic diffusion, and can be unambiguously defined as the attempt by a speaker to reproduce in one language patterns which he has learned in another (p. 363) . . . *it is the language of the learner that is influenced, not the language he learns.*'[19] (p. 370)

The CA hypothesis, on the other hand, states that interference is due to unfamiliarity with L2, i.e. to the learner's not having learned the target pattern, and is manifested in the language he learns.

> We know from the observation of many cases that the grammatical structure of the native language tends to be transferred to the foreign language . . . we have here the major source of difficulty or ease in learning the foreign language. . . . Those structures that are different will be difficult. (Lado, 1957, pp. 58, 59)

Further, Weinreich's definition of interference is not based on which language was learned first:

> Throughout the analysis of the forms of linguistic interference, conventional terms like 'mother tongue', 'first', 'second', or 'native' language were avoided; for from the structural point of view the genetic question . . . is irrelevant. (p. 74)

On the contrary, the native-foreign language distinction is central to Lado's statement.

Types of Evidence   Weinreich's evidence comes from either the study of border and immigrant dialects or the evolution of languages, e.g.

German-English *I come soon home.*
Loss of the old French tense system in Creole (p. 64).

and there are numerous others (see Ch. 2, 3. Grammatical Interference).

Likewise, the data in Haugen's book (some 70 pages—see pp. 482–555) describes 'the various dialects and communities' of Norwegians in America (p. 481). Further, most of this data describes the borrowing of English into Norwegian and the Norwegianization of those borrowings, e.g.

ke'ja kul'le (catch cold)
dres'sa opp (dress up)   (pp. 457–458)

This is the exact opposite of the interference phenomenon the CA hypothesis addresses, that is, the transfer of Norwegian patterns onto English. Haugen does cite three pages of goofs made by Norwegians speaking English. However, they are all either phonological or lexical, e.g.

Oh, he is in the stove (Norwegian *stova* for *living room*)
Tendency to use the unvoiced correlates of [z] and [ž], as in [rowsis] for *roses* and [plešir] for *pleasure.*

Thus, while Haugen and Weinreich describe the languages and dialects of communities, the CA hypothesis refers to the speech of individuals 'who do not usually form speech communities' (Nemser, 1971, p. 120) but whose goal is 'to attempt to speak the language . . . as practised by natives' (Lado, 1957, p. 2).

Functions of Interference   Weinreich stresses the intentional[20] use of interference structures by bilinguals. 'As a mechanism for the reinforcement of expression, the transfer of morphemes flourishes where affective categories are concerned' (p. 34), e.g. diminutives that express endearment, like the Hebrew *-le* derived from Yiddish. He also reports that 'in speaking to a unilingual, the bilingual often tends to limit interference and to eliminate even habitualized borrowings from his speech . . .' (p. 81). Apparently, the bilinguals Weinreich refers to here know two codes—one that includes interference structures and one that does not. Furthermore, they are able to code switch when the situation demands it.

Haugen also mentions the 'deliberate use' by a bilingual of loan translations 'for the sake of enriching his language' (p. 459). (This seems similar to the notion of 'foregrounding' suggested by Gumperz and Hernandez (in press) in their discussion of Chicanos speaking English.)

This use of interference structures is quite different from the CA notion of interference structures as unwanted forms which the L2 learner cannot help but use. The use of interference structures, according to Weinreich and Haugen, is motivated by social factors; in the CA framework it is uncontrollable because the L2 learner has not yet acquired the required L2 habits.

Conditions for Interference   Weinreich's observations of conversations between a bilingual and a monolingual, and between bilinguals, leads him to state that when both speakers are bilingual, interference runs rampant in both directions; when one speaker is monolingual and the other bilingual, interference in the bilingual's speech is 'inhibited'.

> When the other interlocutor is also bilingual, the requirements of intelligibility and status assertion are drastically reduced. Under such circumstances, there is hardly any limit to interference. (p. 81)

Haugen writes:

> Linguistic borrowing . . . is something that has happened wherever there have been bilinguals. It is, in fact, unthinkable without the existence of bilinguals, and apparently inevitable where there is any considerable group of bilinguals. (p. 263)

The CA notion of interference is predicted in quite different circumstances: the less of a bilingual the speaker is, the more interference there will be when he attempts to communicate with speakers of the target language.

In summary, it seems that the work of Weinreich and Haugen, although fundamental to research in language shift, does not speak to the phenomenon of first language interference that we and the CA proponents are concerned with.

What other evidence is there then?

(c) Adult Studies

Jakobovits in his survey of foreign language learning issues (1970) declares that evidence for the assumption of transfer in L2 learning is lacking (see p. 20). In discussing the CA hypothesis, Nemser (1971) writes, 'Direct and systematic examination of learner speech has been largely neglected. . . . Contrastive analysis specialists . . . have been content for the most part to derive empirical support for their formulations from impressionistic observation and intuition.' (p. 121). What evidence there is, which has made the hypothesis seem so intuitively plausible, apparently comes from personal recollection and teachers' accounts of foreigners' different accents in English. Wardaugh (1970) comments that many experienced teachers find themselves unable to reject the CA hypothesis because their experience tells them that a Frenchman is likely to pronounce English *think* as *sink* and a Russian is likely to pronounce it as *tink*.

Most of the valid CA evidence seems to be phonological, and 'studies of second language acquisition have tended to imply that contrastive analysis may be most predictive at the level of phonology, and least predictive at the syntactic level' (Richards, 1970, p. 2).[21]

That there may be some systematically collected evidence for syntactic goofs traceable to L1 is, paradoxically, brought to light by persons whose aim it is to show that other kinds of goofs should be given at least equal attention.

H. V. George (1972) in his book *Common Errors in Language Learning* notes that, from reviewing findings in his students' theses, two-thirds of the goofs collected could not be traced to L1 structure (i.e. one-third could be).

D. Lance (1969) reports that one-third to two-thirds of his adult foreign students' English goofs were not traceable to their native Spanish. In her analysis of French-English goofs, Ervin-Tripp (1970) reaches a similar conclusion.

J. Richards (1971) mentions some examples of transfer goofs from his French-English data, but states that these are only a small portion of his data. He devotes his paper to discussing non-contrastive goof analysis, including performance goofs, overgeneralizations and so forth.

In the same paper, Richards gives an example of an English error a French speaker made which constitutes evidence *against* positive transfer:

composed with (instead of *composed of*)

He remarks, 'Had the French speaker followed the grammar of his mother tongue, he would have produced the correct English form'!

(p. 16). Wolfe (1967) has more evidence for this phenomenon. There is no explanation for this goof type within the CA framework.

Other research on adult L2 goofs (Selinker, 1971; Strevens, 1969; Burt and Kiparsky, 1972) also focuses on non-contrastive goofs.

(d) Child Studies

Though there are no goof analysis studies *per se* on child L2 speech, we have extracted what seems to be relevant information from studies by: Kinzel (reported by Ervin-Tripp, 1970), Valette (1964) and Ravem (1968).

A six-year-old French child studied by Kinzel produced English pronouns that reflected French agreement rules:

> # *She* is all mixed up. (*pendule:* feminine in French, neuter in English)
>
> # I got *her*. (*serviette:* feminine in French, neuter in English)
>
> # Who likes *them*? (*epinards*: count in French, mass in English)[22]

Valette (1964) incidentally reports that in her nine month observational study of L2 French development in a four-year-old American child, the only instance of English transfer was his consistent substitution of *attendre pour* for *attendre* in the sense of 'to wait for'. (No explanation or discussion of transfer is made in the paper.) Interpretation of this data is premature since we have no data on French L1 acquisition and it is possible that children learning French as their native language also make those goofs.

Ravem (1968) documents L1 goofs in the English speech of his $6\frac{1}{2}$-year-old Norwegian child which reflect Norwegian structure:

> # Drive you car to-yesterday?
>
> # Like you ice cream?
>
> # Like you me not, Reidun?

This goof type occurred before the child had acquired *do*. Ravem hypothesizes that the cue for English *yes-no* questions is *do,* which the child had not acquired, and since inverted word order is a frequent and important question cue in Norwegian, which does not have *do*, the child used the Norwegian question cue. Ravem also reports, however, that the child's goofs in his acquisition of negation and *wh*-questions were definitely not traceable to Norwegian. (This is discussed in 3.3.1 below.)

These three studies are the only child L2 studies we know of that present data that can be useful in our discussion.[23]

Valid evidence from the adult and child studies presented above shows that a portion of L2 goofs do reflect L1 structure, confirming in part the product level of the CA hypothesis. However, because a major portion of L2 goofs do not reflect L1 structure, this partial confirmation of the CA product level is not enough to justify the process level which is questionable on theoretical grounds.

2.4 *State of the Contrastive Analysis Hypothesis*

The CA hypothesis in 1972 has come under a good deal of criticism, though no one has rejected it entirely. Many teachers accept it but consider its pedagogical use minimal. Many L2 acquisition theorists have reservations about it,[24] though they seem willing to salvage it, if only partially.

At the product level, the CA hypothesis accounts for a portion of the evidence: that presented by recent goof analysis research on adult L2 syntactic goofs, and that which we have found in three child L2 acquisition studies. It does not account for a major portion of adult L2 syntactic goofs or for the child L2 goofs presented in the next section.

At the process level, the CA hypothesis runs into difficulty—

1. The theoretical base of the hypothesis, which lies in psychological interference theory, is being seriously questioned, if not by L2 acquisition theorists, by psychologists of verbal learning and memory. (See section 2.2 above.)

2. There is evidence against positive transfer. (See p. 154.) If it is true that L2 learners make goofs in L2 that would have been avoided had they followed the rules of L1, the question is raised as to whether negative transfer can be used as an underlying principle that can explain and predict L2 goofs.

3. The use of Weinreich and Haugen's work as 'practical confirmation' of the hypothesis is invalid. (See section 2.3.b above.)

Most of the studies on children's second language acquisition do not speculate about first language interference. They are concerned with the equally compelling other end of the spectrum—that L2 acquisition = L1 acquisition.

3 The L2 Acquisition = L1 Acquisition Hypothesis

3.1 *Statement of the Hypothesis*

With the burst of first language acquisition research in the 60's has come a new interest in second language learning research—that of comparing L2 syntactic development in children with native language acquisition findings. A statement from Dato (1970) sets the scene:

> . . . encouraging results in the search for universals in native language development have led us to explore the existence of similar phenomena in the learning of a second language. (p. 1)

The general hypothesis has been differentiated thus far into three specific hypotheses:

1. L2 syntactic development is characterized by a learning sequence in which 'base structures' are learned first, then increasingly 'transformed structures' are acquired (Dato, 1970).[25]

2. The strategies of L2 acquisition are similar to those of L1 acquisition, e.g. use of word order as the first syntactic rule, omission of functors (Dulay and Burt, 1972).

3. The L2 learning sequence of certain syntactic structures is similar to corresponding L1 syntactic development. So far, the structures studied include *wh*-questions (Ravem, 1970), *yes-no* questions (Ravem, 1968), negation (Milon, 1972 and Ravem, 1968), and plural formation (Natalicio and Natalicio, 1971).

These hypotheses, interesting as they are, span more than we can deal with here. Staying with our plan to discuss only the production of L2 syntax from the point of view of goofs children make, the L2 acquisition = L1 acquisition hypothesis, which is stated in two parts is as follows:

1. Children below the age of puberty will make goofs in L2 syntax that are similar to L1 developmental goofs.

An example of this is the omission of functors which results in a number of specific syntactically unrelated goofs: lack of agreement, lack of tensing, missing determiners, missing possessive markers.

2. Children below the age of puberty will not make goofs that reflect transfer of the structure of their L1 onto the L2 they are learning.

For example, Samoan children should not tend to use Samoan word order in possessive NP constructions (the reverse of English word order) when they are learning English.

3.2 *Theoretical Assumptions*

Proponents of the L1 acquisition = L2 acquisition theory do not spell out their theoretical assumptions. There is usually a paragraph or two rejecting habit theory and affirming that language learning is an 'active' and 'creative' process. Reference is usually made to Noam Chomsky's work and that of Roger Brown, Dan Slobin and their colleagues. The apparent hesitance in spelling out theoretical assumptions may be due to the current state of uncertainty in the field. Ravem takes pains to say, 'the study reported here was not undertaken to test any particular hypothesis relating to certain theories of language learning' (1968, p. 184).

Since we are examining all aspects of the hypothesis, we will attempt to make explicit the assumptions on which the hypothesis must rest:

1. The language learner possesses a specific type of innate mental organization which causes him to use a limited class of processing strategies to produce utterances in a language.

2. Language learning proceeds by the learner's exercise of those processing strategies in the form of linguistic rules which he gradually adjusts as he organizes more and more of the particular language he hears.

One such strategy might be the use of a syntactic rule with a minimum of grammatical redundancy, e.g. word order to express the possessor-possessed relation (# *Daddy dog* for 'Daddy's dog'). In no case would this relation be expressed in English as *Dog Daddy*.

3. This process is guided in L1 acquisition by the particular form of the L1 system, and in L2 acquisition by the particular form of the L2 system.

For example, the strategy of using word order to indicate possession is different in English and Samoan. 'In English ... the relation of possession is expressed by naming first the person who possesses and second the object possessed. In Samoan, the order is just the reverse. In both languages adults mark the construction with grammatical forms as well as word order. Stage I children, whether English-speaking or Samoan-speaking, drop the grammatical form. If English-speaking they use the order Possessor-Possessed, and if Samoan-speaking, the reverse.' (Cazden and Brown, in press, p. 5.)

The present focus of linguistic research is to formulate those principles that generate all and only grammatical sentences. The focus of psychological research is to discover those principles which a learner uses to arrive at the production of grammatical speech. Psycholinguistic language learning strategies appear to be a function of the interplay between linguistic complexity and learning complexity. Some researchers, like Dato, pursue the linguistic complexity factor; some, like Bever in first language acquisition, pursue the learning complexity factor. We are all, in one way or another grappling with the problem that Charles S. Peirce (1957) stressed in his lecture on the 'logic of abduction'—that of searching for the rules of mental organization that limit the class of possible hypotheses a child uses when learning a language.

3.3 Evidence

The first part of the hypothesis—that children below the age of puberty will make goofs in L2 syntax that are similar to L1 developmental goofs—has been shown for three syntactic structures: wh-questions (Ravem, 1970), negation (Milon, 1972, and Ravem, 1968), and plurals (Natalicio and Natalicio, 1971). In each case English L1 studies have produced clear findings, making the comparison straightforward.

The second part of the hypothesis—that children below the age of puberty will not make L2 syntax goofs that reflect their native syntactic structures—has been shown for the following structures: English-Welsh word order in adjective and possessive NP constructions (Price, 1968), Norwegian-English wh-questions (Ravem, 1970), and Norwegian-English negation (Ravem, 1968). Our additional comparison of Japanese negation to Milon's (1972) English L2 data, and of Spanish pluralization to Natalicio and Natalicio's (1971) English L2 data, also confirms this part of the hypothesis for Japanese-English negation and Spanish-English pluralization.

(a) Wh-Questions

R. Ravem (1970) conducted a five month study of his 6½-year-old Norwegian speaking son Rune, using spontaneous speech tape recording plus a translation technique. The main objective of his study was to test the derivational complexity hypothesis in Wh-questions. He found, as did Brown's group (1968) that based on the following rough transformational sequence

    Base ? John will read the book tomorrow
    T-1   John will read the book when?

T-2   When John will read the book?
T-3   When will John read the book?

the child produced T-2 type goofs before acquiring the final *wh-* form. The children's *wh-* goof structure can be described as:

$$S \rightarrow wh\text{-} + (not) + NP + VP$$

L1 (Adam)	*L2 (Rune)*
#What the dollie have?	#What you eating?
#Why not me sleeping?	#Why not me can't dance?
#How he can be a doctor?	#What she is doing?

Briefly, the goof is the absence of the obligatory inversion of aux and subject required by English. Ravem mentions that this is definitely not Norwegian interference as Norwegian requires verb-subject inversion when modal auxiliaries are absent, e.g. *What saying you?* for 'What are you saying?'

(b) Negation

In his six month study of a seven-year-old Japanese child (Ken) learning Hawaiian English, John Milon (1972) reports that the types of negative utterances Ken produced were similar to those produced by Adam, Eve and Sarah in their first two stages[26] (as reported by Klima and Bellugi, 1966). 244 negative utterances were extracted from eight hours of video-tape recordings of 20-minute weekly sessions. His findings, (see page 112), are juxtaposed to Klima and Bellugi's findings.

Briefly, stage 1 places the Neg outside the nucleus; stage 2 places the Neg between the NP and the VP.

Though Milon did not mention the Japanese negation structure, it is in fact different from Ken's structures. Negation in Japanese is a bound morpheme, always attached to the right of the verb stem. Moreover, verbs appear at the end of the sentence.[28] Word order in a Japanese negative sentence would be, for example:

His red shirt + case inflection like + Neg inflection

as opposed to English:

I do not like his red shirt.

Thus, Milon's data shows that Japanese structure is not transferred onto the English negative structures Ken produced, which placed *no* and *not* before the nucleus. Furthermore, in Stage 2 examples.

112 HEIDI C. DULAY AND MARINA K. BURT

	L1 (Adam, Eve and Sarah)	L2 (Ken)
Stage 1:	$S \rightarrow \left\{ \begin{array}{c} no \\ not \end{array} \right\} + $ Nucleus, or Nuc. $\left\{ + \begin{array}{c} no \\ not \end{array} \right.$ # No wipe finger. # Not a teddy bear. # Wear mitten no.	$S \rightarrow \left\{ \begin{array}{c} no \\ not \end{array} \right. + $ Nucleus # Not me. # Not dog. # Not cold.[27]
Stage 2:	$S \rightarrow$ Nom. $+ \mathrm{Aux}^{neg} + \left\{ \begin{array}{c} \mathrm{Pred} \\ \mathrm{Main\ V} \end{array} \right.$ $\mathrm{Aux}^{neg} \rightarrow \left\{ \begin{array}{c} neg^{neg} \\ V \end{array} \right.$ $\mathrm{Neg} \rightarrow \left\{ \begin{array}{c} no \\ not \end{array} \right.$ $V^{neg} \rightarrow \left\{ \begin{array}{c} can't \\ don't \end{array} \right.$ # I don't sit on Cromer coffee. # He not little, he big. # He no bite you.	$S \rightarrow$ Nominal $+ \mathrm{Aux}^{neg} + $ Pred $\mathrm{Aux}^{neg} \rightarrow \left\{ \begin{array}{c} neg^{neg} \\ V \end{array} \right.$ $\mathrm{Neg} \rightarrow \left\{ \begin{array}{c} no \\ not \\ no\ more \end{array} \right.$ $V^{neg} \rightarrow \left\{ \begin{array}{c} no\ can \\ don't \end{array} \right.$ Don't tell teacher OK? # I no queen. # I not give you candy. # I no more five.

Japanese word order, with the verb in final position, is not produced.

Ravem (1968) has similar evidence based on a partial analysis of his data. His son Rune did not produce the Norwegian structure $N + V + (N) + $ Neg, as in:

> Han arbeider ikke (He works not)
> Vi tok det ikke   (We took it not).

Instead, he produced the English L1 acquisition structure $N + $ Neg $+$ VP, as in:

> # I not like that.
> # I not looking for edge. (p. 180)

(c) Plurals

Natalicio and Natalicio (1971) add to our store with their study of the acquisition of English plurals by native Spanish children in Grades 1, 2, 3 and 10. They studied 144 males, 36 in each grade, half native English speakers and half native Spanish speakers, using a test similar to the Berko (1958) 'wug' test. They found that both the native Spanish and the native English speakers acquired the /-s/ and /-z/ plural allomorphs before the /-iz/ (Berko, 1958, and

Anisfeld and Tucker, 1967), though the mean proportion of overall correct responses for native Spanish speakers was lower.

This order of acquisition shows that Spanish L1 structures are not transferred to English L2 speech. Spanish pluralization rules are as follows:

$$V \#^{29} + /s/$$
$$C \# + /es/^{30} \text{ (Da Silva, 1963, p. 17),}$$

i.e. words that end in vowels are pluralized by adding /s/; words that end in consonants add /es/. If transfer from Spanish to English had been operating, the order of acquisition would have been:

/s/ only first,
then /z/ and /iz/ together

because Spanish plurals are all voiceless, and voicing is the new feature English requires.

(d) Word Order in Adjective and Possessive NP Constructions

In his six month study of the acquisition of Welsh by 21 native English-speaking children, Price (1968) reports that the Welsh NP constructions produced by the children reflected Welsh rather than English word order, i.e. they reflected L2 structure rather than L1 structure. The data was collected daily by a classroom observer-teacher who took written notes of the children's utterances at various times during the day. The following table gives Price's striking findings (p. 42).

WELSH (L2)

Pattern	Actual Utterance	English Equivalent[31]
N + Adj	blodyn coch	flower red
N + Adj + Adj	cyw bach melyn	chick little yellow
Poss'd + Poss'r	esgidiau Dadi	shoes Daddy
Poss'd + Adj + Poss'r	blodyn gwyn Karen	flower white Karen
Poss'd + Det + Poss'r	cadair y babi	chair the baby

ENGLISH (L1)

Pattern	Example
Adj + N	a red flower
Adj + Adj + N	a little, yellow chick
Poss'r + Poss'd	Daddy's shoes
Poss'r + Adj + Poss'd	Karen's white flower
Det + Poss'r + Poss'd	the baby's chair

Unfortunately, in this paper Price did not compare Welsh L1 acquisition to the Welsh L2 structures produced by the English-speaking children so this evidence does not speak directly to the first part of the hypothesis.

3.4 *State of the L2 Acquisition = L1 Acquisition Hypothesis*

The L2 acquisition = L1 acquisition hypothesis as stated in studies to date, explicitly refers only to the product level. At this level, the available evidence, discussed above, confirms the hypothesis for children's production of *wh*-questions, negation, plurals, and word order in NP constructions.

With this empirical confirmation of the hypothesis, its theoretical assumptions receive support, at the same time making contrastive analysis theoretical assumptions even less tenable.

However, two weaknesses emerge:

1. What can we say about those structures which have no corresponding L1 data analysis for comparison? Nothing, except suggest the task for 'future research'.

2. There is evidence for interference structures, e.g. Ravem's findings in *yes-no* question formation by a Norwegian child learning English. To account for this, one might make the weak argument that because of the limitations of natural data collection, utterances reflecting, say, subject-verb inversion in *yes-no* questions might have been made by Adam, Eve and Sarah when Brown and his colleagues were not there to collect them.

We would like to make a stronger argument, though, that would require finding an explanation that accounts for both interference-like goofs and non-interference goofs, and that would thus address the process level of children's L2 acquisition.

4 Proposed Second Language Production Strategies

While much of the value of scientific hypotheses lies precisely in their power to yield new and interesting empirically testable consequences, their ultimate virtue, to the extent that they are true, is that they explain known or knowable facts by revealing them to be consequences of underlying principles of great generality. A scientific description therefore cannot stop with a systematic account of observable phenomena but must seek a theory that purports to explain the phenomena, as well as to display them. It is this explanatory goal of science that we have sought to attain in our account. (Halle and Keyser, 1971, p. xiii)

It is this explanatory goal that guides our efforts, rudimentary though they may be at the present time.

4.1 *Statement of the Hypothesis*

We have presented two conflicting theories, each of which has attempted to explain part of the data. Neither as it stands can explain all of the data. Our account will attempt to do so. It relies on the theoretical assumptions we suggested as the base for the L2 acquisition = L1 acquisition hypothesis. We hypothesize that the child's organization of L2 does not include transfer from (either positive or negative) or comparison with his native language, but relies on his dealing with L2 syntax as a system. Within this framework of *process*, we propose to explain the interference-like goofs presented below, as well as some of those which have been presented in section 2.3.d above. This account requires that the goofs be accurately categorizable in the following framework:

1. *Interference-like Goofs*—those that reflect native language structure, *and* are not found in L1 acquisition data of the target language.

For example, #*hers pajamas* produced by a Spanish child reflects Spanish structure, and was not produced by Adam, Eve or Sarah.

2. *L1 Developmental Goofs*—those that do not reflect native language structure, but are found in L1 acquisition data of the target language.

For example, #*He took her teeths off* produced by a Spanish child does not reflect Spanish structure, but an overgeneralization typically produced by children acquiring English as their first language.

3. *Ambiguous Goofs*—those that can be categorized as either Interference-like Goofs or L1 Developmental Goofs.

For example, #*Terina not can go* produced by a Spanish child reflects Spanish structure and is also typical of American children learning English as their native language.

4. *Unique Goofs*—those that do not reflect L1 structure, and are also not found in L1 acquisition data of the target language.

For example, #*He name is Victor* produced by a Spanish child neither reflects Spanish structure nor is found in L1 acquisition data in English.

4.2 *Goof Analysis*

(a) Data

Of the child L2 data presented above (section 2.3.d), only Ravem's data on *yes-no* questions can be categorized in our framework. In addition, we have some pilot data of English L2 speech of native Spanish-speaking children tape recorded by an ESL teacher during free conversation in her first grade ESL class. We also have data collected by G. Williams (1971) during his English conversations with native Spanish-speaking first grade children. Tables 1–4 present all the goof types in the data, along with an example of each type.

Table 1
INTERFERENCE-LIKE GOOFS

GOOF TYPE	GOOF
SPANISH-ENGLISH	
Poss Pro + N number agreement not allowed in English, obligatory in Spanish	# Now she's putting her*s* clothes on.
Omission of obligatory *how* in English, optional in Spanish	# I know to do all that.
Use of infinitive for gerund not allowed in English, obligatory in Spanish	# I finish *to watch* TV when it's four o'clock.
NORWEGIAN-ENGLISH	
Verb-subject inversion not allowed in English, obligatory in Norwegian	# *Like you* me not, Reidun?

Table 2
L1 DEVELOPMENTAL GOOFS

GOOF TYPE	GOOF
SPANISH-ENGLISH	
Irregular plural treated as regular	# He took her teeths off.
Two verbal words tensed; only one required	# I didn't weared any hat.
Accusative Pro for Nominative	# Me need crayons now.
Inappropriate Q form: no aux-NP inversion	# What color it is?

Table 2—*continued*

GOOF TYPE	GOOF
Masc Pro used for Fem	# He didn't come yesterday (answering question about a little girl).
Do-subject agreement missing	# Where does the spiders go?
N-Pro agreement missing	# They're painting his faces (their).
Obj Pro missing	# My mother can fix.
Tense inflection missing	# He say he bring it to school.
Determiner missing	# He say his father buy him car.

Table 3
AMBIGUOUS GOOFS

GOOF TYPE	GOOF
SPANISH–ENGLISH	
Wrong *no* placement; *no/not* distinction; *do* missing (similar to L1 English acquisition in Klima and Bellugi Stage 2, but also obligatory in Spanish)	# He no wanna go. # It no cause too much trouble. # He look like a glass, but no is a glass.

Table 4
UNIQUE GOOFS

GOOF TYPE	GOOF
SPANISH–ENGLISH	
Use of Nom for Poss Pro	# She name is Maria.
Overuse of *do*	# We do got no more book.
Count/mass distinction not expressed correctly	# He got a toys.
	# He got a little bit page (left).
-ing with a modal not allowed	# Now we will talking about . . .
Using simple sentence structure in embedded sentence	# I don't know what's that.

(b) Analysis

The data we have was not systematically collected; therefore, a frequency count is not appropriate. There were, however, few interference-like goofs relative to the number of non-interference goofs.

As stated in **4.1**, our account of L2 syntactic goofs will rely on the general processing strategies we posited as the theoretical assumptions for the L2 acquisition = L1 acquisition hypothesis. Further, in the absence of comprehensive L2 acquisition research and within the framework of this paper, it is not possible to go much beyond

L1 acquisition findings, except for speculations which we take the liberty to present in the final section. Therefore, an explanation of the Unique Goofs listed in Table 4 must await more systematic L2 acquisition research. The Ambiguous Goofs in Table 3 can be explained by both the CA hypothesis and the L2 acquisition = L1 acquisition hypothesis; therefore, they cannot be used as decisive evidence for either. The L1 Developmental Goofs in Table 2 are clearly accounted for by only the L2 acquisition = L1 acquisition hypothesis; therefore, they can be used to confirm it and need not be discussed further. We are thus left with the Interference-like Goofs, which, although they appear to confirm the transfer process posited by the CA hypothesis, are, we think, explainable within the L2 acquisition = L1 acquisition framework. It is this explanation that is presented in this section, namely, that the Interference-like Goofs reflect a strategy similar to one used by children acquiring English as their native language.

L1 learners '. . . "iron out" or correct irregularit[ies] of the language, and incidentally reveal to us the fact that what they are learning is general rules of construction—not just the words and phrases they hear.' (Cazden and Brown in press, pp. 2–3.) For example, children use the past tense inflection (-*ed*) for irregular verbs, such as #*goed* and #*runned* for *went* and *ran*. These have been called 'overgeneralizations'. The explanations offered below are instances of various types of overgeneralization. The specific types of overgeneralizations discussed below have not been found in L1 acquisition data. So in a sense, we have now put *specific* L1 acquisition *structures* aside but have retained L1 processing strategies in our explanation of L2 syntactic goofs.

Spanish-English Interference-like Goofs

> # Now she's putting her*s* clothes on.
> # She putting her*s* pyjamas on.
> # She's gonna brush her*s* teeths.

These goofs look like they reflect modifier-noun number agreement, obligatory in Spanish but not existent in English. However, it is not unreasonable to hypothesize that these are instances of over-generalizing the possessive -s from NP's which are nouns, e.g. *Tim's, Mary's*. (This specific overgeneralization does not appear in English L1 acquisition data, but is consistent with the general strategy.) It is also quite possible that the child was overgeneralizing from the structure [NP is X's], e.g. *It's hers, . . . Tim's*, etc., which is a very common structure of English.

We did not find *bigs houses, talls boys*, etc. which could not have been an English overgeneralization and thus would have been a clear case of Spanish interference. (This is predicted by Stockwell, Bowen and Martin, 1965.)

> #I know to do all that.
> #I finish *to watch* TV when it's 4 o'clock.

These too, reflect typical Spanish complement structures. However, the structure is also typical of English. Replacing *know* and *finish* with *want*, whose frequency of occurrence is undisputed, would yield a structure children produce regularly, e.g., *I want to go to Grandma's*.

Norwegian-English Interference-like Goofs

> #Drive you car to-yesterday?
> #Like you ice cream?
> #Like you me not, Reidun?

These goofs accurately reflect Norwegian structure (see p. 168 above) and usually not American English. However, these children were exposed to English in England, where the verb *have* is permuted: *Has he a job?*, *Have you a cold?* Since *have* is also a verb of very high frequency with children as well as adults, we hypothesize here the generalizing the possessive *s* from NP's which are nouns, e.g. appear in L1 acquisition data, perhaps because the children studied were American and there is less possibility of being exposed to the structure *Have + Subj + Obj* in the United States.[32]

4.3 *Speculations*

The formulation of specific types of production strategies in L2 acquisition has barely begun, so that we can only indicate the direction we hope to pursue. The theoretical assumptions outlined above comprise the starting point and framework for our research efforts. L1 acquisition research provides support and direction. Our next research task, which will include systematic data collection of the speech of two six-year-old Spanish-speaking children learning English, will provide an empirical test for our hypotheses.

So far we are considering the following criteria as a point of departure for the formulation of hypotheses about children's production strategies in L2 acquisition. Each criterion is followed by a hypothesis.

1. *a rule's utility for rich expression with a minimum of grammatical redundancy*
   e.g. word order

Word order alone is sufficient to express the basic semantic relations: agent-action-object, genitive, possessive, locative, negation, etc., as in # *Daddy dog* for 'Daddy's dog'. This has been demonstrated by analysis of children's telegraphese in their native language (Brown, 1971, Bloom, 1970), and by adult telegrams.

In L2 production, word order is used to produce not only simple sentences like those in L1, but also complex sentences relatively early, long before the functors within clauses are acquired, e.g. *He say he bring it to school.*

   e.g. a rule using a minimal number of cues to signal the speaker's semantic intention

Intonation is used alone in the beginning to signal questions. When the *wh-* words are learned, they are used without the additional obligatory aux-subject inversion, which is in fact redundant. In *if-then* clauses, the obligatory congruence of tenses, e.g. present in the *if* clause, future in the *then* clause, is omitted.

We predict that this type of rule will be used earliest and will result in missing functors and missing transformations.

2. *the pervasiveness of a syntactic generalization*
   e.g. the Principle of Transformational Cycle

The Principle of the Transformational Cycle roughly means that certain rules apply to several clauses within a complex sentence in the same way that they apply to a simple sentence, e.g. number agreement, agent deletion, reflexive, *there*-insertion.[33] But, for some sentence types this principle is obligatorily violated, such as in indirect questions where the simple sentence question formation rule does not apply to an embedded question. We don't say:

   #I asked him when would he come.

Instead we say:

   I asked him when he would come.

We predict that if a pervasive principle has been acquired, its use in structures where its violation is obligatory will result in goofs of the type mentioned above.

3. *frequency of a lexical item in the child's speech that entails a specific syntactic structure*

   e.g. *want,* which entails an infinitive complement (M. K. Burt and C. Kiparsky, in press)

This example was discussed in our explanation of the interference-like goofs in our Spanish-English data.

   e.g. *have,* which in British English entails verb-subject inversion in *yes-no* questions   p. 119

This example was discussed in our explanation of the interference-like goofs in Ravem's Norwegian-English data.

We predict that if a child uses a lexical item frequently, he will tend to use the syntactic structure required by it for lexical items which belong to the same form class but which require a different structure.

Much more data will have to be examined in order to formulate these hypotheses more precisely, to find other production strategies, and perhaps to find their respective places in the scheme of second language acquisition.

NOTES

1 The relation between 'production' and 'comprehension' is still opaque to language acquisition researchers. We will thus make no assumptions about the relation and deal only with theories and data about children's speech, rather than about what they are capable of understanding.

2 We are aware of the importance of the influence of social factors and personal motivation on second language learning, but adequate treatment of those factors is also beyond the scope of this paper.

3 Adopted from M. K. Burt and C. Kiparsky's *The Gooficon: A Repair Manual for English.* Rowley, Massachusetts, 1972.

4 We spent many hours, with the help of S. Macdonald, A. Lipson and C. Cazden, searching for a term that would give the reader the connotation of this definition. In the end 'goof' prevailed. The connotations of cuteness or ridicule which 'goof' might evoke are not intended at all. It seems to us that those connotations are less detrimental than the feeling of blame or a vision of red marks on a composition that 'error' and 'mistake' might evoke. Other terms considered were 'deviation' which is a negatively loaded term in social psychology and 'ellipsis' whose mathematical definition connotes exactly what we want to say, but which has been used in linguistics to mean an abbreviated structure.

5 Throughout this paper goofs are marked with a #.

6 These studies include the learning of English by a Japanese child, by a Norwegian child, and by Spanish children; the learning of Spanish and French by American children; along with relevant adult studies.

7 See also Nickel and Wagner, 1968; Banathy, Trager and Waddle, 1966, Upshur, 1962; Lane, 1962; and the introduction to the Michigan Oral Language Series English Guide—Kindergarten 1970.

8 See Fries's Foreword to Lado, 1957, Lado, 1957, pp. 57–59, Upshur, 1962, p. 124, Lane, 1962, Jakobovits, 1970, pp. 194–229, and Sapon, 1971.

9 See especially Rivers, 1964.

10 See Tulving and Madigan, 1970 for a review of the field. See Postman, 1961; Postman, Stark and Fraser, 1968; Postman and Stark, 1969 for full treatment of the theory.

11 The year of 'Postman's optimistic assessment of the health of the [interference] theory . . . at a major verbal learning conference'. (Tulving and Madigan, 1970, p. 470, referring to Postman, 1961.)

12 See also Slamecka, 1969, Melton, 1961 and 1967, and Hart, 1967.

13 See Postman and Stark, 1969; Postman, Stark and Fraser, 1968.

14 See for example Sapon, 1971, and Jakobovits, 1970, pp. 194–221.

15 Italics added.

16 Some anthropological linguists do study the problem of ethnic language retention, however.

17 The theoretical assumptions stated at the beginning of this section have been the subject of intense scholarly debate. We refer the reader to N. Chomsky, 1964; Garrett and Fodor, 1968; Bever, 1968; Bever, Fodor and Garrett, 1968; and Tulving and Madigan, 1970.

18 Italics added.

19 Italics added.

20 By 'intentional' Weinreich apparently means that the speaker chooses one of two options available to him, i.e. he can use items he knows from two languages. Whether the choice is 'conscious' or 'unconscious' is not significant.

21 To do justice to this statement in any way would require an in-depth study of the phonological goofs, their level (deep or surface structure), and their relation to the syntax of the sentences of which these goofs are a part. In addition, the relationship between the phonological processing system and the syntactic processing system would have to be discussed. This is beyond the scope of this paper.

22 Ervin-Tripp, 1970, p. 330.

23 We considered the study by Dato (1970) of American children learning Spanish in Madrid. He includes some samples of Spanish L2 speech that reflect English structure, but each of these samples might also reflect Spanish L1 developmental goofs. In the absence of Spanish L1 acquisition data, there is no way to accurately categorize Dato's data. For example, #*grande oreja* ('big ear') shows wrong adjective placement: in Spanish most adjectives follow the noun they modify, except for a few which may

precede the noun. Adjectives which may appear before the noun may also appear after it, with a different meaning. On the other hand, in English adjectives precede nouns they modify (*green hat*). Though the above goof does reflect the child's L1 (English), we do not know whether in Spanish L1 acquisition children use one adjective position before another. It is interesting that in Dato's published data on the acquisition of the noun phrase, the adjective position goof made was always with *grande*. *Grande* is one of the few adjectives in Spanish that is used both before and after the noun, with a different meaning for each position.

24 These reservations are mostly methodological. The linguistic apparatus necessary to make valid comparisons between languages is still being developed. 'Contrastive analysis has not yet overcome its teething troubles and is still lacking sound theoretical foundations' (Nickel and Wagner, 1968, p. 255). See also Wardaugh, 1970 and Richards, 1971.

25 It is difficult to ascertain what Dato means by 'transformational model' or 'base structures'. He writes, 'our findings indicate that transformational processes as reflected in the utterances of our subjects do indeed have some psychological reality', but he does not compare his descriptions of the intermediate developmental steps with actual generative grammar transformations. He has found however, general trends of increasing complexity across subjects, based on his description of the structures acquired by his subjects.

26 Milon has not completed his analysis of Ken's Stage 3.

27 The two apparent differences are: (i) Ken's utterances as cited in Milon's paper consist of two words, while those of Adam, Eve and Sarah consist of three and four words; (ii) Ken's utterances do not include the structure [Nucleus + Neg], while those of Adam, *et al.* do.

28 See E. Jordan, 1971.

29 # here is the linguistic symbol for 'word boundary'.

30 The third rule—z # + ces (z → c) which is included in most grammar books is omitted because it is phonetically equivalent to the second rule and applies only to spelling.

31 English translation is ours.

32 There is disagreement among informants here, as some speakers of American English consider both versions normal. Perhaps we can only speculate that the *Have* + NP . . .? structure is more commonly used in British English than in American English, and that Rune's parents used it whereas Adam, Eve and Sarah's parents did not.

33 For details see M. K. Burt, 1971, pp. 157–64.

7

Language Acquisition in a Second Language Environment

ROAR RAVEM

Reprinted from IRAL, Vol. VI/2, May 1968, published by Julius Groos Verlag, Heidelberg.

1 Introduction

The present paper is a report on a study of a Norwegian six-year-old child's acquisition of English syntax in a second language environment. The study was undertaken with my son as the informant when I was a student of applied linguistics at the University of Edinburgh in 1966. It arose out of a general interest in language acquisition *per se* and more particularly out of an interest in relating studies of language acquisition to the teaching of foreign languages in kindergartens and at early elementary school stages. The more we know about language learning the more likely we are to be successful in our teaching of a second language. However, the gap between a child acquiring his first language and a child learning a second language, at a time when he already possesses 'language', is likely to be so big that any direct application of our knowledge is difficult, the more so because our knowledge in the first place is still extremely shaky. I hope that the present study will make a small contribution to filling the gap.

Most recent studies of the acquisition of syntax have been concerned with the linguistic competence of the children at different stages of their linguistic development and an effort has been made to write generative grammars for these stages. The investigators have been interested in the obtained data only to the extent that they throw light on the child's system of internalized rules for generating language. According to the language acquisition model suggested by Noam Chomsky,[1] a distinction is made between 'performance'—the actual utterances—and the underlying 'competence' on which performance is based. Chomsky's basic tenet is the notion that linguistic theory should provide an adequate characterization of the native

124

speaker's knowledge of his language, i.e. the native speaker's intuition of what is grammatical in his language should be capable of being described in a logically consistent way. Even if it were possible, in Chomsky's terms, to give a descriptively adequate account of an adult native speaker's linguistic competence, an adequate description of a child's competence is very much more difficult, both because the child's intuition of what is grammatical is not available and also because the child's competence is continually developing.

In the present study no serious attempt has been made to go beyond capturing the syntactic regularities of my informant's speech at the times of observation. An attempt has been made to present some of these regularities in the form of rewrite rules, but as they are based on what appear to be the most productive patterns as shown by performance data, they do not claim to be generalized rules characterizing my informant's competence. They are at best a reflection of it.

The sentences singled out for closer scrutiny were interrogative and negative sentences of the kind that in adult language require a *do*-transformation. These are of particular interest because the comparable sentences in Norwegian are made by inversion of subject noun phrase and verb.

2 Background and Method

My informant, Rune, was $6\frac{1}{2}$ when the study began. He had a rudimentary knowledge of English, acquired during a previous stay in England and from being read to occasionally in English. He had thus been exposed to the language, but had never had any systematic teaching of it. He started school in the middle of January 1966 in Scotland and was allocated to a class of children of his own age-group. Basing one's judgement on a purely subjective impression, one can say that Rune appears to be slightly ahead of his age-group with respect to intelligence and perhaps language development too.

The material was collected from two main sources: free conversation and a translation test. Rune, who is a talkative child, did not seem to be affected by the fact that the conversations were recorded, and thus it was not difficult to elicit utterances from him. With the help of my 11-year-old daughter, who is bilingual in Norwegian and English, we managed to steer the conversation in different directions to elicit from Rune different kinds of sentences, referring to both past, present and future.

The translation test, involving about fifty negative and interrogative sentences requiring an auxiliary in adult speech, was given at regular intervals. The object of the translation experiment was to compare the utterances with the data obtained in free conversation in order to get an indication of the validity of prompted utterances of this kind. The stimulus took the form of a request (in Norwegian) like 'go and ask mother if . . .' or 'tell Ranny that . . .'. The indirect sentence provided Rune with less of a clue to the syntactic structure of *his* sentence than a direct sentence would have done; the clue was further reduced by putting the sentence to him in Norwegian (notably in such cases where *do* is used). By prolonging the time gap between the stimulus and Rune's response it was hoped that the effect of the stimulus as a clue would be further reduced. The validity of the translation experiment was supported by the obtained utterances in free conversation. There were some clear cases of interference from Norwegian, but they were of the same kind as found in the conversation material.

The conversation data were collected at four different 'Times', starting on 31st December 1965 and finishing on 6th March 1966. The translation test was given within a week of the conversation recordings. It was seen to be an advantage to record intensively at 3–4 week intervals rather than more frequently and less intensively.

3 Some findings

Only negative and interrogative sentences have been singled out in the study for analysis. However, some examples of declarative sentences were included for comparative purposes. Our special concern was with Rune's acquisition of *do* as a tense-marker. If Katz and Postal are correct, which they probably are, the only meaning of *do* is to be a carrier of tense.[2] Being semantically empty it does not appear as a morpheme in deep structure and the task of the learner of English is to discover the particular function of *do* as a tense carrier. This might help to explain the reason why *do*-transformations constitute a particular difficulty for foreign learners of English. In this respect *do* has not the same status as the modal auxiliaries, which behave, along with *have* and *be,* roughly in the same way as the equivalent auxiliaries in Norwegian. On this basis we would expect that Rune would acquire these auxiliaries more quickly than *do.* The following examples show that this is in fact the case: *I not like that* (C.1),[3] *eating you dinner to-yesterday?* (T.2), *what you did in Roth-*

bury? (C.3), *climb you?* (C.2) compared with *can I give that to Sooty?* (C.1), *oh, I mustn't take that aeroplane open and . . .* (C.1), *I have try that, 'men'*[4] *I can't do it* (C.1).

3.1 Declarative sentences

The following typical declarative sentences have been included for comparative purposes:

1. All crying.
   We climbing Friday.
   I drawing and do something.
   I fall down again (i.e. prob. *fell*).

2. He can see the moon.
   I will hear what you will say.

3. I have say it.
   I have lost it.
   I have eating and play.

On the basis of data of the kind represented by 1. above we would suggest, very tentatively, the following rule:

$$S \rightarrow NP + \begin{Bmatrix} (be) + V \\ V \end{Bmatrix} + (X) + (adv.t.)$$

Both modals and *have* have been excluded. Rune uses *have* for 'completed' aspect, but the participle morpheme, *-en,* is not normally realized. The only available verb-forms at this stage are, on the whole, verb-stem (V) or V_{ing}. That V and V_{ing} are not free variants, except possibly in 1. above, is indicated by the almost exclusive use of V in sentences with modal auxiliaries. The following obtained sentences uttered in succession illustrate this:

> *I singing out yesterday.*
> *I can sing Blaydon Races for you.*

We can only venture a guess why Rune makes such an extensive use of the *ing*-form of the main verb, more often than not without the auxiliary *be.* Is it because he has been exposed to English at an early stage so frequently in situations where the present progressive is used that he has generalized his own usage on this basis? An interference from Norwegian is out of the question as Norwegian has no expanded tense form.

The concept of tense is available to Rune, but he appears not to have discovered how to realize it in English. Time relations are sometimes expressed by help of an adverb of time as in the obtained sentences *I singing now/yesterday/all the day* (i.e. every day). The non-occurrence of -*ing* with such verbs as *like* and *think* and the fact that *be* occurs optionally only in the context of V_{ing}, not V, might indicate a beginning differentiation between the simple and progressive forms.

3.2 *Negative Sentences*

In adult grammar *do* is used when the verb phrase does not contain another auxiliary verb. As with the modal auxiliaries the negative element, *not*, follows or is attached to *do* and not to V. The sentences below exemplify the similarities between the use of modal auxiliaries and *do* in negative sentences in English as contrasted with Norwegian:

I cannot come.	*Jeg kan ikke komme.*
I could not come.	*Jeg kunne ikke komme.*
He does not work.	*Han arbeider ikke* (he works not).
We did not take it.	*Vi tok det ikke* (we took it not).

Since *do* is not yet available at Time 1, one prediction would be that Rune, in keeping with Norwegian structure, lets *not* follow the main verb and produces sentences of the form $NP + VP + not$. What we find, however, are such sentences as *I not like that, one is not crying, I not looking for edge*. The negative sentences at this stage correspond to the pattern for declarative sentences. We need only insert *not* after the subject NP in our formula.

3.3 *Interrogative Sentences*

The following types of interrogative sentences, all of them requiring *do* in adult grammar, were studied: 1. sentences beginning with a question word (*what, when,* etc.), 2. sentences requiring *yes* or *no* as an answer, 3. negative versions of 2, 4. negative questions beginning with *why.*

Again we find a high degree of syntactic similarity between English and Norwegian in the use of modal auxiliaries and *have* ('ha'), but there is no equivalent to *do* as shown by the following examples:

1. What did he say?	*Hva sa han?*
	(What said he?)
2. Did you do it?	*Gjorde du det?*
	(Did you it?)

3. Don't you like ice-cream?   *Liker du ikke iskrem?*
   (Like you not ice-cream?)
4. Why don't you like ice-cream?   *Hvorfor liker du ikke iskrem?*
   (Why like you not ice-cream?)

A reasonable prediction would be that Rune at Time 1 would make use of Norwegian syntactic structure to form English sentences of the types in brackets above, i.e. by inversion of subject NP and V. If *do* is semantically empty, these sentences differ from adult grammar only in their transformational history. They would sound foreign, but would be perfectly understandable.

As we shall see later this happens to both affirmative and negative versions of *Q-yes/no*-sentences, but interestingly enough not to *Q-wh*-sentences. These seem to be generated on the basis of the rule for declarative sentences with a prefixed *Q-wh* morpheme. If we take the sentence 1. *What you reading to-yesterday?* (T.1) to represent a simple tense sentence and 2. *What she (is) doing now?* (C.1) to represent progressive tense, they both retain the word order $NP + V$ of declarative sentences.[5] Both sentence types then appear to have developed from the same basic pattern, that of declarative sentences. We could illustrate this hypothesis by help of the following structural description.

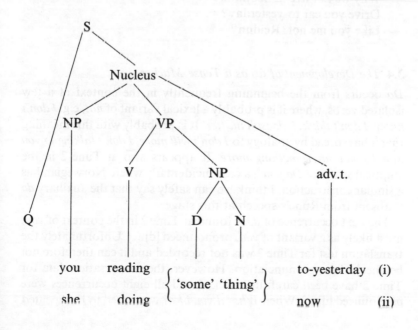

| | you | reading | ⎰ 'some' 'thing' ⎱ | to-yesterday | (i) |
| | she | doing | | now | (ii) |

On the basis of this pattern we could make various predictions about the line of development for 1. and 2.

That Rune, like L1 learners, makes use of the pattern of the declarative sentence in *Q-wh*-sentences is, as we have already pointed out, rather surprising in view of the inversion of subject NP and V in Norwegian. It would be reasonable to expect both 1. and 2. to come out as *What reading you to-yesterday?* and *What doing you now?* This happens with *yes/no*-questions, where typical examples are *Climb you?* and *Like you food?* Again we could speculate as to whether Rune in these types of sentence makes use of inversion as a question signal from lack of a question word. Negative *yes/no*-questions and negative *why*-questions are structured differently, but on a par with the respective affirmative sentences. These sentences were included in the Translation test only at Time 3. The *Q-why-Neg*-sentences proved much more resistant to the *do*-transformation than the other types of sentence included in the study. Typical sentences before the introduction of the *do*-transformations are:

I singing out yesterday.
I not sitting on my chair.
What you reading to-yesterday?
Why we not live in Scotland?
Drive you car to-yesterday?
Like you me not, Reidun?

3.4 *The Development of* do *as a Tense Marker*

Do occurs from the beginning frequently in the context of a few isolated verbs, where it is probably a lexical variant of *not*, e.g. *I don't know, I don't think, it doesn't matter*. It is probably with this meaning that it has spread by analogy to *I don't will more, I don't talking to you* and *I don't say something more*. It appears also at Time 2 in the elliptical sentence *Do you?*, a case incidentally where Norwegian has a similar construction. I think we can safely say that the auxiliary *do* is absent from Rune's speech at this stage.

The next occurrence of *do* is found at Time 2 in the context of *you*, most likely as a variant of *you*, pronounced [dju:]. Unfortunately the translation test for Time 2 was not recorded and it can therefore not be checked for pronunciation. However, the conversation data for Time 2 have been carefully checked and all eight occurrences were pronounced [dju:]. When *What d'you like?* was asked to be repeated slowly, Rune repeated it as *'What 'you 'like*. It is not unthinkable that *do* is acquired by children by first being a variant of *you*.

Time 3 is a transition stage. *Do* is clearly emerging as a tense carrier. The fact that Rune is now in the middle of a process of acquiring *do* is likely to be responsible for the greater lack of stability found at this stage than at the other times of observation. It is as if Rune is searching for a morpheme to attach tense to. The following examples illustrate the vacillation:

> I not sitting on the chair.
> I don't sit on the chair.
> What d'you do to-yesterday?
> What d'you did to-yesterday?
> When d'you went there?
> What you did in Rothbury?
> What you do—in the hayshed?
> Like you ice-cream?
> Did you drive car to-yesterday?

By Time 4 *do* has clearly emerged as a separate element, with both a present and past tense form. *Did* is more often than not used in sentences requiring the past tense, but there are also examples which show that the distinction is not fully established. Where *do* occurs it is almost invariably followed by the infinitive form of the main verb.

Contrary to the findings of Susan M. Ervin,[6] there does not appear to be any significant time lag between the introduction of *do* into negative and interrogative sentences in Rune's case. This might be accounted for, however, by Rune's greater linguistic maturity and faster rate of learning.

At this stage *yes/no*-questions, both negative and affirmative, also fall into line with *Q-wh*-sentences as shown by the following examples: *Did you not see on TV to-yesterday?* as compared with the Time 3 *See you not on TV to-yesterday?* and *Did you not say it to daddy?, Don't you like me, Reidun?* as compared with the Time 3 *Say it you not to daddy?, Like you me not, Reidun?* Except for the *Q-why-Neg*-sentences, which throughout the time of study have consistently been of the type *why + NP + not + VP* (or alternatively *why + not + NP + VP*), the other structures under study should at Time 4 be capable of being described by a single set of related rules, as is the case in adult grammar.[7] These are by no means as stable as in adult grammar. Rune still frequently produces sentences which syntactically correspond to earlier structures.

4 Conclusion

The study reported here was not undertaken to test any particular hypotheses relating to certain theories of language learning. The only purpose was to conduct a study within the framework of recent L1 syntax studies to find out something about developmental sequence as compared with first language learners.

Recent first language syntax studies have shown that children exposed to a language at an early age internalize rules with the aid of which they are able to generate sentences. Attempts have been made with some degree of success to give a characterization of the sets of rules that are operative at various stages of development. The studies have shown that a large measure of creativity enters into the process of language acquisition.

The situation of the learner of a second language is clearly different from that of the L1 child. The most obvious difference is that the task of the foreign learner is not to learn 'language', which he already possesses and the knowledge of which must affect his acquisition of a second language. The process of learning the second language might therefore conceivably be qualitatively different. Nor is he very often exposed to 'primary linguistic data' in the sense that an L1 learner is, but rather to carefully graded language items presented in small doses for a few hours a week.

The present study has, I believe, shown what we would expect to find, namely that a normal six-year-old child at all levels of language is greatly facilitated by the linguistic competence he already possesses through his first language. The six-year-old's greater maturity makes for a faster rate of learning. The first language, especially when it is as closely related to English as Norwegian is, is a source the learner can draw on. The detrimental effect of first language interference can only be assessed properly after the learner has achieved a good command of the second language.

What is perhaps more striking is the extent to which second language acquisition in an environment where no formal instruction is given seems to be a creative process not unlike that of first language acquisition. The similarities between Rune and L1 learners in the developmental sequence of negative and interrogative sentences are in many ways more revealing than the differences.

It does not follow from this that the appropriate methodology for teaching a foreign language at an early stage is to expose the children to a 'language bath' and let them develop for themselves internalized generative rules which ultimately develop into those of adult grammar. We do not know if second language acquisition can be speeded up by the children being exposed to selected and linguistically graded language patterns. And even if we have accepted that language learning is not merely a question of habit formation and reinforcement of correct responses, we cannot exclude the possible transfer value of well-established basic sentence patterns, especially if they are acquired in contextualized situations.

Perhaps a larger measure of language exposure and a freer scope for creative and self-corrective language learning than permitted by a graded course would be appropriate in early foreign language teaching in a school setting. Only a series of carefully controlled experiments could provide an answer to this question.

NOTES

1 Chomsky, 1965, ch. 1.

2 Katz and Postal, 1964, p. 8.

3 C refers to Conversation data, T refers to Translation. The number refers to Time of recording.

4 Norwegian for *hut*. Rune made use of Norwegian vocabulary items frequently and without hesitation, as if they were available English words. One interesting observation is that, even at Time 1, before he knew any written English (or Norwegian), the Norwegian words were often given an English pronunciation. Somehow he was able to translate from one phonological system into another. Examples are: *tak*/tɑ:k/(roof), pronounced by Rune as /teik/; *ratt*/rɑt/(steering wheel) pronounced as /ræt/.

5 The only justification for letting 1. represent a simple tense sentence is the fact that this and similar sentences in the translation test later develop into simple past tense sentences of adult grammar.

6 Ervin, 1964, p. 184.

7 To find out what had happened to *Q-why-neg*-sentences after the termination of the study, Rune was asked (January '67) to translate some of these from Norwegian. In addition to some earlier structures, such as *Why not Ranny come home?*, most of them were in the main in keeping with adult grammar, e.g. *Why do we not live in Oslo?*, *Why doesn't we go to Oslo?*. But also the obtained *Why didn't mummy don't make dinner?* was attested by Rune as correct.

8

The Development of *Wh*-Questions in First and Second Language Learners*

ROAR RAVEM

Originally published as an occasional paper by the Language Centre, University of Essex.

1 Introduction

Roger Brown (1968)[1] reports the result of an analysis of *Wh*-questions in the speech of the three children whose language development has been studied by him and his associates at Harvard University.[2] The analysis was made to determine whether or not there was evidence in the spontaneous speech of pre-school children that the transformational rules of current generative-transformational grammar also figure in the child's competence, in other words, if the intermediate hypothetical strings in a transformational analysis correspond to stages in the child's development of *Wh*-questions. Such hypothetical intermediates are not, usually, actualized in adult forms and hence not available to the child for imitation. If they occurred in the speech of children at a certain stage of development, it would suggest that transformational grammar has managed to capture psychologically real operations, and it would throw further doubt on an empiricist explanation of language acquisition, since these intermediate structures are not exemplified in the language data the child is exposed to.

2 The Grammar of *Wh*-Questions

Table 1 presents examples of types of sentences that I shall be concerned with in this report, here given in their adult form.

* I am indebted to my superior, Dr Terence Moore at the Language Centre, University of Essex, for critical comments and advice on this paper. He is, however, not responsible for the views expressed and my possible misinterpretation of Professor Brown's views.

Table 1

When will John come?
What was Mary saying?
Where has he gone?
How do you like it?
Why did John leave?
Who did Mary see?
Who saw John?

In the current transformation analysis the sentences in Table 1 are derived transformationally from a final derived phrase marker (a terminal string of symbols derived by phrase structure rules). The leftmost symbol will be an abstract interrogative morpheme (Q), followed by the subject noun phrase (NP) and the verb phrase (VP). Each of these major constituents will dominate a hierarchy of minor constituents. Thus the VP will contain an AUX, which contains tense (T) and a verbal auxiliary constituent. It will further include to the right of AUX a main verb (V) and an NP when the sentence requires a direct object. If the sentence requires an adverbial (ADV), this will be generated to the right of the VP. The constituent to be questioned, either the subject NP or the object NP or the ADV, will have associated with it an abstract dummy element (WII).[3] Before lexical insertion, a simplified underlying string for a sentence like

When will John read the book?

would look like this:

Q NP AUX V NP WH-ADV (time)

For convenience we will render it as:

Q John will read the book WHEN

In this example the constituent ADV has been questioned. If an NP is questioned, we get either *Q John will read WHAT* or *Q WHO will read the book*.

To derive the normal question, two transformations are required (disregarding the transformation that deletes Q), namely, (1) a 'preposing transformation', which moves the constituent with the WH-feature to a front position (this transformation applies vacuously when it is the subject NP that contains the WH-feature), and (2) a 'transposing transformation', which moves (the first element of) the auxiliary in front of the subject NP. *Q John will read*

WHAT will by (1) be changed into

> *WHAT John will read?*

and further by (2) into

> *WHAT will John read?*

If morpho-phonemic rules were applied to the underlying non-transformed strings, sentences like the following would result:

> *John will read what?*
> *John will read the book when?*
> *Who will read the book?*

If we assume that the stages in language acquisition mirror the transformational derivation in transformational grammar, we would expect to find sentences in the child's grammar that are basically of this form. I shall therefore refer to it as the first Hypothetical Intermediate (H.I.1).

It should be noted, however, that the H.I.1 is not identical with Brown's 'Occasional Question' (1968, p. 279). In Brown's treatment the *Wh*-word is spoken with heavy stress and rising intonation. He gives the following example. 'If someone said: "John will read the telephone book" one might respond "John will read *what*?" '. This would not in my analysis constitute an example of H.I.1. As a question it is semantically different from a normal question in that the constituent that is questioned is already known and the question expresses a disbelief or astonishment.[4] The sentence we would expect to find, if our assumption were correct, would be one with normal interrogative stress and intonation.

The next stage of development would be one in which morpho-phonemic rules were applied to an underlying string after preposing, but in the absence of transposing. This would result in sentences like:

> *What John will read?*
> *When John will read the book?*

I shall refer to this type as the second Hypothetical Intermediate (H.I.2). It corresponds to the Hypothetical Intermediate found to be a general feature of the grammar of the three children studied by Brown and his associates.

Diagram 1 is meant to illustrate some of the features relevant to our discussion of the underlying structures of *Wh*-questions as they might be represented in a child's grammar. The *Q* symbolizes the

DIAGRAM 1

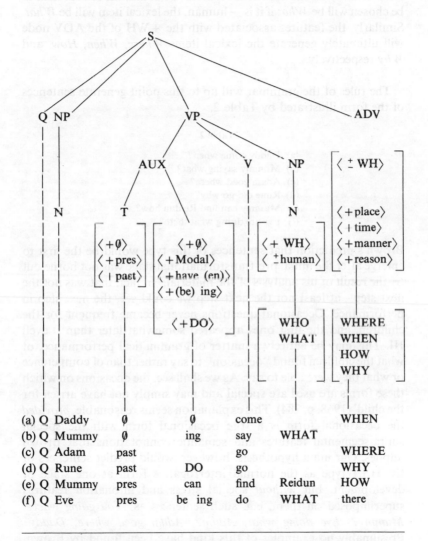

The diagram has been designed for expository convenience; details have therefore been omitted and notational conventions violated. (a)–(f) exemplify structures underlying the hypothetically intermediate strings (H.I.1) in Table 2.

fact that a sentence is to be interpreted as a question; the constituent to be questioned has received the feature +WH. If the constituent at the NP node has the additional feature +human, the lexical item to be chosen will be *Who*; if it is −human, the lexical item will be *What*. Similarly, the features associated with the +WH of the ADV node will ultimately generate the lexical items *Where, When, How,* and *Why* respectively.

The rules of the grammar will up to this point generate sentences of the form illustrated by Table 2.

Table 2

(a) Daddy come when?
(b) Mummy saying what?
(c) Adam goed where?
(d) Rune did go why?
(e) Mummy can find Reidun how?
(f) Eve are doing what there?

Brown's prediction that sentences of this type would be the first to emerge after the initial pre-transformational stage was not borne out by the result of his analysis of the material. 'In fact, that was not the next step—at least not the next step we could see, the next step in performance. Occasional questions never became frequent for the children, and the first ones appeared somewhat later than [Level] III. This may be entirely a matter of grammatical performance, of what the children found "occasion" to say rather than of competence or what they were able to say. As we shall see, the occasions on which these forms are used are special and may simply not have arisen for the child' (1968, p. 284). This explanation seems reasonable, *provided* the occasional form is a true occasional form with the special supra-segmental features and semantic connotations that Brown implies. Our main hypothesis, however, would predict sentences of the H.I.1 type as the normal interrogative form at one stage of development, but *without* special stress and intonation features superimposed on them, e.g. such sentences as: *You going where, Mummy?, Eve doing what, Adam?, Adam goed where, Daddy?* Presumably no examples of this kind have been found by Brown, which means that neither Brown's hypothesis about occasional questions nor mine about H.I.1 has been confirmed by Brown's study.[5]

The story is different for our H.I.2, which is the string resulting from a preposing transformation. An actualization of this string would change the sentences in Table 2 to those in Table 3.

Table 3

(a) When Daddy come?
(b) What Mummy saying?
(c) Where Adam goed?
(d) Why Rune did go?
(e) How Mummy can find Reidun?
(f) What Eve are doing there?

The sentences in Table 3 are not actual sentences from a corpus, but they are—with the possible exception of (d)—plausible children's sentences. All the three children in the study reported by Brown used sentences of the preposing type, so here at least the hypothesis is not disconfirmed.

3 Own Study[6]

The findings to be described in this survey are based on a preliminary analysis of the emergence of *Wh* questions in the speech of two Norwegian children learning English as a second language in a naturalistic setting, i.e. in an English-speaking environment comparable to that of first language learners, with the exception that Norwegian is usually spoken at home.

The two studies have been longitudinal-observational and the corpora consist of tape-recorded interviews and various informal experiments, mainly translation and imitation tests.

My informants have been my son, Rune, and my daughter, Reidun. Rune was $6\frac{1}{2}$ when the study began and he had a rudimentary knowledge of English from a previous stay in Great Britain. The material for this study was collected over a period of five months, with fairly intensive recordings at 3–4 week intervals. For a report based on part of the corpus see Ravem (1968).

My present study is a follow-up of the previous study, but has mainly concentrated on my daughter's acquisition of English. She was three years and nine months old when the study began in September 1968. At that time she had no knowledge of English. Her Norwegian language development has on a subjective impression been normal and average. Her articulation has been exceptionally clear in both languages, which has facilitated transcriptions and made them more reliable.[7] The recordings were made at weekly intervals up to July 1969, each interview averaging one hour.

The interlocutors have been either our eldest, bilingual daughter, my wife and myself, native English-speaking adults, or playmates. The interviews have been arranged without being deliberately structured, as I wanted the speech during the sessions to be as spontaneous as possible. The most rewarding situations with regard to amount of data have been with peers or members of the family. As we were conscious about what we were looking for, we could steer the conversations in different directions and thereby elicit responses of the kind we were interested in. The translation tests have proved a useful instrument for eliciting the types of sentences I wanted, and their validity has been supported by obtained utterances in free conversation.

The collection of material was resumed after a break of two months, when the family were in Norway. Intensive recordings were made immediately before and after the break, as I was interested in the degree of forgetting that might have occurred during the two months. This, however, is only an incidental aspect of the study. Reidun seemed essentially to have caught up with her agemates by July 1969, but the collection of material has continued since in a less systematic fashion. I have only recently started analysing the corpus and the present report is based on only a portion of it.

4 Results and Discussion

There is no *prima facie* evidence why a child acquiring a second language should go through a similar development as first language learners. Nor incidentally, is it obvious that essentially the same path is followed (the same strategy chosen) by all learners of their mother tongue. Although a comprehensive study, the investigation by Brown and associates is to my knowledge the only complete longitudinal study of interrogative and negative sentences to date, and it comprises only three children. It is therefore quite conceivable that the picture will be more varied as more studies have been undertaken.

Nevertheless, as the actual data in Tables 4 and 5 show there are striking similarities between my own material and data from the study by Brown and associates (Table 6), and it is not likely that this is altogether accidental. (If one set out to search for differences, these would probably be equally striking, but less surprising.) I have not yet found any examples corresponding to our H.I.1; nor have I found any of Brown's occasional questions, with their associated stress and intonation contour, in spite of the fact that they are quite frequent in the speech of the interlocutors (my wife and myself).

Table 4
Wh-questions from Rune Times 1–4

Time 1
What is that?
What are mean? (what does mean mean)
Where is that /britʃ/? ('brikke')
What you eating?
What he's doing?
What she is doing?
What—you going to build tomorrow?
Where dem drink?
Why you say that before? (for)

Time 2
(c. 2 wks
later)
What Jane give him?
Rannveig, what dyou doing to yesterday on school?
What dyou like?
   (Adult: Say that again clearly)
'What 'you 'like?
What you think Pappy—name is?
What is—Mummy doing not?
(T)[1] What you doing to-yesterday?
(T) What dyou do to-yesterday?
(T) What you going to do tomorrow?
(T) What-uh-time-uh-clock Rannveig come back?
   (when; fut. re.)
(T) What you talking to to-yesterday? (who)
(T) – Translation test.

Time 3
(3–4 wks
later)
What . . . you knitting?
What he's doing?
What is he doing?
What dyou do the last week before you be—did—'bli'—ill?
(T) What dyou reading to-yesterday?
What you did in Rothbury?
What dyou did to-yesterday in the hayshed?
How did you do—have do—you—do—what you do on school last week?
When dyou went there? (In response to: Ask her when she went there)
Why the baby crying?
Why he come for a cup of coffee?
Why dyou must have table—and chairs?
Why drink we tea and coffee?
(T) Why we not live in Scotland?
(T) Why not Mummy make dinner?

[1] (T) stands for Translation Test.

Time 4   What you did after Ranny go to bed? (In response to: Ask Dad what he
(c. 3 wks   did.)
later)   What did you more—that night?
             What did you talk to them? (say/talk about)
      (T)   What do you doing to-yesterday?
      (T)   What did you do to-yesterday?
             When you go to bed? (past reference)
      (T)   What do you going to do tomorrow?
      (T)   Who you talking to to-yesterday?
      (T)   Why not that go up? (that window)
             Why not Mummy make meat today? (from Nor. *mat* = food)

Table 5

Wh-questions from Reidun

Months: weeks
  of exposure
  to English

3:1   What this? (What colour is this)
4:0   Where find it? (in response to: Ask her . . . where you can find it)
        Where *jeg kan jeg* find it—apples? (*jeg* = I; *kan* = can)
4:4   Whats that?
        Hvor er—my Mummy? (where is)
5:3   Whats her doing?
        Whats *er* her doing? (*er* = is/are)
        Where *er* hers Mummy?
        Why that the bed *er* broken? (prob.: why (is it) that)
6:0   What that is?
        Why it—Humpty Dumpty sat on a horse?
6:2   What call that man?
        What—name that man?
        Why that man have that on?
        Whats that—is?
        Why—uh—him have got like that? (a jacket like that)
        Why her don't stand there?
        Hvem er that? (who)
        Whos that?
        Whos that is?
        Whosis that is?
        What her going to make? (or: goingto?)
        Whats her baking?
6:3   Which one you want?
        What you want?
        What do you want? (or: doyou)
8:0   Who is that?
        Why you can't buy like that shoes?
        Where is it, then?
        Whats are they?

Why him have got a motor?
Why you can't—why you couldn't take it here? (i.e. bring)
What I got on?
Why I got that white dress on?
Mummy, where—where was you—are?
Where my penny?
9:3   What they got on they eyes?
What are he doing now, then—that man?
Why isn't that lady in there?
Why can't you touch with your—with your hand?
Which colour have we got, then?
Whats those two man doing?
What they doing?
Why hasn't she—got same as us?

Table 6

Wh-questions from the study by R. Brown and associates*

Stage 2	Where my mitten?
	Where me sleep?
	What the dollie have?
	What book name?
	Why you smiling?
	Why not me sleeping?
	Why not . . . me can't dance?
Stage 3	Where's his other eye?
	Where I should put it when I make it up?
	Where my spoon goed?
	What I did yesterday?
	What he can ride in?
	What did you doed?
	Why the Christmas tree going?
	Why Paul caught it?
	Why he don't know how to pretend?
	Why kitty can't stand up?
	Which way they should go?
	How he can be a doctor?
	How that opened?
	How they can't talk?

Brown's discussion of the role the occasional form might play in helping the child to see the relationship between different, but

*The examples are taken from E. S. Klima and U. Bellugi (1966). Klima and Bellugi's Stages do not correspond to Brown's Levels. Stage 2 appears to correspond roughly to Level III.

equivalent, question forms; the relation of the *Wh*-word to various pro-forms, such as *it* and *there*; and to learn the membership of a constituent, such as NP, is an interesting and plausible attempt to show that there is more in the language data the child is exposed to than meets the ear and that one might profitably look again at what might be exemplified in the input before one jumps to 'innateness' conclusions. However, the discussion would appear to be much less relevant to L2 acquisition, where the abstract categories and relationships are already known to the child through his first language. The learning task of my children may have been more of the order of learning how these relations, or whatever, are realized in the second language.

It appears, then, that transformational grammar has captured a stage in the child's development of *Wh*-questions; but this is not the same as saying that it has captured a psychologically real operation. The latter is what Brown, in effect, assumes. 'We believe that these questions, in general, were derived by a single preposing transformation out of underlying strings with dummy elements . . .' (1968, p. 286). The preposing transformation cannot be given a psychological status without at the same time assuming some kind of psychological reality for the underlying string (H.I.1). If this were not the case, there would be no preposing operation to carry out. It is for the hypothesis unfortunate that no sentences have been obtained that could be said to be either an actualization of the occasional question or of our H.I.1.

While entertaining the hypothesis of a preposing operation, Brown goes on to discuss the evidence for and against it. The *Wh*-questions in his corpus fall into two classes, one which he calls 'Preposing Weak' and another which he calls 'Preposing Strong'. A general characteristic of children's early speech is the omission of inflections and of minor word classes (functors), which results in what has been referred to as 'telegraphic' speech (Brown and Fraser, 1963). The class for which the evidence for a preposing transformation is weak consists of children's sentences that could have been learned as a reduction of adult speech to 'telegraphese', as shown by the following examples, where the omitted words are in parenthesis:

What (do) you want?
How (will) you open it?
What (is) his name?

The second class of *Wh*-questions are those for which the evidence for a preposing operation is strong, since they cannot be arrived at by telegraphic reduction. This is the case where the verb is inflected or where the questions include auxiliaries or the verb *be*, for example:

What he wants?
How he opened it?
What you will want?
Why you can't open it?
What his name is?

Before we consider the validity of the evidence for a preposing operation, it might be profitable to ask why one would want to suggest a hypothesis of this kind in the first place. If I understand Brown correctly, the argument seems to run something like this: The children had prior to Level III produced large numbers of *Wh*-questions, with all the *Wh*-words in initial position, but there was reason to believe that the questions were constructions or routines of some non-transformational type.[8] At Level III, however, there is ample evidence that the *Wh*-word replaces missing elements in the sentence, both locative adverbials and subject and object noun phrases. The child is capable of responding appropriately to questions calling for different constituents and is also able to produce such questions. 'It seems then that the constituents were organized as such and that the children were able to take a *Wh*-word supplied by a parent as the signal to supply an appropriate constituent member' (1968, p. 284).

The child's 'knowledge' can thus be accounted for by transformational grammar; but why would one expect to find that this knowledge—for which there is independent evidence—should be demonstrated in the child's language as an actualization of either the occasional question or H.I.1? Brown expected to find it since the occasional question 'only requires that the dummy element (which becomes a *Wh*-word) be selected from the constituent and supplied in place' (*ibid.*). I did not expect to find it, since the child has already for a long time used *Wh*-words in initial position and since the *Wh*-word normally appears in the same position in the adult model. What I am uneasy about in Brown's analysis, is that it appears to tie position learning of a fairly simple kind too closely to a much more abstract form of learning complex interrelationships. We can independently establish that the child possesses knowledge of the kind made explicit by transformation grammar and choose to describe it in those terms, and, for example, say that the child 'knows' that *what* in *What you want?* is the direct object of *want* and that it is related to an indefinite pro-form in the declarative sentence *You want 'some thing'*. It seems to me that it is quite legitimate to assume this knowledge and at the same time propose hypotheses to account for the order of constituents in *Wh*-questions of the preposing type in the child's speech.

One such hypothesis suggests itself, namely that the *Wh*-word remains in initial position and is followed by a 'nucleus' which retains the word order of a declarative sentence according to the child's grammar at any time.[9] This hypothesis does not purport to account for more than word order; nor is there more involved, it seems to me, in Brown's class of weak evidence. The evidence for preposing is weak exactly because it allows for an explanation in terms of selective imitation of an adult model and leaves unanswered such questions as how the child is able to question different constituents or can see the relationship between discontinuous constituents, such as the verb and the direct object in *What you want?*

The Preposing Weak class constitutes weak evidence for preposing only if the 'strong' evidence that Brown alleges does exist. If one is willing to concede an alternative explanation which is not in terms of an 'underlying grammatical network' for the Preposing Weak class, one should do this also for the class of strong evidence. On the alternative hypothesis (*Wh*-Nucleus) the strong evidence will turn out to be no stronger than the weak evidence; the hypothesis does not, in fact, distinguish between them. Sentences like *What he wants?* or *Why you can't open it?* cannot be derived from adult models alone, but the 'nucleus' of the sentence (or what remains of it) preserves the word order of the declarative sentence. When the child acquires inflections and auxiliaries in declarative sentences these will also—although usually somewhat later, which may complicate the analysis—be incorporated in *Wh*-questions as well. This alternative explanation does not affect the hypothesis that the child reduces adult speech in a systematic way and induces general rules on the basis of this reduction; but by adopting reduction as the only criterion, one is forced into setting up a separate class of Preposing Strong evidence, which is not required by the alternative hypothesis.

I like to believe that Tables 4 and 5 show, fairly conclusively, that the intermediate sentence type without transposing (inversion) is a feature also of my informants' acquisition of English as a second language. That they already knew the transposing transformation from Norwegian does not seem to have had much effect. Admittedly, the majority of the sentences obtained before inversion became general were of the Preposing Weak type, and hence could have resulted from reduction alone. Even if that were the case, one would have to account for the many clear cases of lack of inversion, such as:

What that is?
What she is doing?
What you did in Rothbury?
Why that man have that on?

A difficulty in deciding whether or not the lack of transposing represents a necessary developmental stage is the fact, which Brown also notes (*ibid.*, p. 285), that by the time the child produces sentences of the Preposing Strong type, he might already have gone a long way to acquiring the adult form with inversion. There are several examples in Table 5 that show how Reidun oscillates between different alternatives, e.g.

(6:2) *Hvem er* that? (Who is that)
Whos that?
Whos that is?
Whosis that is?

It does not seem unreasonable to expect that my children would have made use of inversion from the beginning by applying the rules for Norwegian. There are isolated examples from both Rune and Reidun where this is in fact the case, e.g.

Why drink we tea and coffee? (Rune)
Where livd (i.e. live) Catherine and Richard? (Reidun)

but they remain isolated cases. Lack of inversion was a feature of Reidun's Norwegian at an intermediate stage in her development as well, so we seem to have to do with a rather general phenomenon.[10] Since the use of the auxiliary *do* is specific to English, I will return to the acquisition of it later; I only want to point out here that there is strong evidence that *dyou* in Rune's speech, probably throughout Time 3, was a variant of *you*. The examples with *dyou* in Table 4 are therefore only apparent counter-examples of transposing.

5 The Development of the AUX node

Diagram 1 shows that the AUX is the most 'crowded' node on our tree. It contains some morphemes that are lexical and others that are realized as inflections, for example, present or past tense, past participle (en), and present participle (ing). There are a number of combinatorial possibilities, some as complicated as, for example:

>   *Past   Modal   have   en   be   ing*

Even without considering the cognitive problems involved in acquiring tense and aspect, the linguistic mechanisms themselves are complicated enough, and it is therefore to be expected that the full range of auxiliary morphemes and their distribution will be late in developing. There is probably room for some individual variation in the order in which children develop the AUX node, but the general picture is from no auxiliary at all through stages of approximations to adult grammar. I have not yet done any detailed analysis of the development of the auxiliary in my children, but it seems to resemble in many important respects the development in first language learners.

The main function of *do* is to be a carrier of tense.[11] The task of the learner of English is to discover this particular function of *do*. Since the use of *do* is specific to English, the second language learner is faced with very much the same learning problem. *Do* has been included in Diagram 1 as a verbal element of AUX, because it shares some of the distributional characteristics of the Modals. We could therefore on this basis predict that *Wh*-questions at the H.I.2 stage would have the form of sentence (d), *Why Rune did go?,* in Table 3, namely:

>   WH   NP   Tense-DO V

When *do* was introduced in affirmative *Wh*-questions as a tense carrier, Rune used inversion, for example:

>   *What did you do before you get to bed?*

With Reidun the situation is not clear-cut. There is still much material that has not been analysed, and although a couple of her affirmative *Wh*-questions have inversion of *do* and the subject NP, the translation tests show isolated examples of non-inversion, e.g.

>   (8:4) *Where we did livd for we come here?* (for = before).

I would have tended to interpret the few examples of non-inversion of *do* and subject NP in *Wh*-questions found so far as possible performance mistakes had it not been for Reidun's widespread use of *do* in declarative sentences, which might suggest a prior (or optional) rule of non-transposing also in *Wh*-questions with the auxiliary *do*. Examples are:

(9:1) I did have jelly.

(9:2) My Mummy did make lunch for them. You did take me, didn't you?

. . . and she did say 'yes', she did.

We did saw that in the shop.

Nuclear stress is in none of the entries on *did,* so there is no question of an emphatic form. Menyuk (1969, p. 73) gives an example from first language learners of both an affirmative sentence with *do* and a *Wh*-question without inversion:

I did read that motor boat book.

Where the wheel do go?

6 *Why* and *Why not* Questions

Although formally identical to other *Wh*-questions of the preposing type, Brown (1968, pp. 286–7) found reason to suspect that *Why*- and *Why not*-questions were not derived 'by a single preposing transformation out of underlying strings with dummy elements' when they were first introduced by Adam, one of his three informants. Adam's responses did not give evidence that he related his questions to a missing constituent, but rather to his mother's antecedent declarative, e.g.:

MOTHER	ADAM
I see a seal.	Why Adam see seal?
I don't see anything.	Why not you see anything?
You can't dance.	Why not me can't dance?

The underlying constituent that is questioned in *Why (not)*- questions is the indefinite pro-form 'for some reason'. The answers to such questions are clauses involving causal or teleological explanations introduced by 'because' or 'in order that'. It is therefore not implausible that *Why (not)* -questions are introduced at a later stage than other question types and that there is no clear relationship between the interrogative word and the questioned constituent in these questions when they first appear in the child's speech. In Adam's case it seems likely that he had some vague notion about causality, but that he is dependent upon an antecedent declarative sentence, which he largely echoes (using his own grammar) and to which he preposes *Why* or *Why not*. As for the two other children in the study, they did not start producing *Why (not)* -questions till they had reached the stage when they could give appropriate answers to them.

This appears, from a survey of parts of my corpus, to have been the case also with Reidun. Early *Why*-questions did not receive an appropriate response.

> RUNE: Why do you put the telephone on the front seat?
> (3:2) REIDUN: Yes.

Reidun's acquisition of *Why*-questions and their appropriate responses cannot in the same way as for first language learners be related to her cognitive development, that is, to 'learning what explanation is'. She knew this, relative to her age, and had used the Norwegian equivalents for some time.

As Table 7 shows, all Reidun's early sentences lack inversion. The first attested occurrences of *Why*-questions were in the fifth month of exposure to English. One half-hour recording at 6:3 had no less than 27 *Why*-questions and 8 *Why (not)*-questions. In the same recording there were three 'because'-responses and two embedded 'because'-clauses. The *Why (not)* -questions corresponded both to Brown's Preposing Weak and Preposing Strong types. Since Reidun had by now acquired auxiliaries and inflections required by the Preposing Strong class, a large percentage of her sentences were of this type.

Table 7

Why (not)- questions from Reidun

Months: weeks
of exposure
to English

6:2	Why that man have got it?
	Why uh that horses have that—that on—foot?
	Why—that man are over there?
	Why her don't stand there?
7:2	Why that man take—hang clothes on the—on the boat?
	Why that go up?
7:3	Why you can't eat it?
8:0	Why I sitting there?
	Why Daddy hold me?
	Why we can't go to London now—today?

8:2   Why has him lotsome pockets?
Why them have got some—lotsome pockets?
Why 'de' got those on?
Why can't I have it?
Why you've got those paper?

(T) 8:4   Why . . . Rune . . . isn't here?
Why Toto don't cry?
Why Andy Pandy don't sleep yet—now?
Why Daddy don't 'lag' (i.e. make)—eat lunch tomorrow?
(i.e. yesterday)

(T) 9:2   Why isn't Rune here?
Why doesn't Toto . . . cry?
Why isn't Andy Pandy sleeping?
. . . Why didn't Daddy—make lunch—yesterday?

9:2   Why have you got it on?
Why must I sit on the floor?
Why is it too hot?

The first clear case of inversion in the material so far analysed occurred at 8:2, viz.,

Why has him lotsome pockets?

which was followed soon after by the non-inverted

Why them have got some—lotsome pockets?

At 8:4 most of the *Why (not)-* questions in the translation test were of the Preposing Strong type, and none of them had undergone transposing:

Why Toto is in him room?
Why we don't go to Norway?
Why Daddy haven't got hat on?
Why I must bath all—all day? (i.e. every day)

The change took place at about 9:0 months of exposure, possibly affecting the copular sentences first. By 9:2 all the entries in the translation test had inversion (but not all *Wh*-questions):

Why is Toto up his room?
Why don't we go in Norway?
Why haven't Daddy got hat on—his head?
Why must I—bath all day?

Because of the many occurrences of transposing noticed during the interview session a few days later (9:2), some elicited imitation items were added at the end of the session, such as:

> Father: Why you didn't go to Colchester?
> Reidun: Why didn't you go to Colchester?

> Father: Why she has got trousers on?
> Reidun: Why have you got trousers on?

> Father: Why Mummy doesn't sit on the table?
> Reidun: Why doesn't Mummy sit on the table?

It appears, then, that the transposing operation took place over a short period of time and seems to have affected both affirmative and negative *Why*-questions with different auxiliaries simultaneously.

All Adam's early negative *Why*-questions were declarative sentences preposed by *Why not*. The introduction of an initial *Why not* has tentatively been suggested by Bellugi as a developmental stage in the formation of negative questions, which might in turn have been responsible for the temporary use of double negation by the children, such as, *Why not me can't dance?*[12] As the examples cited from Reidun show, the basis for her negative *Why*-questions is *Why* followed by a negative nucleus, and I have found no double negatives at this stage.

Rune, however, produced negative questions of both types, either

> *Why   Nucleus   neg*

or

> *Why not   Nucleus*

for example:

> Why you not come home?
> Why not that window go up?

Either type was produced throughout Times 3–5 in a crude translation test, apparently in a random fashion. Although there is little data on *Why not*-questions from Rune's first stay in Great Britain, there is supporting evidence in the—as yet unanalysed—data from the beginning of his second stay to suggest that they were alternative patterns. Although the auxiliary *do* had appeared in Rune's *What*-questions at Time 4, there were no occurrences of *do* in the elicited *Why not*- questions. This might be accidental, or due to the fact that negative questions are more complicated, involving a negative transformation in addition.

Rune's further development could have been based on either of the structures *Why Nucleus (neg)* or *Why not Nucleus,* exemplified by *Why you not like ice-cream?* and *Why not you like ice-cream?* If the next stage in Rune's development involved the introduction of *do* without transposing—which would be conceivable, taking the timing of the two operations in Rune's speech into account—we could predict sentences of either or both of the following kind:

(i) Why you don't like ice-cream?
(ii) Why not you don't like ice-cream?

Although 'there are a few unprocessed tape-recordings from the period between Time 5 (the end of March 1966), when my study was discontinued, and July 1966, when our first stay in Great Britain was terminated, I have no analysis as yet of Rune's speech from that three-month period. However, when preparing my report (1968) in January 1967, I devised some translation test items for Rune in order to find out what had happened to his *Why*-questions after he had been away from English for half a year. I expected that I would find non-inverted sentences, mainly of type (i) above. As shown by the following examples, this expectation was not borne out:

Why do we not live in Oslo?
Why doesn't we go to Oslo?
Why doesn't Reidun cry?
Why did you not draw that letter to Grandma? (i.e. write)

There were a few occurrences of more primitive structures, such as, *Why not Ranny come home?,* as well as double negatives, the status of which is difficult to ascertain, for example, *Why didn't Mummy don't make dinner to-yesterday?* (They could reflect a combination of transposing with a negative nucleus; or they could simply be performance mistakes. No attempt was made at the time to find out.)

These examples show that Rune had by this time acquired both the *do*-transformation and the transposing transformation. What is not clear is whether he went through a prior stage of using non-inverted sentences with *do*. In this connection it is interesting—and possible revealing—that most of the negative *Why*-questions found $1\frac{1}{2}$ years later, at the beginning of Rune's second stay in Great Britain, were in the majority of cases of the structure predicted in 1967, namely, non-transposed sentences with *do* (in addition to a fair number of more primitive structures):

Why you don't like and going skiing?
Why you don't going to school to-yesterday?
Why Mummy don't play piano now?

It is tempting to speculate that I have accidentally captured an intermediate stage in Rune's development of *Why not*-questions— a productive rule between the last test in March 1966 and the termination of Rune's first stay in Great Britain in June 1966. If so, does it suggest that the process of 'forgetting' has been the reverse of learning—a regressive process?

  Why don't you like ice-cream?
→ Why you don't like ice-cream?
→ Why you not like ice-cream?

7 Conclusion

The purpose of this paper has been to present some of my findings concerning the development of *Wh*-questions in two Norwegian children acquiring English as a second language and relate them to those of a similar study of first language acquisition. The presentation has been somewhat biased in that I have chosen to concentrate on the similarities between first and second language learners. Taking the age and maturity levels into consideration and the fact that my children already know one language, the similarities are quite striking and not necessarily what one would expect.

  The findings have been discussed in the light of the hypotheses put forward by Brown (1968). Brown has been concerned with confirming or disconfirming a development of *Wh*-questions in children which reflects the transformational derivations in transformational-generative grammar, in order to find out if these might be said to represent psychologically real operations. Brown is cautious in his interpretation of the evidence and recommends that it might be wise to have a second look at empiricist explanations, as they might still throw light on the process of language acquisition.

  Although I think nothing conclusive can be said about the psychological reality of the transformational rules discussed in the paper, the transformational description itself has made it possible to set up testable hypotheses. Whether Brown is right or not in his tentative conclusions is of less importance. At the present stage of inquiry into child language development it is of interest to find out what the regularities are across children with regard to the order of emergence of linguistic structures, irrespective of whether or not the development can be predicted from linguistic theory. What we need is a more comprehensive language learning theory, which also takes into account general cognitive factors and not only linguistic mechanisms.

NOTES

1 See also R. Brown *et al.* (1969) and Ursula Bellugi (1965).

2 The team has included also Ursula Bellugi, Colin Fraser, Dan Slobin, Jean Berko Gleason, and David McNeill.

3 The constituent itself dominates indefinite elements, such as: 'some thing'. 'at some place'. For a treatment of questions, see J. J. Katz & P. M. Postal (1964), pp. 79–117.

4 J. J. Katz & P. M. Postal (1964), pp. 108–112, discuss the distinction between ordinary questions and 'echo questions' (Brown's 'occasional questions') and propose the introduction of an Emphasis Marker in deep structure to account for this difference.

5 Nor has it so far been confirmed by the Language Acquisition Research Project at the University of Edinburgh, according to Elisabeth Ingram, 'Language development in children' (mimeo).

6 My research project is supported in full by the Norwegian Research Council for Science and the Humanities.

7 The equipment used has been a Tandberg stereo tape recorder Model 64 × with a footswitch rewind-playback control and a Tandberg tape recorder Model 13, which is a cartridge machine for a one channel repeater system. The two can be connected. Further equipment consists of two Tandberg TM 4 microphones and two headphones AKG, K 50 for stereo and mono respectively. Apart from a few recordings on a portable mono tape recorder, all recordings have been stereo recordings, with a tape speed of $7\frac{1}{2}$ i.p.s. The sound has been of a very high quality.

8 For a justification of this analysis, see U. Bellugi (1965).

9 A description in terms of a prefixed NEG or Q morpheme followed by a Nucleus is used in Klima & Bellugi (1966) for the early stages, but is not proposed as a hypothesis to account for the word order in sentences of the preposing type.

10 The same general similarities have been found in the development of negative sentences between my informants and those of Brown and associates. A brief discussion is included in Ravem (1969).

11 *Cf.* Katz & Postal (1964), p. 8.

12 Bellugi (1965), p. 119. See also Klima & Bellugi (1966), pp. 203–4 and 'The Growth of Transformations' in McNeill (1966), particularly p. 60.

PART FOUR

Error Analyses of
Adult Language Learning

In this section we deal with the methodology of error analysis, particularly as it is applied to the analysis of the adult learner's syntax in a second language. Corder presents a model based on a distinction between an *idiosyncratic* dialect (the learner's personal, unstable, developing grammar) and a *social* dialect (the target language which is the dialect of a social group). He illustrates the possible relationships between the learner's idiosyncratic dialect and the target social dialect, and compares these with a number of other *X dialect/social dialect* relationships, such as that evidenced in a piece of poetry, in the speech of a young child, or in the speech of an aphasic. Corder attributes greater importance to the relationship *mother tongue/learner's dialect* than others might; he does however acknowledge that there are other variables involved.

Richards, while acknowledging the influence of the mother tongue on the learner's language, documents a number of other common features of the learner's dialect, often ignored in discussions of learner's errors. These are referred to as intralingual and developmental errors and reflect the general characteristics of rule learning, such as overgeneralization, incomplete application of target language rules, failure to learn the conditions under which rules apply, and the development of false concepts. Some of these are seen to be reinforced by common teaching procedures. Jain sees the learner's language as manifesting a general learning strategy to simplify the syntax of the language he is learning. He suggests that the motivation to add new rules to one's idiosyncratic dialect may decline, once a degree of proficiency has been achieved for the language to function adequately as an operational tool, and illustrates the concept of overgeneralization as a learning strategy (cf. discussion of instrumental and integrative motivation in Richards and Sampson). Jain is concerned with reconstructing the learner's interlanguage, when hypothesis testing (i.e. further learning) has largely stopped (cf. Selinker, *fossilization*).

9

Idiosyncratic Dialects and Error Analysis

S P CORDER

Reprinted from IRAL, Vol. IX/2, May 1971, published by Julius Groos Verlag, Heidelberg.

What has come to be known as 'Error Analysis' has to do with the investigation of the language of second language learners. I shall be taking the point of view in this paper that the language of such a learner, or perhaps certain groupings of learners, is a special sort of dialect. This is based on two considerations: firstly, any spontaneous speech intended by the speaker to communicate is meaningful, in the sense that it is systematic, regular and, consequently is, in principle, describable in terms of a set of rules, i.e. it has a grammar. The spontaneous speech of the second language learner is language and has a grammar. Secondly, since a number of sentences of that language are isomorphous with some of the sentences of his target language and have the same interpretation, then some, at least, of the rules needed to account for the learners' language will be the same as those required to account for the target language. Therefore the learner's language is a dialect in the linguistic sense: two languages which share some rules of grammar are dialects.

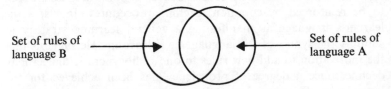

Set of rules of language B ————→ ←———— Set of rules of language A

Languages A and B are in a dialect relation. (I am not here concerned whether or not all languages can be regarded as being in this relation.)

It is, of course, usual to apply a further non-linguistic criterion to a language in order to establish its dialect status, namely that it should be the shared behaviour of a social group, i.e. that it should con-

stitute a 'langue' in the Saussurean sense. In this sense the language of
a learner may or may not be a dialect. I shall return to this point later.
For the time being, however, I shall make a distinction between the
dialects which are the languages of a social group (I shall call these
social dialects) and the dialects which are not the languages of social
groups (I shall call these idiosyncratic dialects). The justification for
calling the latter dialects is therefore a linguistic one and not a social
one. You may say that the dialects I am talking about are already
adequately identified under the name *idiolects*. I would maintain that
this is not the case. An idiolect is a personal dialect but which
linguistically has the characteristic that all the rules required to
account for it are found somewhere in the set of rules of one or
another *social* dialect. An *idiolect* can be said to be some sort of a
mixture of dialects.

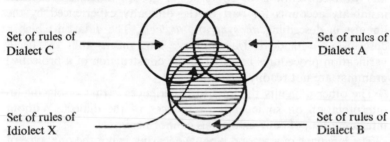

Set of rules of
Dialect C

Set of rules of
Dialect A

Set of rules of
Idiolect X

Set of rules of
Dialect B

From the diagram we can see that Idiolect X possesses rules drawn
from three overlapping social dialects but does not possess any rules
which are not rules of any one of these dialects. If all these social
dialects are 'included' in a language D then Idiolect X is a dialect
of language D in the conventional sense.

This state of affairs is different in the case of what I am calling
idiosyncratic dialects. In these, some of the rules required to account
for the dialect are not members of the set of rules of any social
dialect; they are peculiar to the language of that speaker.

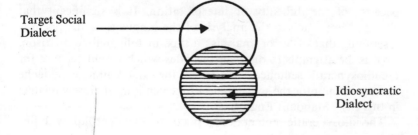

Target Social
Dialect

Idiosyncratic
Dialect

All *idiosyncratic dialects* have this characteristic in common that some of the rules required to account for them are particular to an individual. This has, of course, the result that some of their sentences are not readily interpretable, since the ability to interpret a sentence depends in part upon the knowledge of the conventions underlying that sentence. The sentences of an *idiolect* do not therefore present the same problems of interpretation since somewhere there is a member of that social group who shares the conventions with the speaker.

It is in the nature of *idiosyncratic dialects* that they are normally unstable. The reason for this is obvious. The object of speech is normally to communicate, i.e. to be understood. If understanding is only partial, then a speaker has a motive to bring his behaviour into line with conventions of some social group, if he is able. This instability accounts for part of the difficulty experienced by the linguist in describing *idiosyncratic dialects*. The data on which a description is made is fragmentary. This means that the usual verification procedures required in the construction of a projective grammar are not readily available.

The other difficulty the linguist experiences is that of placing an interpretation on some of the sentences of the dialect. Without interpretation, of course, analysis cannot begin.

The language of a second language learner is not the only type of *idiosyncratic dialect*. 'Error Analysis' is not applicable only to the language of second language learners. One class of *idiosyncratic dialects* is the language of poems, where this cannot be accounted for wholly in the terms of the rules of some social dialect. As Thorne (1965) says: 'given a text like Cummings' poem "Anyone lived in a pretty how town" containing sequences which resist inclusion in the grammar of English, it might prove more illuminating to regard it as a sample of a different language, *or a different dialect,* from Standard English' (My italics).

That the language of this poem is idiosyncratic is evident, if only because of the difficulty of interpretation. It is significant that Thorne's approach to the analysis of the language of the poem is essentially that of 'error analysis', a type of bilingual comparison. That is, he attempts to discover the rules which would account for the idiosyncratic sentences[1] in terms of the same syntactic model he uses to account for the social dialect to which it most closely relates: in this case, Standard English.

The idiosyncratic sentences of a poetic text can perhaps with justice be called *deliberately deviant*, since the author presumably knows the conventions of the standard dialect but chooses not to obey them (cf. Katz, 1964). His deviances are motivated. This means that the ability to interpret the text is dependent upon the knowledge of the semantic structure of the related standard dialect. In this sense poetic dialects are 'parasitic' upon standard dialects.

Another idiosyncratic dialect one might consider is the speech of an aphasic. This, too, in the happiest circumstances, is an unstable dialect, but presents the same problem of interpretation to the linguist. Whether it would be just to call the idiosyncratic sentences of an aphasic deviant is, however, less certain. We must assume that he was, before his disease, a native speaker of some social dialect, but he cannot be said to be deviating deliberately, and it is difficult to know in what sense he can be said still to 'know the rules' of that dialect.[2]

Perhaps we may provisionally characterize the idiosyncratic sentences of the aphasic as *pathologically deviant*.

The third class of *idiosyncratic dialects* is that of the infant learning his mother tongue. It too presents typical problems of interpretation, in an even more acute form perhaps, than either of the other two classes. I am open to correction here, but I would guess that the single factor which makes the problem of describing child language so intractable is that of placing a plausible interpretation (let alone a correct interpretation) upon a child's utterances. This idiosyncratic dialect is also obviously unstable.

The fourth class of *idiosyncratic dialects* is that of the learners of a second language. Everything I have said about idiosyncratic dialects in general applies to his language. It is regular, systematic, meaningful, i.e. it has a grammar, and is, in principle, describable in terms of a set of rules, some sub-set of which is a sub-set of the rules of the target social dialect. His dialect is unstable (we hope) and is not, so far as we know, a 'langue' in that its conventions are not shared by a social group (I shall return to this point later) and lastly, many of its sentences present problems of interpretation to any native speaker of the target dialect. Selinker (1969) has proposed the name *interlanguage* for this class of idiosyncratic dialects, implying thereby that it is a dialect whose rules share characteristics of two social dialects or languages, whether these languages themselves share rules or not. This is an open question and has to do with the problem of language universals.

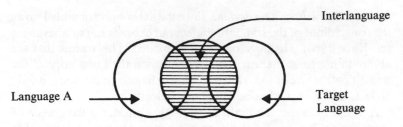

Interlanguage

Language A

Target
Language

An alternative name might be *transitional dialect,* emphasizing the unstable nature[3] of such dialects.

I have suggested that it would be reasonable to call the idiosyncratic sentences of a poet's dialect *deliberately deviant,* since the writer is assumed to know the conventions of a social dialect and that he deliberately chooses not to follow them. Similarly I have suggested that the aphasic's idiosyncratic sentences might be called *pathologically deviant* since he too was presumably a speaker of some social dialect before his disease. We cannot, however, refer to the idiosyncratic sentences of a child as deviant, since he, of course, is not yet a speaker of a social dialect; and indeed it is not usual (until he goes to school) to call a child's sentences deviant, incorrect or ungrammatical. For precisely the same reason I suggest it is misleading to refer to the idiosyncratic sentences of the second language learner as *deviant.* I also suggest that it is as undesirable to call them *erroneous* as it is to call the sentences of a child erroneous, because it implies wilful, or inadvertent breach of rules which, in some sense, ought to be known. Whereas, of course, sentences are idiosyncratic precisely because the rules of the target dialect are not yet known.

The only sentences in anyone's speech which could, I suggest, with justice be called *erroneous* are those which are the result of some failure of performance. These may contain what are often called slips of the tongue, false starts, changes of mind, and so on. Hockett (1948) refers to these as lapses. They may be the result of failures in memory. A typical example in English would be: 'That is the problem which I don't know how to solve it' (Reibel, 1969). Interestingly such erroneous sentences do not normally present problems of interpretation. The reason that suggests itself for this is that there may be, in any social dialect, 'rules for making mistakes'. Here, clearly, is a field for investigation (Boomer and Laver, 1968). But we are not yet in a position, I think, to set up a fifth class of idiosyncratic dialects to account for the regularities of erroneous sentences. The noticeable thing about *erroneous* sentences is that they are normal readily corrected or correctable by the speaker himself. This coul be a defining criterion for erroneous sentences. It would, of course, be applicable to some sentences of the second language learner. Such sentences could be accounted for as being cases of *failure* (for whatever reason) to follow a *known* rule, in contradistinction to what I am calling idiosyncratic sentences, which involve no failure in performance and which cannot be corrected by the learner precisely because they follow the only rules known to him, those of his transitional dialect.

But so long as we do not make the mistake of assuming that the idiosyncratic sentences of a learner of a second language are simply the result of performance failure, that is, that he knows the rules of the target language but has, for some reason or other failed to, or chosen not to, apply them, then there is no harm in talking about *error* or *correction*.

My principal reason for objecting to the terms *error, deviant* or *ill-formed* is that they all, to a greater or lesser degree, prejudge the explanation of the idiosyncrasy. Now, one of the principal reasons for studying the learner's language is precisely to discover why it is as it is, that is, to explain it and ultimately say something about the learning process. If, then, we call his sentences deviant or erroneous, we have implied an explanation before we have ever made a description.

There is an even more compelling reason for not calling the idiosyncratic sentences of a learner *ungrammatical*. While it is true that they cannot be accounted for by the rules of the target dialect, they are in fact *grammatical* in terms of the learner's language.

I have suggested that the idiosyncratic dialects I have identified differ from social dialects in that some of the rules needed to account for them are not members of the set of rules of any social dialect, that they are in fact idiosyncratic rules, not shared rules. It is, however, possible that while these dialects are not 'langues', in the sense that their conventions are not shared by any social group identifiable according to the criteria of the sociologist, nevertheless the idiosyncratic rules are not unique to an individual but shared by others having similar cultural background, aims or linguistic history. There is such a term as 'poetic language' or 'poetic dialect' to designate that dialect which possesses certain features found only in poetry. However, such a dialect is part of the 'langue' of the community whose poetry it is and presents no difficulties of interpretation. Such a sentence as: 'And hearkened as I whistled the trampling team beside' is perhaps unique to verse in modern English but can be accounted for by a convention accepted by all English speakers. This is not true, however, of 'Up so many bells . . .' of Cummings' poem. This is not part of the poetic dialect of English, is difficult of interpretation and I doubt whether the rules which accounted for it would account for any other poetic utterances by any other poet. It is fully idiosyncratic.

The situation is, I think, different in the case of the other three classes of idiosyncratic dialects. Aphasics do not form a social group in any sociological sense, and yet there is strong evidence to suggest that the idiosyncracies of their speech may be classified along a number of dimensions (Jakobson, 1956). No one would, of course, attempt to describe the speech of aphasics unless he believed that some general statements of classification were possible. The object of such investigations is to find what relations there are between the medical signs, symptoms, history and the set of rules needed to account for the idiosyncratic aspects of the aphasic's speech.

Similarly, no one would undertake the study of child language acquisition unless he had reason to believe that all children in a certain dialect environment followed a course of development which was more or less similar (Smith and Miller, 1968). There would be little point in describing the speech of *a* three-year-old unless it was expected ultimately to throw light on the speech of *the* three-year-old. Therefore, there is an underlying assumption that the language of all three-year-olds in a certain language environment will have certain features in common.[4]

May it be that the situation is similar in the case of the learner of a second language? It is certainly the case that teachers work on the assumption that a group of learners having the same mother tongue and having had the same experience of learning the second language speak more or less the same interlanguage at any point in their learning career, and that what differences there are can be ascribed to individual variation in intelligence, motivation and perhaps attitude. This belief is inherent in the notion of 'teaching a class' as opposed to an 'individual', and indeed, it is difficult to see how one could proceed otherwise.

Can we assume that such learners all follow a similar course of development in acquiring a second language? We certainly do all we can to see that they do. That is what a syllabus is for. It is a map of the route the learners are to follow. But supposing it were possible for the learner to select his own route, can we assume that he would follow the route we have mapped out for him? We simply do not know, since no one has ever tried to find out. We lack totally any information about the development of individual learners of a second language outside the classroom situation, and indeed it is difficult to imagine how such a study could be made. But one thing is clear: the longitudinal study of the language development of a second language learner would rely heavily upon the techniques of what we are calling 'error analysis' just as the longitudinal study of the infant learning his mother tongue depends on the analysis of his idiosyncratic sentences (Brown and Frazer, 1964). Furthermore, I believe that until we do attempt to undertake the longitudinal study of the free-learning second language learners, we shall not make much headway with finding out how people learn second languages.

I shall now turn to a general consideration of the methodology of describing what I have called an idiosyncratic dialect, and which, in part, is 'error analysis' as we are calling it. I have already suggested that this methodology is not uniquely applicable to the dialects of second language learners but is valid for all idiosyncratic dialects.

The dialect is *une langue* in the Saussurean sense. It is therefore a methodological mistake to concentrate only on those sentences which are overtly idiosyncratic. The superficially well-formed sentences in terms of one social dialect (the target dialect in the case of the learner) are just as important as those which are overtly idiosyncratic. They too tell us what he knows. Furthermore, as I have suggested above, the 'value' to be assigned to 'well-formed' forms is only discoverable in terms of the whole system of his dialect. Thus, for example, a well-formed 'plural' or an apparently 'proper' use of the definite article can only be understood in relation to his 'ill-formed' plurals or his use of other determiners.

This means that all the learner's sentences should in principle be analysed. This is all the more necessary since many of his apparently 'well-formed' sentences may have a derivation different from that assigned by the rules of the target dialect. Thus the sentence: 'After an hour it was stopped' was only recognized as idiosyncratic when the context showed that *it* referred to the *wind* and that therefore the target dialect interpretation was unlikely and in fact the translation into the target language was: 'After an hour it stopped'. A similar case in poetic dialect is: 'Anyone lived in a pretty how town' where the syntactic parallel is not with 'Someone lived in a pretty old town' but 'John lived in a pretty old town', i.e. *Anyone* is a proper name in that poetic dialect, and not an indefinite pronoun, and *how* is an adjective and not an interrogative adverb.

The first stage in 'error analysis' then is *recognition of idiosyncracy*. We can enunciate a general law. *Every sentence is to be regarded as idiosyncratic until shown to be otherwise.* As I have suggested, a learner's sentence may be superficially 'well-formed' and yet be idiosyncratic; these sentences I shall call *covertly idiosyncratic*. They may also, of course, be *overtly idiosyncratic,* in that they are superficially 'ill-formed' in terms of the rules of the target language, or they may, of course, be neither. If the 'normal' interpretation is acceptable in context, then that sentence is not for immediate purposes idiosyncratic. If, however, the sentence appears superficially well-formed in terms of the rules of the target language but nevertheless cannot be interpreted 'normally' in context, then that sentence is *covertly idiosyncratic* and a plausible interpretation must be placed upon it in the light of the context. We then have what I call a *reconstructed sentence* to compare with the original. A reconstructed sentence is, roughly speaking, what a native speaker of the target language would have said to express *that* meaning in *that* context, i.e. it is a translation equivalent.

Let us take another possibility: that the sentence is *overtly idiosyncratic,* that is, it is superficially 'ill-formed' according to the rules of the target language. We must then ask whether a plausible interpretation can be placed upon it in the context. If it can, well and good, and we can proceed to make a 'well-formed' reconstructed sentence to compare with the original. If we cannot readily make a plausible interpretation of the overtly idiosyncratic sentence then our problem is much greater. Somehow or other we must attempt to make a plausible interpretation. We can first see whether, by reference to the mother tongue of the learner, we can arrive at such an interpretation. If the mother tongue is not known then the analysis of that sentence may have to remain in abeyance until we have learned more of the idiosyncratic dialect of the learner. If, however, the mother tongue is known, we may be able, by a process of literal translation, to arrive at a means of interpreting the sentence plausibly. If we can do that, then, by translating the mother tongue sentence back into a well-formed sentence of the target language, we have available a reconstructed sentence which once again we can compare with the original overtly idiosyncratic sentence of the learner.

The end point of the process of identifying idiosyncracy and the

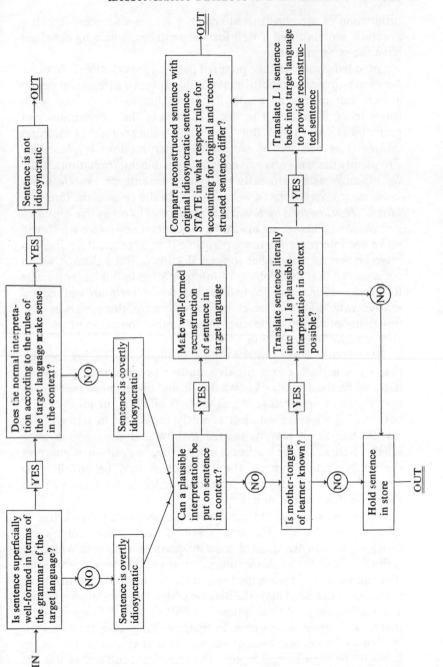

ALGORITHM FOR PROVIDING DATA FOR DESCRIPTION OF IDIOSYNCRATIC DIALECTS

production of a reconstructed sentence is two sentences: the idio-syncratic sentence and a well-formed sentence, which *by definition* have the same meaning.

I need hardly say that the picture I have given is idealized. At every decision point in the algorithm it is unlikely that a categorical yes/no answer can readily be made. The first decision as to the 'well-formedness' is in itself a problem in view of the indeterminacy of grammar (Lyons, 1968). But more acute is the problem of interpretation. How can we be sure when interpretation is plausible? Frequently there may be two equally plausible interpretations. Take for example such an overtly idiosyncratic sentence as: '*He didn't know the word so he asked a dictionary*'. In the context the interpretation '*He asked for a dictionary*' is perhaps as likely as '*He consulted a dictionary*'. There is not always in the context any factor which will make one interpretation more plausible than another. Recourse can often be had to the mother tongue, if known. But I think it worth pointing out that the problem of interpretation looms larger outside the classroom than in. The teacher has almost certainly learned the idiosyncratic dialect of his class and, of course, there is always the possibility of asking the learner in his mother tongue to provide an authoritative interpretation.

The recourse to the mother tongue of the learner (in his absence, that is) is in fact also a highly intuitive process and, of course, depends on the degree of knowledge of that dialect possessed by the investigator. Furthermore, we cannot assume that the idiosyncratic nature of the learner's dialect is solely explicable in terms of his mother tongue; it may be related to how and what he has been taught. Here again the teacher is in a privileged position to interpret the idiosyncratic sentence, though teachers may be unwilling to admit that idiosyncracy can be accounted for by reference to what they have done or not done!

 We have now arrived at the *second stage:* accounting for a learner's idiosyncratic dialect. The first stage, if successfully completed, provides us with the data of a set of pairs of sentences which by definition have the same meaning, or put another way, are transla-tion equivalents of each other: one in the learner's dialect, the other in the target dialect. This is the data on which the *description* is based. The methodology of description is, needless to say, fundamentally that of a *bilingual comparison*. In this, two languages are described in terms of a common set of categories and relations, that is, in terms of the same formal model. The technical problems of this are well known and I do not wish, or need, to go into them here.

The *third stage* and ultimate object of error analysis is *explanation*. Whereas the two previous stages have been linguistic, the third stage is psycholinguistic, inasmuch as it attempts to account for how and why the learner's idiosyncratic dialect is of the nature it is. We must, I think, all agree that there could be no reason to engage in error analysis unless it served one or both of two objects. *Firstly,* to elucidate what and how a learner learns when he studies a second language. This is a theoretical object (Corder, 1967); *secondly,* the applied object of enabling the learner to learn more efficiently by exploiting our knowledge of his dialect for pedagogical purposes. The second objective is clearly dependent on the first. We cannot make any *principled* use of his idiosyncratic sentences to improve teaching unless we understand how and why they occur.

It is a generally agreed observation that many—but not necessarily all—the idiosyncratic sentences of a second language learner bear some sort of regular relation to the sentences of his mother tongue.[5]

This is a phenomenon which no one would dispute. It is the explanation of this phenomenon which is open to discussion. One explanation is that the learner is carrying over the habits of the mother tongue into the second language. This is called *interference* and the implication of this term can only be that his mother tongue habits prevent him in some way from acquiring the habits of the second language. Clearly this explanation is related to a view of language as some sort of habit structure.

The other explanation is that language learning is some sort of data-processing and hypothesis-forming activity of a cognitive sort. According to this view his idiosyncratic sentences are signs of false hypotheses, which, when more data is available and processed, either by direct observation or by statements by the teacher, i.e. corrections and examples, enable the learner to reformulate a hypothesis more in accordance with the facts of the target language (cf. Hockett, 1948).

It is not surprising that people holding the habit formation theory of learning, which has been the most prevalent theory over some decades now, showed no particular interest in the study of the learner's idiosyncratic sentences. They were evidence that the correct automatic habits of the target language had not yet been acquired. Their eradication was a matter of more intensive drilling in correct forms. What the nature of the error might be was a matter of secondary importance since it would throw no interesting light on the process of learning. Sufficient that they were there, indicating that the learning task was not yet complete. Theoretically, if the teaching process had been perfect, no errors would have occurred.

The alternative view would suggest that the making of errors is an inevitable and indeed necessary part of the learning process. The 'correction' of error provides precisely the sort of negative evidence which is necessary to discovery of the correct concept or rule. Consequently, a better description of idiosyncratic sentences contributes directly to an account of what the learner knows and does not know at that moment in his career, and should ultimately enable the teacher to supply him, not just with the information *that* his hypothesis is wrong, but also, importantly, with the right sort of information or data for him to form a more adequate concept of a rule in the target language.

It is not, I think, therefore, a pure coincidence that an increased interest in error analysis at the present time coincides with an increased interest in formulating some alternative hypothesis to the habit-formation theory of language learning.

NOTES

1 Strictly speaking, of course, all the sentences of the poem are idiosyncratic, since the dialect is idiosyncratic and as de Saussure says: '*la langue est un système dont tous les termes sont solidaires et où la valeur de l'un ne résulte que de la présence simultanée des autres*'. This means that apparently 'non-idiosyncratic' sentences should not receive the same interpretation as they would if they were sentences of Standard English. This is so because the value of any term in a system is a function of all the terms in the system and since by definition his system is different, then the value of all the terms is idiosyncratic, even when surface realization appears the same. I shall, however, hereafter use the term 'idiosyncratic sentence' to refer to any sentence which superficially is not a sentence of any social dialect and also any sentence which, while it superficially resembles a sentence of a social dialect, cannot receive the interpretation that such a sentence would receive in that dialect.

2 We may note in passing that one of the problems of describing an aphasic's speech is an absence of information about the precise nature of his dialect before illness.

3 Theoretical objections to the concept of Interlanguage (or Transitional Dialect) apply with equal force to the concept of 'a language'. Both are, of course, unstable. The concept of *état de langue* underlies all descriptions of languages. The objections to the concept of interlanguage have weight only inasmuch as they are regarded as practical objections to the feasibility of making comprehensive descriptions of an *état de dialecte*, because of the

paucity of data available in most cases. The same practical problems beset workers in the field of child language acquisition, of course.

4 An interesting speculation is whether three-year-olds can understand each other better than adults understand them or than they can understand adult speech.

5 For an interesting discussion of idiosyncrasies which may derive from the methods or materials of teaching or arise in the process of learning from the nature of the target language itself see Richards (1971).

10

A Non-Contrastive Approach to Error Analysis*

JACK C RICHARDS

Reprinted from English Language Teaching, *Vol. 25, 3, June 1971, published by Oxford University Press, London.*

* This article is based on a paper presented at the TESOL convention held at San Francisco in March 1970. I am grateful to William F. Mackey, Bernard Spolsky and John Macnamara for comments on earlier versions of it.

1 Introduction

The identification and analysis of interference between languages in contact has traditionally been a central aspect of the study of bilingualism. The intrusion of features of one language into another in the speech of bilinguals has been studied at the levels of phonology, morphology and syntax. The systems of the contact languages themselves have sometimes been contrasted, and an important outcome of contrastive studies has been the notion that they allow for prediction of the difficulties involved in acquiring a second language. 'Those elements that are similar to the (learner's) native language will be simple for him, and those areas that are different will be difficult.'[1] In the last two decades language teaching has derived considerable impetus from the application of contrastive studies. As recently as 1967, Politzer affirmed: 'Perhaps the least questioned and least questionable application of linguistics is the contribution of contrastive analysis. Especially in the teaching of languages for which no considerable and systematic teaching experience is available, contrastive analysis can highlight and predict the difficulties of the pupils.'[2]

Studies of second language acquisition, however, have tended to imply that contrastive analysis may be most predictive at the level of phonology, and least predictive at the syntactic level. A recent study of Spanish-English bilingualism, for example, states: 'Many people

172

assume, following logic that is easy to understand, that the errors made by bilinguals are caused by their mixing Spanish and English. One of the most important conclusions this writer draws from the research in this project is that interference from Spanish is not a major factor in the way bilinguals construct sentences and use the language.'[3]

This paper focuses on several types of errors, observed in the acquisition of English as a second language, which do not derive from transfers from another language. Excluded from discussion are what may be called interlanguage errors; that is, errors caused by the interference of the learner's mother tongue. A different class of errors are represented by sentences such as *did he comed, what you are doing, he coming from Israel, make him to do it, I can to speak French.* Errors of this nature are frequent, regardless of the learner's language background. They may be called intralingual and developmental errors. Rather than reflecting the learner's inability to separate two languages, intralingual and developmental errors reflect the learner's competence at a particular stage, and illustrate some of the general characteristics of language acquisition. Their origins are found within the structure of English itself, and through reference to the strategy by which a second language is acquired and taught.[4] A sample of such errors is shown in tables 1-6 (see Appendix). These are representative of the sort of errors we might expect from anyone learning English as a second language. They are typical of systematic errors in English usage which are found in numerous case-studies of the English errors of speakers of particular mother tongues. They are the sort of mistakes which persist from week to week and which recur from one year to the next with any group of learners. They cannot be described as mere failures to memorize a segment of language, or as occasional lapses in performance due to memory limitations, fatigue, and the like.[5] In some learners they represent final grammatical competence; in others they may be indications of transitional competence.

2 Sources of the present study (see Tables 1–6)

Tables 1–6 are taken from studies of English errors produced by speakers of Japanese, Chinese, Burmese, French, Czech, Polish, Tagalog, Maori, Maltese, and the major Indian and West African languages.[6] From these sources I have selected those errors which occurred in a cross-section of the samples. By studying intralingual and developmental errors within the framework of a theory of second language learning, and through examining typical cases of the teaching of the forms from which they are derived, it may be possible to see the way towards teaching procedures that take account of the learner's strategy for acquiring a second language.

3 Types and causes of intralingual and developmental errors

An examination of the errors in tables 1–6 suggests that intralingual errors are those which reflect the general characteristics of rule learning, such as faulty generalization, incomplete application of rules, and failure to learn conditions under which rules apply. Developmental errors illustrate the learner attempting to build up hypotheses about the English language from his limited experience of it in the classroom or textbook. For convenience of presentation, tables 1–6 will be discussed in terms of: 1. over-generalization, 2. ignorance of rule restrictions, 3. incomplete application of rules, 4. false concepts hypothesized.

4 Over-generalization

Jakobovits defines generalization or transfer as 'the use of previously available strategies in new situations. . . . In second language learning . . . some of these strategies will prove helpful in organising the facts about the second language, but others, perhaps due to superficial similarities, will be misleading and inapplicable'.[7] Over-generalization covers instances where the learner creates a deviant structure on the basis of his experience of other structures in the target language. For example (see table 1, 1.3.4.8), *he can sings, we are hope, it is occurs, he come from.* Over-generalization generally involves the creation of one deviant structure in place of two regular structures. It may be the result of the learner reducing his linguistic burden. With the omission of the third person -*s*, over-generalization removes the necessity for concord, thus relieving the learner of considerable effort. Dušková, discussing the omission of third person -*s*, notes 'Since (in English) all grammatical persons take the same zero verbal ending except the third person singular in the present tense . . . omissions of the -*s* in the third person singular may be accounted for by the heavy pressure of all other endingless forms. The endingless form is generalized for all persons, just as the form *was* is generalized for all persons and both numbers in the past tense. . . . Errors in the opposite direction like *there does not exist any exact rules* may be explained either as being due to hypercorrection . . . or as being due to generalization of the 3rd person singular ending for the 3rd person plural.'[8]

Over-generalization is associated with redundancy reduction. It may occur, for instance, with items which are contrasted in the grammar of the language but which do not carry significant and obvious contrast for the learner. The *-ed* marker, in narrative or in other past contexts, often appears to carry no meaning, since pastness is usually indicated lexically in stories, and the essential notion of sequence in narrative can be expressed equally well in the present — *Yesterday I go to the university and I meet my new professor.* Thus the learner cuts down the tasks involved in sentence production. Ervin-Tripp suggests that 'possibly the morphological and syntactic simplifications of second language learners correspond to some simplification common among children (i.e. mother tongue speakers) learning the same language'.[9]

Certain types of teaching techniques increase the frequency of over-generalized structures. Many pattern drills and transform exercises are made up of utterances that can interfere with each other to produce a hybrid structure:

Teacher	Instruction	Student
He walks quickly.	Change to continuous form	*He is walks quickly.*

This has been described as overlearning of a structure.[10] At other times, *he walks* may be contrasted with *he is walking*, *he sings* with *he can sing*, and a week later, without any teaching of the forms, the learner produces *he can sings, he is walks.*

5 Ignorance of rule restrictions

Closely related to the generalization of deviant structures is failure to observe the restrictions of existing structures, that is, the application of rules to contexts where they do not apply. *The man who I saw him* (table 3, 2) violates the limitation on subjects in structures with *who*. *I made him to do it* ignores restrictions on the distribution of *make*. These are again a type of generalization or transfer, since the learner is making use of a previously acquired rule in a new situation. Some rule restriction errors may be accounted for in terms of analogy; other instances may result from the rote learning of rules.

Analogy seems to be a major factor in the misuse of prepositions (table 4). The learner, encountering a particular preposition with one type of verb, attempts by analogy to use the same preposition with similar verbs. *He showed me the book* leads to *he explained me the book; he said to me* gives *he asked to me; we talked about it,* therefore *we discussed about it, ask him to do it* produces *make him to do it; go with him* gives *follow with him.* Some pattern exercises appear to encourage incorrect rules being applied through analogy. Here is part of a pattern exercise which practises *enable, allow, make, cause, permit.*

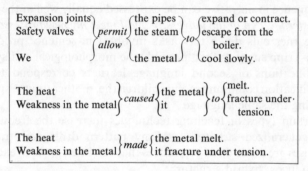

It is followed by an exercise in which the student is instructed to complete a number of statements using verbs and prepositions from the table: *The rise in temperature—the mercury—rise up the tube. The risk of an explosion—the workers—leave the factory. The speed of the train—it—leave the rails on the curve. . . .*

From a class of 23 with mixed language backgrounds, no fewer than 13 produced sentences like *The rise in temperature made the mercury to rise up the tube.* Practising *make* in the same context as *allow it to, permit it to, enable it to,* precipitates confusion. Other instances of analogous constructions may be less easy to avoid. Table 3, 2 includes *this is not fit to drink it, the man who I saw him.* By analogy with the learner's previous experience of subject + verb + object constructions, the learner feels that there is something incomplete about *that's the man who I saw,* and so adds the object, after the verb, as he has been taught to do elsewhere.

Failure to observe restrictions in article usage may also derive from analogy, the learner rationalizing a deviant usage from his previous experience of English. This may happen even when the mother tongue is close to the English usage. F. G. French gives the following example of how a common article mistake is produced by

rational analogy.[11] In English we say *The sparrow is a small bird.*
Sparrows are small birds. Since the statements are exactly parallel, a
logical substitute for the second language would be *The sparrows
are small birds.* In Burmese, the equivalents would be

sa gale thi	nge thaw	nget	pyit thi
The sparrow	small	bird	is

and in the plural

sa gale mya thi	nge thaw	nget mya	pyit kya thi
The sparrows	small	birds	are

Instead of following the form of the mother tongue, however, the
learner, having first produced *The sparrows are* from *The sparrow is,*
sees a parallel between *sparrows* and *birds,* and produces the common error *The sparrows are the small birds.* A similar example is
noted by Aguas, from Tagalog-speaking students.[12]

6 Incomplete application of rules

Under this category we may note the occurrence of structures whose
deviancy represents the degree of development of the rules required
to produce acceptable utterances. For example, across background
languages, systematic difficulty in the use of questions can be
observed. A statement form may be used as a question, one of the
transformations in a series may be omitted, or a question word may
simply be added to the statement form. Despite extensive teaching
of both the question and the statement forms, a grammatical question
form may never become part of competence in the second language.
Redundancy may be an explanatory factor. The second language
learner, interested perhaps primarily in communication, can achieve
quite efficient communication without the need for mastering more
than the elementary rules of question usage. Motivation to achieve
communication may exceed motivation to produce grammatically
correct sentences. A further clue may be provided by classroom use
of questions.

The use of questions is a common teaching device. Typically they
are used, not to find out something, but as a means of eliciting
sentences. Alternatively, the statement form may be used as a means
of eliciting questions through a transform exercise. Classroom
observation suggests that the use of questions may be unrelated to
the skills it is meant to establish. Here are some examples:

Teacher's Question	Student's Response
Do you read much?	*Yes, I read much.*
Do you cook very much?	*Yes, I cook very much.*
Ask her what the last film she saw was called.	*What was called the last film you saw?*
What was she saying?	*She saying she would ask him.*
What does she tell him?	*She tell him to hurry.*
What's he doing?	*He opening the door.*
Ask her how long it takes.	*How long it takes?*
Will they soon be ready?	*Yes, they soon be ready.*
How much does it cost?	*It cost one dollar.*
What does he have to do?	*He have to do write the address.*
What does he ask his mother?	*He ask his mother for the address.*

As the above sample illustrates, when a question is used to elicit sentences, the answer often has to be corrected by the teacher to counteract the influence of his question. Some course-books proceed almost entirely through the use of questions; others avoid excessive use of questions by utilizing signals to indicate the type of sentence required. These may reduce the total number of deviant sentences produced.

7 False concepts hypothesized

In addition to the wide range of intralingual errors which have to do with faulty rule-learning at various levels, there is a class of developmental errors which derive from faulty comprehension of distinctions in the target language. These are sometimes due to poor gradation of teaching items. The form *was,* for example, may be interpreted as a marker of the past tense, giving *one day it was happened* (table 1, 2) and *is* may be understood to be the corresponding marker of the present tense: *he is speaks French* (table 1, 1). In table 2, 4 we find the continuous form instead of the simple past in narrative; elsewhere we encounter confusion between *too, so,* and *very,* between *come* and *go,* and so on. In particular instances I have traced errors of this sort to classroom presentation, and to presentation which is based on contrastive analysis of English and another language or on contrasts within English itself.

Here is an example of how the present continuous came to be understood as a narrative tense. The simple present tense in English is the normal tense used for actions seen as a whole, for events which develop according to a plan, or for sequences of events taking place at the present moment.[13] Thus the sports commentator's *Now Anderson takes the ball, passes it to Smith . . .* and the cooking demonstrator's *I take two eggs, now I add the sugar. . . .* How do we find this use represented in textbooks for teaching English as a second language?

Typically one finds that the continuous form has been used for these functions instead. A recent audio-visual course contains many sequences like the following: *The lift is going down to the ground floor. Ted is getting out of the lift. He is leaving the office building. Ted is standing at the entrance of the office building. He is looking up at the sky . . .*

This is not a normal use of English. The usual tense for a sequence of events taking place 'at the moment' is the present tense, the continuous tense being used only when a single event is extracted from a sequence, the sequence itself being indicated by the present forms. This presentation of the continuous form led a number of students to assume that the continuous form in English is a tense for telling stories and for describing successions of events in either the present or the past.

The reasons for the occurrence of untypical verb-uses in many course-books appears to be related to a contrastive approach to language teaching. In this example, the course-designer has attempted to establish the use of the continuous form in a context in which the present form is appropriate. It is often felt that a considerable amount of time should be devoted to the continuous form, since it does not exist in most learners' mother tongues. Excessive attention to points of difference at the expense of realistic English is a characteristic of much contrastive-based teaching. My experience of such teaching confirms Ritchie's prediction: 'A course that concentrates too much on "the main trouble spots" without due attention to the structure of the foreign language as a whole, will leave the learner with a patchwork of unfruitful, partial generalizations . . .'[14]

Many courses progress on a related assumption, namely, that contrasts within the language are an essential aid to learning. 'Presenting items in contrast can lighten the teacher's and the student's work and consequently speed up the learning process.'[15] Here are some examples of actual learning from materials thought out in terms of contrast.

George notes that a frequent way of introducing the simple and continuous forms is to establish the contrast:

is = present state, $is+ing$ = present action.[16]

The contrast is in fact quite false to English. When the past is introduced, it is often introduced as a past state. *He was sick.* This lays the groundwork for the learner to complete the picture of present and past in English by analogy:

is = present state, $is+ing$ = present action,

was = past state $\therefore$ $was+ing$ = past action.

Thus *was* or *was+ing* may be used as past markers. Used together with the verb $+ed$ this produces such sentences as *he was climbed the tree.* Interpreted as the form for 'past actions' it gives *I was going down town yesterday* instead of *I went down town yesterday.*

Table 3.4 shows examples of the confusion of *too, so,* and *very.* Other substitutions are common, such as the use of *teach* for *learn,* of *do* for *make,* of *come* for *go,* of *bring* for *take.* Learners often feel that the members of such pairs are synonyms, despite every attempt to demonstrate that they have contrastive meanings. Such confusion is sometimes attributable to premature contrastive presentation.

Here are the occurrences of *too* and *very* in a first reader which tells the story of a group of children who light a fire in the snow in front of an old house: *The house is empty because it's old . . . I'm very cold. England is too cold . . . The fire is very big . . . It's very big. It's a very big fire. The firemen are going to put water on the fire because it's too big.*

The course designers intended to establish a contrast between *too* and *very,* but in so doing they completely confuse the meaning of the two forms. From the presentation—and from the viewpoint of a young learner—they have the same meanings. Thus we have the parallelism between:

It's too big and it's dangerous.
The fire is dangerous. It's very big.

How could a child, following such a presentation, avoid saying *This is a too big house? Too* would be more safely taught out of association with *very,* and in contexts where it did not appear to be a substitute for *very,* as, for example, in a structure with *too+* adjective+infinitive—*this box is too heavy to lift.*

Other courses succeed in establishing confusion between *too, so,* and *very* by offering exercises like these:

1. Reword the following sentences, using *too*. *This coffee is so hot that I can't drink it. I've got so fat that I can't wear this dress now* . . .
Example: *This soup is very hot. I can't drink it. This soup is too hot (for me) to drink.*
2. Remake these sentences using *too*. *This hat is very big; he's only a little boy. This grammar is very difficult; a child can't understand it.*
This type of exercise leads to the errors in table 3, 4. The common confusion of *since* and *for* (table 4, 4) is sometimes reinforced by similar exercises, such as those which require choosing the correct preposition in sentences like:

> *I have been here (for/since) a week.*
> *We have been in Canada (for/since) 1968.*

Constant attempts to contrast related areas of English can thus have quite different results from those we intend. As yet, there is no substantial confirmation that a contrastive approach to teaching is likely to be *a priori* more effective than any other approach. Classroom experience and common sense often suggest that a safer strategy for instruction is to minimize opportunities for confusion by selecting non-synonymous contexts for related words, by treating them at different times, and by avoiding exercises based on contrast and transformation.

8 Conclusions

An analysis of the major types of intralingual and developmental errors—over-generalization, ignorance of rule restrictions, incomplete application of rules, and the building of false systems or concepts—may lead us to examine our teaching materials for evidence of the language-learning assumptions that underlie them. Many current teaching practices are based on the notion that the learner will photographically reproduce anything that is given to him, and that if he does not, it is hardly the business of the teacher or textbook writer. It has been remarked that 'Very surprisingly there are few published descriptions of how or what children learn. There are plenty of descriptions of what the teacher did and what materials were presented to the children, but little about what mistakes the children made and how these can be explained, or of what generalizations and learning strategies the children seem to be developing. . . .

It may be that the child's strategy of learning is totally or partially independent of the methods by which he is being taught.'[17]

Interference from the mother tongue is clearly a major source of difficulty in second language learning, and contrastive analysis has proved valuable in locating areas of interlanguage interference. Many errors, however, derive from the strategies employed by the learner in language acquisition, and from the mutual interference of items within the target language. These cannot be accounted for by contrastive analysis. Teaching techniques and procedures should take account of the structural and developmental conflicts that can come about in language learning.

APPENDIX

Tables 1–6—Typical Intralingual and Developmental Errors

Table 1

Errors in the Production of Verb Groups

---

1. *be + verb stem* for *verb stem*

We are live in this hut
The sentence is occurs . . .
We are hope . . .
He is speaks French
The telegraph is remain . . .
We are walk to school every day.

---

2. *be + verb stem + ed* for *verb stem + ed*

Farmers are went to their houses
He was died last year
One day it was happened
They are opened the door

---

3. Wrong form after *do*

He did not found . . .
He did not agreed . . .
The man does not cares for his life
He did not asks me
He does not has . . .

---

4.   Wrong form after modal verb

Can be regard as . . .
We can took him out
I can saw it
It can drawing heavy loads
They can used it
It can use in state processions
She cannot goes
She cannot to go
They would became
We must made
We can to see
We must worked hard

---

5.   *be* omitted before *verb + stem + ed* (participle)

He born in England
It used in church during processions
They satisfied with their lot
He disgusted
He reminded of the story

---

6.   *ed* omitted after *be + participle verb stem*

The sky is cover with clouds
He was punish
Some trees are uproot

---

7.   *be* omitted before *verb + ing*

They running very fast
The cows also crying .
The industry growing fast
At 10.30 he going to kill the sheep

---

8.   *verb stem* for *stem + s*

He alway talk a lot
He come from India
She speak German as well

Table 2

Errors in the Distribution of Verb Groups

---

1.   *be + verb + ing* for *be + verb + ed*

I am interesting in that
The country was discovering by Columbus

---

2.   *be + verb + ing* for *verb stem*

She is coming from Canada
I am having my hair cut on Thursdays

---

3.   *be + not + verb + ing* for *do + not + verb*

I am not liking it
Correct rules are not existing
In French we are not having a present continuous tense and we are not knowing
    when to use it

---

4.   *be + verb + ing* for *verb + ed* in narrative

. . . in the afternoon we were going back. On Saturday we were going down
    town, and we were seeing a film and after we were meeting my brother

---

5.   *verb stem* for *verb + ed* in narrative

There were two animals who do not like each other. One day they go into a
    wood and there is no water. The monkey says to the elephant . . .

---

6.   *have + verb + ed* for *verb + ed*

They had arrived just now
He had come today
I have written this letter yesterday
Some weeks ago I have seen an English film
He has arrived at noon
I have learned English at school

---

7.   *have + be + verb + ed* for *be + verb + ed*

He has been married long ago
He has been killed in 1956

---

8.   *verb (+ ed)* for *have + verb + ed*

We correspond with them up to now
This is the only country which I visited so far

---

9.   *be + verb + ed* for *verb stem*

This money is belonged to me
The machine is comed from France

Table 3

Miscellaneous Errors

1.	Wrong verb form in adverb clause of time
	I shall meet him before the train will go
	We must wait here until the train will return

2.	Object omitted or included unnecessarily
	We saw him play football and we admired
	This is not fit to drink it
	This is the king's horse which he rides it every day
	That is the man who I saw him

3.	Errors in tense sequence
	He said that there is a boy in the garden
	When the evening came we go to the pictures
	When I came back I am tired

4.	Confusion of *too, so, very*
	I am very lazy to stay at home
	I am too tired that I cannot work
	I am very tired that I cannot go
	When I first saw him he was too young
	Honey is too much sweet
	The man became so exhausted and fell on the floor

Table 4

Errors in the Use of Prepositions

1.	*with* instead of	∅	met with her, married with her
		from	suffering with a cold
		against	fight with tyranny
		of	consist with
		at	laughed with my words

2.	*in* instead of	∅	entered in the room, in the next day
		on	in T.V.
		with	fallen in love in Ophelia
		for	in this purpose
		at	in this time
		to	go in Poland
		by	the time in your watch

3.	*at* instead of	$\emptyset$	reached at a place, at last year
		by	held him at the left arm
		in	at the evening; interested at it
		to	went at Stratford
		for	at the first time

4.	*for* instead of	$\emptyset$	serve for God
		in	one bath for seven days
		of	suspected for, the position for Chinese coolies
		from	a distance for one country to another
		since	been here for the 6th of June

5.	*on* instead of	$\emptyset$	played on the piano for an hour
		in	on many ways, on that place, going on cars
		at	on the end
		with	angry on him
		of	countries on the world
		to	pays attention on it

6.	*of* instead of	$\emptyset$	aged of 44, drink less of wine
		in	rich of vitamins
		by	book of Hardy
		on	depends of civilisation
		for	a reason of it

7.	*to* instead of	$\emptyset$	join to them, went to home, reached to the place
		for	an occupation to them
		of	his love to her

Table 5

Errors in the Use of Articles

1.	Omission of *the*	
	(a) before unique nouns	Sun is very hot
		Himalayas are . . .
	(b) before nouns of nationality	Spaniards and Arabs . . .
	(c) before nouns made particular in context	At the conclusion of article
		She goes to bazaar every day
		She is mother of that boy
	(d) before a noun modified by a participle	Solution given in this article
	(e) before superlatives	Richest person
	(f) before a noun modified by an *of*-phrase	Institute of Nuclear Physics

2. *the* used instead of ∅

(a)	before proper names	The Shakespeare, the Sunday
(b)	before abstract nouns	The friendship, the nature, the science
(c)	before nouns behaving like abstract nouns	After the school, after the breakfast
(d)	before plural nouns	The complex structures are still developing
(e)	before *some*	The some knowledge

3. *a* used instead of *the*

(a)	before superlatives	a worst, a best boy in the class
(b)	before unique nouns	a sun becomes red

4. *a* instead of ∅

(a)	before a plural noun qualified by an adjective	a holy places, a human beings, a bad news
(b)	before uncountables	a gold, a work
(c)	before an adjective	. . . taken as a definite

5. Omission of *a*

before class nouns defined by adjectives	he was good boy
	he was brave man

Table 6

Errors in the Use of Questions

1. Omission of inversion

What was called the film?
How many brothers she has?
What she is doing?
When she will be 15?
Why this man is cold?
Why streets are as bright as day?

2. *be* omitted before *verb + ing*

When Jane coming?
What she doing?
What he saying?

3.   Omission of *do*

Where it happened?
How it looks like?
Why you went?
How you say it in English?
How much it costs?
How long it takes?
What he said?

---

4.   Wrong form of auxiliary, or wrong form after auxiliary

Do he go there?
Did he went?
Did he finished?
Do he comes from your village?
Which road did you came by?

---

5.   Inversion retained in embedded sentences

Please write down what is his name.
I told him I do not know how old was it
I don't know how many are there in the box

NOTES

1 Lado, 1957, p. 2.

2 Politzer, 1967, p. 151.

3 Lance, 1969.

4 Cf. Cook, 1969; Stern, 1969; Menyuk, 1969.

5 Corder, 1967, pp. 161–9.

6 Major sources for Tables I–IV are: French, 1949; Dušková, 1969; Arabski, 1968; C. Estacia, 1964; Bhaskar, 1962; Grelier; Aguas, 1964.

7 Jacobovits, 1969, p. 55.

8 Dušková, *ibid.*

9 Ervin-Tripp, 1969, p. 33.

10 Wolfe, 1967, p. 180.

11 French, *ibid.*, p. 9.

12 Aguas, *ibid.*, p. 49.

13 Hirtle, 1967, pp. 40–1; Close, 1959, p. 59.

14 Ritchie, 1967, p. 129.

15 Hok, 1964, p. 118.

16 George, 1962, pp. 18–31.

17 Dakin, 1969, pp. 107–11.

11

Error Analysis: Source, Cause and Significance*

M P JAIN

The realization that the second language learner's errors are potentially important for the understanding of the processes of second
language acquisition, and consequently the planning of courses
incorporating the psychology of second language learning, is a
current focus in the literature on modern language teaching. But
what is not clear is (a) how to arrive at principled means for account-
ing for errors which will more fully determine their source and cause
than contrastive study of the contact languages, (b) how to interpret
their significance in a meaningful conceptual framework, and (c)
whether, because of these methodological difficulties, it is possible
to effectively use error evidence in a linguistically oriented and/or
learning theory based programme of language teaching. These are
questions which cannot be covered in a single paper; nor are there
any ready answers to them.

What this paper attempts to do is to reinforce the position that
the conceptual framework for the study of error source and significance based on contrastive study of the contact languages is fragmentary and therefore inadequate; it overlooks many errors that
the learner seems to make notwithstanding his language background.[1] With the help of confirming evidence from learners'
performance data,[2] the paper highlights what may be called L_1[3]
independent errors, deliberately excluding from discussion errors
uniquely traceable to L_1 interference, and thus draws attention to
some L_1 independent sources of errors. That in any one bilingual
situation all such L_1 independent errors may and do not occur does
not invalidate the hypothesis, because different L_1 independent

* This is a revised version of a paper written in June 1969 for the Department
of Applied Linguistics, University of Edinburgh. I am grateful to Larry
Selinker of the University of Washington for comments on earlier versions
of it; to P. H. G. Gibbs and L. H. M. Clift of the British Council for
comments on this version.

variables related to second language learners operate differently in each second language learning situation. Learning strategies, different training procedures, individual differences of teachers, learners, text books—all seem to operate to make each learning situation different from the other. Inevitably, L_1 independent errors across diverse language backgrounds differ to the extent that these variables operate differently. In presenting error evidence[4] here, an attempt is made to avoid simple inventories, for inventories are essentially unrevealing if they do not explain why the listed errors are made. Of the many factors causing L_1 independent errors, learning strategies, teaching techniques, folklore about the second language, the age of bilingualism, i.e. the period over which the second language has been used by the speech community to which the learner belongs, the learner's sociolinguistic situation, are some of the more easily identifiable variables. In this paper the emphasis is on some learning and teaching strategies; the other factors have only been touched upon in passing, because they represent problems for which we do not have systematic knowledge. The paper seeks to suggest that there is a system in learners' errors in spite of their apparent arbitrariness in performance data, but this method cannot be captured through a simple binary opposition between systematic and non-systematic errors.[5] Finally, though the evidence is limited, the paper offers some tentative observations about the significance of learners' errors: what light they seem to throw on the psychology of second language learning and what implications they carry for language pedagody.

If then errors are traceable to both L_1 and other-than-L_1 sources, a single conceptual framework uniting both these sources alone seems to provide a meaningful frame for inquiry into error source and error significance. Not that it is an easy task: errors do not seem to submit themselves to any precise systematic analysis; the division between errors traceable to L_1 interference and those that are independent of L_1 interference is not invariably clearcut; the phenomenon of errors caused by the cross-association of both L_1 and L_2 also seems to exist; the identification and establishing of various L_1 independent interference factors is far from easy; the learner's psychological processes of second language learning in terms of learning strategies can at best be marginally inferred from his performance data. Beset though the task is with numerous methodological difficulties, it appears that some tentatively useful direction is feasible for fruitful explorations in this area.

An analysis of the data under review, from tables 1 to 8, suggests that learning and teaching strategies, severally and in conjunction with each other, through interaction with the surface structure of English and the teaching situation, constitute some of the necessary and essential conditions for the learner to generate certain classes of sentences. In any language learning situation, from that of a child learning his native language to that of an adult learning a second language, the learning strategy to reduce speech to a simpler system seems to be employed by every learner: both the native child and the second language learner have a 'telegraphic' stage. We do not know if speech reduction in first language learning and adult second language learning is qualitatively the same. What is of importance to us is that this strategy is employed by the second language learner; some of its characteristic features are identifiable through his performance data, both errors and non-errors.[6] Though both the native child and the second language learner use a developmental process of speech reduction, at one stage in their learning they diverge: the native child 'expands' his 'reduced system'[7] to give it a one to one correspondence with the accepted adult system of his speech community; the second language learner with varying degrees of adjustment continues to operate it as a reduced system. If the reduction diverges widely from the target language and operates at all levels of syntax, his second language performance data are marked with errors of diverse kind; if, however, the reduction is selective and does not seriously violate the target language system, his second language performance data may be comparatively free from errors. So, what obtains is a cline both with respect to second language learners and their performance: at one end of the scale, i.e. the bottom end, are those whose performance data are marked with a high degree of deviancy and at the other end are those whose performance data are marked with little or a very low degree of deviancy; in between these two points, there is a whole range of learners whose performance data vary from high to low degrees of deviancy.

The reduction of the target language to a simpler system seems to be best effected through generalizations, which are very often restricted in nature, and thus carry within them potential errors through over-application of these generalizations. Table 1 lists errors which are the product of the over-application of the generalization that says that nouns in English are either count or uncount; that the former are used both in the singular and the plural—the singular form is preceded by the indefinite article 'a' and the plural is marked by plural morphemes; that the latter have no plural form, nor are they marked by 'a'. Hence the following occur in the learner's performance data:

1. They have bought a new chair.
2. They have bought new chairs.

And also:

3. She wants drinking water.
4. She wants some drinking water.

'Chair' and 'water', like many other members of the class N, neatly conform to the generalization. A rule strategy of this type does not however block the following if the learner is writing to convey a plural sense apparently under pressure from non-linguistic environmental cues. (The asterisk marks a 'wrong' sentence.)

* 5. Entry will be by tickets.
* 6. He is a man of his words.
* 7. She is always finding faults with me.

To avoid the plural he has to sub-categorize certain 'count' nouns as 'uncount' for these specified contexts. In the face of his overwhelming experience with 'word', 'ticket' and 'fault' in the second language corpus as 'count' nouns, and also in terms of the teaching strategy, this sub-categorization is particularly difficult: the heavy pressure of these nouns as 'count' occurrences nearly rules it out. Occasional appearances of these words in the singular do not therefore become 'significant' for him. The generalization that they are count constitutes for him the 'creative'[8] aspect for their use. It also accounts for the plural forms of 'leg', 'pass', 'book', 'boy', and 'stone' (table 1, section 1). Thus, whenever the situational context seems to demand a plural idea, the generalized rule produces 8 as well as 9 unless of course the use of 'word' in idiomatic expressions is deliberately learnt outside the generalization:

8. He had no words to express his gratefulness.
9. He will not go back upon his words.

The nonce singular form occurrence of these 'count' words in a context where non-linguistic features of the situation apparently demand the plural, e.g.

10. He sent the message by word of mouth.

may be a product of rote learning, or mere reproduction of a heard utterance, or a teaching strategy listing some useful exceptions to the generalization. Such nonce occurrences do not invalidate the basic point that is being made: the 'creative' use of count words like 'word', 'ticket', 'fault', 'leg', 'pass', 'book', 'boy', 'stone' is being controlled by the generalization that they are 'count' and such a generalization has errors built into it for contexts such as 5, 6, 7, 9[9] and the others cited in table 1, section 1.

Similarly, classed under the category 'count' because of their usual occurrence as 'count' nouns in English and not sub-categorized for these idiomatic expressions, the singular form of 'child', 'arm', 'lip' seem to attract 'a' in the following because this is what the generalization demands (table 1, section 2).

*   11. To defeat him is a child's play for me.
*   12. It is advisable to keep your enemies at an arm's length.
*   13. They don't practise the ideal of democracy; they only pay
        a lip service to it.

Examples in table 1, section 3 show that the same generalization brings about the absence of 'a' in front of 'noise', 'rest', 'temperature', 'fire' because the learner through his overwhelming experience of these words in English in a vast number of situations and also through teaching instruction has classed them as 'uncount':

*   14. Please don't make noise.

As 'a' comes to be associated with count nouns in the singular implying 'one', the generalization eliminates 'a' in front of such words as 'hundred', 'few', 'little', 'thousand', 'million' (table 1, section 4) into which numerically or in terms of bulk, the meaning of more than one is so distinctly woven:

*   15. At the ceremony about hundred people were present.
*   16. He says that power is centralized in few hands.

The English language may maintain the contrast between 'few' and 'a few', 'little' and 'a little', but for the learner thinking in terms of the generalization productive of good results the contrast is not 'significant'.

These errors unambiguously demonstrate that they are the products of his effort to learn English on its own terms and not through equivalents in the mother tongue.

Errors in the opposite direction also occur; the plural morpheme on the noun seems out of place when the singular through 'one' is so overtly indicated as in the following (see table 1, section 5):

* 17. It is one of the interesting book I have read.

As a majority of noun occurrences for number in the surface structure of English are regularly governed by this 'count-uncount' generalization, the economy-seeking second language learner readily adopts it for all occurrences, excluding at best a few nouns only which have been given the status of 'exception' through a particular teaching strategy or a popular school grammar. With this generalization crystallized as a rule, and no longer a mere hypothesis open to further modification, the learner multiplies his experience a thousand times on its basis in the 'creative' mode, with on the whole good communication results. It is possible that L_1 may facilitate the categorization of some of the nouns in the category 'count' rather than the other. What is more important is that once they are categorized, their occurrences in the learner's English is governed by this generalization. Subsumed under the category 'count', the nouns 'work', 'bedding', 'fruit', 'scenery', 'hair', 'luggage', 'equipment', 'data', 'criteria', 'criterion', 'phenomenon', 'paper', 'information', (see table 1, sections 6 and 7) take plural morphemes or 'a' according to what sense the learner wishes to convey:

* 18. She has a very important work to do.
* 19. We have many important works to finish today.
* 20. He offered a fruit to the deity.
* 21. The doctor has advised him to eat plenty of fruits.
* 22. I pulled out a white hair from my head this morning.
* 23. Her hairs are black.

It is possible that the errors in 18 and 20 are due to L_1 interference, but it is difficult to explain the errors in 19 and 21 on the same count, particularly when the pull of the mother tongue in these contexts should have forced the singular form of 'work' and 'fruit'. The learner is not operating merely in terms of the mother tongue equivalents. Similarly, one may attribute 'a' in 22 to·the mother tongue, and this time the interference proves a blessing in disguise, but we are again put to great difficulty in explaining 'hairs' in 23 on the same ground because the mother tongue in this context would demand the singular form.

The 'count-uncount' generalization seems to have other ramifications too. The learner's experience of the regularity of -s and -es marking on the plural form of count nouns is further reinforced through this generalization and he seems to infer that nouns ending with them are count and in the plural[10] and conversely the removal of these plural markers would turn them into singular count nouns.[11] Hence he writes:

*   24. The girls need three more scissors.
*   25. She wants to buy a scissor.

even though the word he meets and is taught is 'scissors'. It is possible to suggest that the occurrence of 'three' in 24 and 'a' in 25 is due to L_1 interference but then the omission of -s from 'scissors' on the same ground is difficult to defend. In spite of the likely cross-association from L_1 the suggestion here is that like many other members of the class N, 'scissors' is also being handled by the same generalization and hence the particular forms produced. (For other examples see table 1, sections 8 and 9.)

The strategy to generalize -s as the plural marker is markedly evident from the learner's use of such plurals as 'datas', 'criterias', 'phenomenas' even though he has not met them in the corpus of the second language, nor do they seem to be influenced by the L_1 system. What seems to happen is that at times the learner is confronted only with one form of these words—'data', 'criteria', 'phenomena'—simply because of the 'register' bias of the second language corpus to which he is exposed, e.g. scientific and technical writings, and then wishing to convey the plural sense he adds -s according to his generalization.

*   26. On the basis of these datas we draw the following conclusion.
*   27. You must examine your criterias once again.

If, however, the other forms of these words constitute his language experience, the plural forms then are: 'criterions', 'phenomenons'; 'datums' has not appeared in the scripts of the learners under discussion probably because 'datum' is used in very restricted texts and does not seem to be part of their lexicon; 'data' is the only form they have consistently met with and its plural form according to their grammar is 'datas'.

Generalizations of several inflexions based on a fairly high degree of regularity in the surface structure of English are common both for foreign learners and native children.[12] Most second language learners in mastering this area of English, like native children, drift through various stages by successively modifying restricted generalizations through 'exceptions' or sub-classification in the direction of the accepted standard of an ideal speaker of English; but for some learners the generalizations prematurely acquire the status of rules. These rules, used creatively, are over-generalized and give rise to the many inflexional errors so well known to second language teachers: mouse : 'mouses'; machinery : 'machineries'; equipment : 'equipments'; hit : 'hitted'; dig : 'digged'. Because of their productive character they are very often a source of interesting novel creations; e.g.

*   28. Witnessers and supporters also thought of utilizing their energy . . .

*   29. A discussion started about pick-pocketers.

*   30. He is a big cheater.

If the 'count-uncount' generalization constitutes the 'creative' aspect for number and also the use of 'a' for members of the class N, the generalization that the verb must agree with the subject determines the number of the verb. Hence, if the learner's grammar generates 'datas', 'criteria'—'criterias', 'scissor'—'scissors', the subject-verb agreement generalization leads to:

*   31. The datas given in the table are very revealing.

*   32. This criteria is questionable.

*   33. The criterias are objective.

*   34. This scissor is of good quality.

*   35. These two scissors are of better quality.

Similarly, as 'police' is not overtly marked for number and neither the teaching strategy nor the school grammar has given it the status of 'exception', the generalization systematically determines the singular verb:

*   36. The police was unable to control the rioting mob.

The errors in table 2 are the product of the generalization that all members of the class *verb* in English are either transitive or intransitive, and for the progressive aspect they are marked with *-ing* on the surface. Hence the occurrences:

37. They are drinking tea.

38. They are playing chess.

39. They are running.

A grammar of this type will not block the following:

* 40. I am having a very heavy workload this semester.
* 41. We make mistakes because we are not knowing the rules.

Nor will it block many others listed in table 2, unless some of the members of the class V are sub-categorized. While the *-ing* marking of 'have' in 40 and 'know' in 41 has no parallel in L_1 in contexts like the ones above, 'like', 'feel', 'get' can be used in the progressive form in L_1 in some of the contexts of the utterances given in the table. Yet to treat their occurrence in the progressive form as arising because of negative transfer would amount to underestimating the pull of generalization, which seems to be the basis for the learner to multiply his experience in the use of the members of the class V in the progressive aspect.

In order to avoid errors of over-application of restricted generalizations, the learner has to bring the latter in one-to-one correspondence with the facts of English. This involves a great deal of sub-classification at all syntactic levels. For example, to make the *-ing* marking on members of the class V coterminous with the facts of English, the over-generalized rule that verbs are either transitive or intransitive and take *-ing* for the progressive aspect has to be modified to accommodate a sub-class of verbs, generally called 'stative' verbs. But the process of sub-classification is not that straightforward because some 'stative' verbs occur in the progressive aspect in certain contexts, e.g.:

42. The dog was smelling the abandoned shoe.

So even in this apparently simple area further sub-classification is involved. It is not only difficult to set up sub-classes;[13] it is uneconomical. Further and further sub-classifications appear to bring to the learner very insignificant returns; they account for less and less members of the class V: the learner therefore seems to be discouraged by the 'law of diminishing returns'. The cost of storing and retrieving these sub-classes seems to be out of all proportion to his limited aim in using English as a tool of communication. As part of a reduction strategy aimed at learning economy, he by and large ignores sub-classes and subsumes them in highly generalized rules.

In a second language teaching situation the learner alone is not engaged in this process. In fact all other components in the teaching situation—teaching materials, teaching techniques, popular school grammars, teaching and learning goals—are attempting to bring about learning economy through reduction of the second language along one dimension or another. Limited vocabulary, limited structures, abridged and simplified texts, simplified and very often oversimplified school grammar books are attempts in the same direction. Thus simplified generalizations would seem to be built into a second language teaching situation. For example, there would hardly be a teaching course that does not base itself on the 'count-uncount' generalization; nor is there a teaching technique which dispenses with it. We all know that this type of generalization is a helpful teaching device[14] but it does not truly reflect the nature of the second language. In fact nearly all count nouns are potentially uncount.[15] But the learner has very little choice in rejecting a restricted generalization, if that is the only one available; for if he does so he faces the problem of missing the generalization and consequently learning is affected.

The learner does not generalize along the dimension of structural regularities alone. Other kinds of regularities also seem to be learned. Some generalizations seem to be derived from a high degree of consistency between form and function in the surface structure of English. For example subject-verb inversion is nearly an invariant property of the interrogative sentence, while subject-verb order nearly always marks declarative sentences. If the learner, then, generalizes that a sentence overtly marked in the initial position with the question word or the anomalous finite alone has the privilege of subject-verb inversion, and gives it the status of rule, he is not far from capturing a very frequent feature of the English language in terms of a form related to a particular function. A generalization along these lines rules out inversion in the following as the question word is not prefixed to these sentences (see table 3):

*   43. Under no circumstances we will accept these terms.
*   44. They didn't like it; nor I liked it.
*   45. He was unhappy at the development; so I was.

Yet another way in which the learner generalizes from his experience of this sentence type is to associate the question word with the subject-verb inversion. Either his own experience with this sentence type or a particular teaching strategy or both may facilitate the generalization. Over-generalized to indirect questions, the rule leads to errors of the type cited in table 4:

*   46. Now I see why did he behave like this?

Certain generalizations seem to be encouraged by particular teaching strategies, some of them in turn are influenced by the learner's age and/or the sociolinguistic situation of the learner. For example in the English language situation in India, the written word through books, newspapers, journals and magazines is dominant—the spoken word is largely derived from it. The whole of the English language is reduced to a uniform style—the rigid written code. The result is what has been described as 'dictionary-oriented and Nesfield-possessed English.'

As part of the strategy of reducing language to a simpler system, if both learner and teaching strategy eliminate 'register' differences from the second language, the reduction results in utterances of the following type:

47. She has five lovely offspring.
48. The teacher reprimanded the boy.
49. I hope you'll attend the party with your spouse.
50. I purchased this pencil yesterday.
51. She is donning a beautiful hat.

These are mainly stylistic oddities, very often with no syntactic consequences.

How a particular teaching strategy, rooted in the age of bilingualism of a country, can encourage a restricted generalization is seen from what is discussed below. Certain types of teaching exercise are part of the English language teaching tradition in India. The one referred to here is called 'exercise in direct and indirect narration'. This exercise asks the learner to change sentences from direct to indirect speech. Sentences on the following pattern figure predominantly in exercise materials modelled on it; first the examples:

52. My father said, 'It is time to go away.'
53. My father said that it was time to go away.
54. He has told you, 'I am coming.'
55. He has told you that he is coming.
56. He will say, 'The boy was lazy.'
57. He will tell them that the boy was lazy.
58. All men declare, 'He has never been defeated.'
59. All men declare that he has never been defeated.

Through such examples the learner is asked to convert the following types of sentences from Direct to Indirect:

60. We said to him, 'The weather is stormy, and the way is long.'
61. The teacher told us, 'The prize will be presented tomorrow.'
62. We heard him say, 'I will agree to what you propose . . .'
63. My son exclaimed, 'Someone has taken the book I was reading.'
64. He made a promise, 'I will come, if I can.'

What is to be noted is that by its very nature the exercise plays up 'that' as a clause marker. The exercise in the reverse direction, i.e. from indirect to direct narration, also tends to emphasize it. The learner is asked to convert sentences of the following type from Indirect to Direct:

65. He made them understand that he would soon return.
66. They affirmed that he was the best worker they had seen.
67. He admitted that he had not worked so hard . . .
68. He heard them say that he did not deserve the prize.
69. He promised them that he would do it as soon as he could.

To these are added examples of the following type:

70. He reminded me, 'When the cat is away, the mice play.'
71. He reminded me that when the cat is away, the mice play.
72. Pilate replied to the Jews, 'What I have written, I have written.'
73. Pilate replied to the Jews that what he had written, he had written.[16]

Exposed to this language data, coupled with text lessons organized around the principle of one-thing-at-a-time in which the 'that-clause' is again separately highlighted as a 'teaching' point, the learner seems to induce that 'that' is an invariant clause marker for 'noun clauses'. In terms of relative position of 'that' to other items in the sentence, it implies that the clause after the verb is to be preceded by 'that'. His non-error performance data as well seem to bring out this 'that' fixation; his utterances are cluttered with 'that'. Take the following sequence:

74. He conceives that with the help of science . . . He conceives that with the help of the Bokanovsky's process . . . He shows that all the discomforts . . . He thinks that . . . He saw that . . . The fact that . . .

When the learner adds to this generalization, another generalized inference that words like 'when', 'why', 'how', 'where', express such concepts as 'time', 'reason', 'manner', 'place' and are therefore meaning carriers, the result is that his grammar produces 75 and 76:

75. I think that you are right.
76. I know that you have done your best.

and also 77 and 78 with 'that' as clause marker and 'how' and 'why' as meaning carriers.

* 77. This shows that how sensitive he is.
* 78. It is now that I have realized that what books really have done for me.

Multiplying his experience on the generalization that 'that' is the invariant noun clause marker and 'why', 'how' and other *'Wh'* words are meaning carriers, he makes errors of the type listed in table 5. Through exercises on the pattern of 70–73 highlighting 'that what', 'that when', combinations like 'that how', 'that why', 'that whether' seem to gain further legitimacy.

Using 'that' with this high degree of generality as a noun clause marker in combination with the generalization of subject-verb inversion for *Wh* words and/or anomalous finites in the front position, he produces (table 5, section 2):

* 79. He points out that how will he escape punishment.
* 80. He asks that is it possible to expect work from a blind man?

The shift from the period to the question mark in 80 seems to be the product of indecision about whether the resultant sentence is interrogative or declarative.

Sometimes the learner over-generalizes because of interference between items in the second language. From 'say about', 'speak about', 'write about', he seems to generalize and say:

* 81. In this poem Wordsworth has described about nature.

Verbs like 'conceive', 'describe' (see table 6, section 1) seem to attract 'about' more easily probably because they are closer in meaning to verbs which do take 'about'.

When the learner adds to this the generalization of 'that' as a noun clause marker and of *Wh* words as meaning carriers, the result is (table 6, section 2):

* 82. In this poem Wordsworth has described about nature that how it will mould Lucy.

The errors in table 7 highlight the learner's failure to observe the restrictions on the co-occurrence of items within a sentence. Restrictions are of two types: lexical and grammatical. Lexical restrictions deal with the co-occurrence of wholly lexical items; they rule out the co-occurrence of some words with others because of the incompatibility of pairs of words, e.g.

*   83. He drives a scooter.

Grammatical restrictions, on the other hand, determine the occurrence of items in grammatical contexts; they do not permit certain words to enter at all into certain grammatical constructions. Thus

*   84. We want that Hindi should be the medium of instruction.

is not acceptable because 'want' cannot be followed by any subordinate clause.

Very often the learner's failure to observe these two types of restriction is attributed to L_1 interference, particularly in sentences such as 83 and 84. However, the violation of the grammatical restrictions in the following sentence (for more examples see table 7) cannot be defended on the same ground:

*   85. She delivered a male child.

The failure hardly seems to stem from L_1 interference. What is being suggested here is that most of these errors are rooted in the same learning strategy of speech reduction as discussed earlier in relation to many other errors. By not going into the idiosyncratic properties of individual words, the learner cuts down the tasks of subcategorizing. It may, however, be noted that the burden of subcategorizing at the level of grammatical and lexical restrictions on the co-occurrence of items is highest. While a rule that verbs are either transitive or intransitive takes care of many members of the class V, the rule, for example, that 'deliver' is to be used in the passive and followed by 'of' takes care of a single member. But as rules at the level of restrictions very often reflect the idiosyncratic property of individual words, they cannot be used in the 'creative' mode; so the failure to apply them correctly may only result in nonce errors.

So far we have discussed errors which seem to fall into definable patterns; they show a consistent system, are internally principled and free from arbitrariness: they are therefore systematic. These systematic errors may be looked upon as rule-governed for they follow the rules of whatever grammar the learner has.

Table 8 presents errors which do not exhibit a rule-patterned consistent system: they are not always internally principled; yet they are not totally arbitrary. At this point it may be useful to distinguish between two types of restricted generalizations: those however partial or inefficient, which have acquired the status of rules with the learners; and those which have come to stay as hypotheses. The generalizations discussed above are all in the nature of rules. Generalizations which are in the process of becoming rules are not relevant to the discussion here because throughout this paper we are talking about learners who after 11 to 14 years of instruction have reached a stage when they are no longer 'testing their hypotheses' about the second language; they have arrived at a system, whatever it is. What is being proposed here is that certain generalizations remain, for one reason or another, hypotheses, and the learner is unable to give them the status of rules; they are therefore open to unsettling influences. The result is that though the learner may have seemingly arrived at a hypothesis, he is not able to apply it with any degree of consistency in handling his performance data. These are areas of indeterminacy[17] in his syllabus which give rise to systematic-unsystematic errors: they are henceforth in this paper called asystematic errors as opposed to systematic and unsystematic or non systematic errors. To appreciate the nature of these errors, it seems best to reproduce a sequence of utterances from a learner's performance data:

> In the meantime the driver stopped the engine. He tried to start it again when the conductor whistled. Engine did not start. In the meantime conductor decided to check the bus. Conductor asked me about my ticket; I had not bought it by then. I asked the conductor for the ticket. By now engine was on; then he whistled and bus went away.

There is no apparent rule-governed consistency with which the article is applied or missed in front of 'engine', 'conductor' and 'bus'.

What seems to happen is that the learner has arrived at no firm generalization for the use of the definite article in English, not even a partial generalization with the status of rule. And yet, he seems to operate with some hypothesis that members of the class N alone can be preceded by the article, for it is not used in front of members of any other class; but what the hypothesis does not seem systematically to settle for him is where to use the article and where to miss it out when he has to make the choice for members of the class N. If language is taken to be rule-governed behaviour, then performance data of this type in these selected areas would constitute language-like behaviour. In other words he has no productive control of article usage, not even that type of control which he shows in areas where he has over-generalized. The result is: asystematic errors. It is in the context of such errors that it is difficult to state precise rules for the occurrence of errors in the learner's performance data. However, he has some kind of receptive control of these indeterminate areas, largely owing to the total context of the utterance or discourse.

It appears that in a particular learning situation for the learner there are too many cues to frustrate his reaching a firm generalization. Teaching techniques, the learner's experience with the second language—the facts of surface structure at times may completely obscure the generalization—the popular school grammar, folklore about the second language, the learner's sociolinguistic situation, the various practices and traditions regarding the second language usage obtaining in a bilingual situation, all may promote certain selected areas of indeterminacy in the learner's syllabus. For example, let us take the learning situation in which both the school grammar and the teaching techniques offer for article use the following generalization; 'a' is to be used before singular count nouns, but it should not be used in front of 'abstract' nouns. Examples:

86. It is a big white egg.
87. It is a toy train.
88. I see a man in the distance.
89. It is a good story.
90. You can buy a pencil; she can buy a pen.
91. He is a painter.
92. This is a bus, that's a doll, and that's a cat.
93. They jumped for joy.
94. Books give pleasure.

Before the proffered generalization crystallizes into a rule, if the learner is confronted with the data of the following type, a sort of 'cognitive clutter' occurs:

86a. The child likes egg.
87a. We'll go by train.

88a. Man is selfish.
89a. What sort of story is this?
90a. Between pencil and pen there is a distance of about one foot.
91a. As painter, he is not so well known.

92a. Captions: | bus | | doll | | cat |

93a. A thing of beauty is a joy forever.
94a. It is a pleasure to see you.

The so-called count nouns in the singular are not, and the uncount nouns are, preceded by 'a'; this is in direct contradiction to what the generalization says. Fortunately, the rule and its contradictions for 'a' do not occur in this sharply defined matching fashion. The situation with respect to 'the' is much more ambiguous and misleading. In the face of this copious contradiction between the proffered generalization and his language experience the learner fails to generalize with any degree of definiteness or finds it difficult to accept the proffered generalization as a rule. This then constitutes one of the typical situations for indeterminacy. The folklore that article use in English is very difficult and is governed by no rules, the tradition and practice in the bilingual's speech community where a majority of second language learners operate the article system with indeterminacy may further worsen the situation. So much so that under such punishing circumstances, he may adopt an escapist strategy of choosing new forms, which do not parallel either language,[18] or may operate selected areas of the second language with some kind of hit or miss strategy. Once again it may be noted that these errors are not uniquely traceable to interference from the L_1 system; it is, however, possible that along with other factors L_1 features may also contribute to indeterminacy.

It seems that because of the apparent copious opposition between rules and arbitrariness manifested in the surface structure of English, certain areas within the structure of English are more facilitative of indeterminacy than others. In many English-as-a-second-language teaching situations, three such typical areas are: articles, prepositions and the tense system. The major difficulty about them is that they do not submit themselves to any easy generalization or overgeneralization based on some consistent regularity; the system of the second language in these areas demands a combination of decisions at several levels of syntax. Teaching techniques, popular grammars, teaching materials along with teachers and learners despair of any systematic rules in these areas: 'learning' is 'hoped' to take place through the learner's 'experience' of and 'practice' in the second language. Quite often the 'hope' is not fulfilled because this kind of indeterminacy seems to mar the learner's ability to infer linguistic forms, patterns and rules from new linguistic contexts.

Articles, prepositions and the tense system in English, however, do not exhaust the likely areas of indeterminacy. A teaching strategy or any one or more of the other error-causing L_1 independent variables referred to above may transfer this opposition between rules and arbitrariness to many other areas, even though the surface structure of English may not so obviously carry it for the learner, making it difficult for him to accept the proffered rule or to induce it. This is apparent from the learner's clause handling in the four paragraph sequence quoted in table 8, section 2. In spite of his appropriately using 'that' in the first sentence of the first paragraph, 'how' in the first sentence of the second paragraph, 'what' in the second sentence of the fourth paragraph as clause markers, the learner's use of 'that' after *arise, becomes* and *is a problem* seems to show that his grammar has not been able to spell out for him the grammatical restrictions which hold for the 'that' clause, nor has it made the use of 'how' and 'what' explicit as clause markers because it still permits ungrammatical occurrences of 'that what' and 'that how'. Through error examples of this nature it is not unreasonable to suggest that these are not random errors; they seem to be the product of indeterminacy in the learner's syllabus with respect to construction rules for noun clauses.

Besides systematic and asystematic errors, the learner, like the native speaker, seems to make unsystematic errors too. They are the slips of the tongue or pen caused purely by psychological conditions, such as intense excitement, and/or physiological factors, such as tiredness, which change from moment to moment and from situation to situation: errors under these circumstances are *ipso facto* unsystematic. From the pedagogic point of view, one may usefully dismiss them as 'mistakes'.[19] As these 'mistakes' are not central to the discussion in this paper, they have not been considered.

From the above explanation of the source and cause of errors certain implications for language acquisition and language pedagogy follow.

1. Errors discussed under the category of systematic errors seem to establish that in certain areas of language use the learner possesses construction rules. The debatable question whether rules should be

taught or not is irrelevant in this context: he is using rules. Because of some kind of limitation in rule schemata, the rules give rise to errors of over-application. The relevant question, then, is: which rules, at a particular stage of learning with his adopted learning strategies and rule schemata should prove facilitative both for corrective and additional learning?[20]

Stripped of the shell of formalism and metalanguage, recent advances in linguistic theory providing us with more powerful generalizations than have previously been possible, seem to hold the answer.

2. With respect to asystematic errors, the inescapable conclusion seems to be that in the indeterminate areas of language use concerned, the learner's capacity to generalize must improve, for progress in learning a language is made by adopting generalizations and stretching them to match the facts of the language. The teacher, classroom instruction, teaching materials, his own 'inductive language learning ability'—all seem to have failed him. Therefore, teaching strategies and materials must provide him with a stronger inclination and better ability to formulate rules. How this can be done[21] is outside the domain of this paper.

3. All of the restricted generalizations that the learner is employing for language use are not of equal status, for their error-causing potentialities. Those which do not cover the broadest facts of the second language and can be used in the 'creative' mode, are more productive of errors (cf. errors in tables 4, 5.1, 5.2, 6.2). On the other hand, generalizations which are in larger agreement with the second language facts are less productive of errors (cf. tables 2, 3, 6.1). Relatively speaking, the latter require marginal corrective adjustment. Similarly, generalizations which are not productive in nature, e.g. with respect to restrictions on the co-occurrence of items within a sentence, do not generate many errors (cf. table 7). Thus errors would help determine which areas in the learner's English need more attention and what type of attention.

4. For errors which are rooted in restricted generalizations, investment of energies in the mere correction of actual errors would not seem to be very rewarding.[22] What is required is to tackle the restricted generalization itself; to establish for the learner that a broader generalization is more 'significant' than the former; that a rule schema for sub-classes, if they are not covered by his generalized rule, has to be provided for. This cannot be achieved through mere correction of errors or an error-based 'remedial programme'; nor

through intensive drills of correct forms. Depending upon the nature of the error-causing generalizations, it may be absolutely essential to re-examine and modify teaching techniques, the presentation of the corpus of the primary linguistic data, the disabusing of the learner's language acquisition device of the heresies of 'popular' but erroneous generalizations. If placed in this larger context, the correction of actual errors would have meaning.

5. The fact that errors cited in this paper are from the performance data of those who have studied English from 11 to 14 years, would suggest that their learning has largely stopped. Their competence is marked partly by indeterminacy and partly by restricted generalizations crystallized into rigid rules hardly open to revision in the face of new evidence. In areas of language use where the learner possesses rules, he is no longer discovering the second language; he has arrived at a system. And howsoever inadequate his rules may be from the standpoint of the accepted grammar of the native speaker, he uses them in the 'creative' mode and his sentences are grammatical in terms of his own grammar. This is the point where it seems reasonable to hypothesize that the 'input' in terms of learning the L_2 system is not what is available for going in but what he takes in through his over-generalized rules.[23] If learning is to take place in these areas, teaching materials with an explicit mechanism in them to motivate the learner to test his 'rules' and 'see' their inadequacies would seem to be required. An implicit faith in this kind of approach is not to regard errors as exemplifiers of 'linguistic sin' to be subjected to 'intensive remedial drill'; rather it is to consider them as an essential condition of learning, providing the teacher with clues on how to take the learner from limited rule schemata to more generalized ones, establishing the latter as more 'significant' than the former.

APPENDIX

Table 1

---

1.   To convey the idea of plurality, the underlined 'count' nouns are pluralized leading to errors.

Entry will be by tickets.
He is a man of his words.
She is always finding faults with me.
He will not go back upon his words.
Don't pull my legs.

Admission will be regulated by passes.
He finished books after books.
Boys after boys shouted for the same demand.
The Delhi Fort is made of red stones.

---

2.   Classed in the category 'count', the underlined singular nouns attract 'a'.

To defeat him is a child's play for me.
It is advisable to keep your enemies at an arm's length.
They only pay a lip service to Gandhian ideas.

---

3.   Classed in the category 'uncount', the underlined nouns are not preceded by 'a'.

You are not expected to make noise here.
He was running temperature yesterday.
We decided that after each two hours we would stop and take rest.
When we reached the camp, the first thing we did was to light fire.

---

4.   'A' is dropped in front of the underlined nouns because they so obviously imply the meaning of more than one.

At the ceremony about hundred people were present.
He says that power is centralized in few hands.
After thinking little I decided to break the ties.
Even thousand repetitions will not help.
About million times I must have reminded you.

---

5.   As the underlined nouns are so overtly modified by 'one', they are used in the singular.

It is one of the interesting book I have read.
It was one of those hot day in June.
A journey by a D.T.U. bus is one of the most tiring journey.
He is one of the most interesting man I have ever met.

---

6.   Subsumed under the category 'count', the underlined nouns are pluralized to express a plural sense.

We have many important works to finish today.
In all we had about 15 beddings. (Instead of bed rolls.)
The doctor has advised him to eat plenty of fruits.
The mountain city abounds in beautiful sceneries.
They were carelessly throwing the luggages of the passengers.
All the new equipments are kept in that room.
On the basis of these datas we draw the following conclusion.
You must examine your criterias once again.
She likes fruits.
She has very black hairs.
What are your criterions for deciding the prize?

This study describes some rare phenomenons in the field of magnetism.
Let me have two papers. (Instead of two sheets of paper.)
These informations are not very reliable.
Her hairs are black.

---

7. Subsumed under the category 'count', the underlined nouns are preceded by 'a' (also underlined) to convey the sense of 'one'.

She has a very important work to do.
Each one of you is advised to carry a bedding with you.
He offered a fruit to the deity.
As you enter this mountain city, you are greeted by a beautiful scenery.
You can't charge so much cartage for carrying one luggage only.
A sound criteria is to be fixed for judging it.
For the time being I want a paper and a pencil.
He was irritated to find a hair in his food. (Though the source of error in other sentences in this section of the table, 'a' here turns out to be an acceptable usage.)

---

8. Subsumed under the category 'count', the underlined nouns are preceded by numerals (also underlined) to give the idea of number.

These are two very good news you have brought.
The girls need three more scissors.
You may buy two woollen trousers.
I always carry two spectacles with me, one for reading and the other for general use.
In the theft we lost about 15 clothes.

---

9. To use the 'count' nouns of his grammar in the singular, the learner drops the plural marker -s and puts 'a' in front of the noun.

She wants to buy a scissor.
It seems to be a new trouser.
Why didn't he buy a new spectacle?
In the theft they seemed to have lost only one clothe.
It's a good news.
(The -s seems to stick because of the meaningful contrast between 'news' and 'new' in the learner's English.)

Table 2

Verbs are marked with -ing for the progressive aspect.

I am having a very heavy work-load this semester.
We make mistakes because we are not knowing the rules.
The main reason for my leaving the hostel was that I was not liking the food.

I was feeling as if I was in a hell.
I was having deep breathes. . . .
I was feeling almost strangled.
I had been feeling rather gay.
I was really getting too terrified.
Are you noticing these changes in his behaviour.
I was seeing all this happen in front of my own house.
All these days, I have been desiring to meet you.
I was getting shocks after shocks.
One bus was standing at the bus stop but it was out of order.

Table 3

As the 'subject-verb inversion' is 'the property of the interrogative sentence', the inversion is ruled out in sentences which have the statement form.

Under no circumstances we will accept these terms.
They didn't like it; nor I liked it.
He was unhappy at the development; so I was.
No sooner they reached the stop than it started.
Only then I realized how many people were present at the fair.
Hardly it was possible for us to finish the project report in time.
Only after his brother's persuasion he gave up his stand.
Seldom he makes such silly remarks.
Rarely you see such a vintage performance.
I thought the movie was disgusting, and so my friend thought.

Table 4

Subject-verb inversion for the question word.

Now I see why did he behave like this.
We don't know why are we taught so many courses.
I don't understand why should we do so much chemistry as part of the engineering course.
Tell us how do you account for this type of curriculum?
Can you tell us how is he going to settle the matter?

Table 5

---

1. 'That' is used as a noun clause marker and *Wh* words are treated as meaning carriers.

This shows that how sensitive he is.
It is now that I have realized that what books really have done for me.
At this stage Louka asks Sergius that for whom he has got higher love.

God will ask him that why he did not make any use of his talents.
In these lines the poet has described that how the nature will guide the little girl.
He tells us that he has moments when he considers that how he became blind.
He knows well that what a blind man can do.
His behaviour indicates that whom he likes more.
He thought that how people behaved in romantic ways.
He says that when he thinks that whether God wants hard work from a blind man, the answer is 'no'.
He further says that what can be done when one's death has been decreed by God.
It looks to him very strange that why man should fear death.
It is fantastic that how a blind man can write so well.
It is wonderful that how they have been able to explore the outer space.
Since it is not predictable in most of the cases that who is going to fall ill. . . .

2.   'That' is used as a noun clause marker, and the subject-verb inversion for the question word or the anomalous finite.

He points out that how will he escape punishment?
He asks that is it possible to expect work from a blind man?
But then he deeply thinks that does God expect work from a blind man?
Then he complains to God that does God demand full work from them who are blind?
Do you think that will God punish a blind man for not doing his work?
Now it is clear that why will God not punish him?

Table 6

1.   Mutual interference between items in English.

In this poem Wordsworth has described about nature.
He has explained to him about the whole matter.
In this way Huxley conceives about the future of the modern world.

2.   Mutual interference between items in English in conjunction with 'that' and *Wh* generalizations.

He explains to Raina about the battle that how they were attacked.
In this poem Wordsworth has described about nature that how it will mould Lucy.

Table 7

Miscellaneous items used without the grammatical restrictions that go with them.

She delivered a male child this morning.
You didn't avail of the opportunity.

We enjoyed at the theatre for two hours.
The music from the adjoining room sounds melodiously.
It smells sourish.
I know swimming.

Table 8

1. Asystematic errors with respect to article use. Underlined Ns and NPs show
    that the article is used and missed in front of them rather 'asystematically'.

A. In the meantime the driver stopped the engine. He tried to start it again
    when the conductor whistled. Engine did not start. In the meantime
    conductor decided to check the bus. Conductor asked me about my ticket;
    I had not bought it by then. I asked the conductor for the ticket. By now
    engine was on ; then he whistled and bus went away.

B. After a long wait a bus came and conductor shouted . . . I also rushed to
    catch bus like others.
    The bus stopped at third bus stop and the trouble arose. At last conductor
    asked me to get down. But the trouble was not finished yet. The conductor
    was crying from the door. . . .

C. I started from hostel to go to see a movie. When we were still waiting at
    bus stop . . . I could only get some space to keep my one leg on foot-board
    . . . I had to request conductor   At last bus moved. The bus stopped at
    a bus stop with a jerk. All the time I was trying to balance myself on the
    footboard. I was more worried about movie.

D. But it is not possible to attain 100% integration or disintegration of
    society. So the degree of integration must be specified, e.g. in terms of
    religion. The religion is for the integration of the society, e.g. take Hindu
    religion. So different elements of society of Hindus show the integration of
    the society.

E. Malinowaski (sic) considered individual as the functioning unit. He held
    that an individual had primary as well as derived needs. Malinowaski's
    approach was criticized by a French Scholar, Emile Durkheim. He said
    we would not be able to account for the diversified nature of societies if
    individual is taken as the starting point. Instead of taking the individual
    as the functional unit, he took society as the unit. He said though individuals
    constituted a society but society did not die with the exit of an individual.
    According to him individual was not indispensable. . . .

2. Asystematic errors with respect to noun clause construction.

A. The first problem means that the productive resources available to man are
    limited and the demand for commodities is unlimited, so it is a problem
    that what should be produced with the given limited resources so as to
    satisfy the demand. . . .
    The other problem is how to produce the commodities that we have to
    produce. . . .
    The third problem is that suppose somehow we have produced the com-

modity, then who will consume it?. . . .
The same reason can be used to produce different commodities and once
it is decided what to produce, the problem arises that how to produce
them because the resources are limited. . . .The production is comparatively
less than the demand for it, so the problem becomes that how to dis-
tribute among people the commodities produced.

NOTES

1 See French, 1949; Corder, 1967, pp. 161–70; Wolfe, 1967, pp. 179–82;
Lee; Dušková, 1969, pp. 11–36; Richards, 1971, pp. 204–19; Afolayan,
1971, pp. 220–29; George, 1971, pp. 270–77.

2 The data (see Appendix, Tables 1–8) pertain to the written scripts in
English of Indian students at the university level who have had 7 to 11
years' instruction in English at school. At the university they are to receive
2 to 3 years' more instruction. Of the learners who figure in this study, some
are about to complete and some have just completed their last phase of
formal instruction in English, the total instruction period varying from 9
to 14 years from learner to learner. From now onwards they have to cope
with English on their own in whatever situation they wish or have to use it.

3 In the context of this paper Hindi is L_1, the learner's first language or
mother tongue; English is L_2, the second or foreign language.

4 In collecting the evidence the context of each error was taken fully into
account. For economy of presentation, errors from 1 to 8 have been
cited devoid of the context of the discourse; while in Table 8, because of
the nature of the errors, they have been cited in longer stretches of the discourse.

5 Cf. S. P. Corder, *ibid.*, p. 166: 'The opposition between systematic and non-
systematic errors is important.' Also see Dušková, *ibid.*

6 Non-error performance data do carry evidence for reduction. For example, between two free variants, *Help me to lift the box* and *Help me lift
the box*, if a learner has made a choice for the one and not the other, he is
reducing speech but without creating possibilities for errors as he does
when he settles on a restricted generalization and stretches it through
over-application. See the discussion below.

7 See Klima and Bellugi, 1966.

8 Used here in the Chomskian sense. Chomsky, 1965.

9 It is interesting to note that if the second language learner were to act
under the pull of the mother tongue, the mother tongue would ensure the
singular form of 'ticket' and 'word' in 5, 6 & 9.

10 They aid the identification of nouns for number. Cf. Brown, 1957, pp. 1–5.

11 See Ervin, 1964. She points out how under the pressure of a learned rule,
i.e. adding 'ed' for the past, the irregular forms of past tense like 'came',
'went', 'sat', often correctly produced early on in the child's development
are dropped and forms like 'comed', 'goed' and 'sitted' are generated.

12 For the production of inflexions in the 'creative' mode in native children see Berko, 1958, pp. 150–77.

13 Hill, 1967.

14 For example, *The Advanced Learner's Dictionary of Current English*, uses it.

15 See Hill, 1967.

16 All these examples are cited from Nesfield, 1953.

17 It does not, however, mean that all areas of indeterminacy cause errors. For example if the learner is not certain between 'on an average' and 'on the average', the choice of either will be correct. Further, in many indeterminate areas these are alternative escape routes; e.g. if he is uncertain about: He insists on my doing it., he can say: He insists that I do it.

18 See Wolfe, 1967, p. 181.

19 For this distinction between 'errors' and 'mistakes', see Corder, 1967, pp. 166–7.

20 See Jakobovits, 1967, pp. 77–8.

21 For some useful discussion in this area see Jakobovits, 1967, pp. 78 80.

22 Cf. Ritchie, 1967, p. 129.

23 See Corder for his insightful observation on input-output relationship in the case of the second language learner, 1967, p. 165.

Bibliography

Afolayan, A. 'Contrastive Linguistics and the Teaching of English as a Second Language.' *English Language Teaching*, **XXV**, 1971, 220–9.

Aguas, E. F. *English Composition Errors of Tagalog Speakers*. D.Ed. diss., UCLA, 1964.

Alatis, James (ed.). *Bilingualism and Language Contact: Anthropological, Linguistic, Psychological and Sociological Aspects*. Monograph Series on Languages and Linguistics, **23**, Washington, 1970.

Alford, N. D. *Research Report on some Aspects of the Language Development of Pre-School Children*. Brisbane, 1970.

Allen Jones, J. 'English Language Teaching in a Social/Cultural Dialect Situation.' *English Language Teaching*, **XXII**, 3, 1968, 199–204; **XXIV**, 1, 1969, 18–23.

Allsopp, Richard. 'The English Language in British Guinea.' *English Language Teaching*, **XII**, 2, 1958, 59–65.

Anisfeld, M. and Tucker, C. R. 'English pluralization rules of six-year-old children.' *Child Development*, **38**, 1967, 1201–18.

Arabski, J. 'A Linguistic Analysis of English Composition Errors Made by Polish Students.' *Studia Anglica Posnaniensia*, **I**, 1 and 2, 1968, 71–89.

Ashton-Warner, Sylvia. *Teacher*. New York, 1963.

Bamgbose, A. 'The English Language in Nigeria.' In Spencer, 1971.

Banathy, B., Trager, E. C. and Waddle, C. D. 'The use of contrastive data in foreign language course development.' In A. Valdman (ed.), *Trends in Language Teaching*. New York, 1966.

Bazell, C. E. *et al. In Memory of J. R. Firth*. London, 1966.

Bellugi, Ursula. 'The Development of Interrogative Structures in Children's Speech.' In K. Riegel (ed.), *The Development of Language Functions*, Ann Arbor: Michigan Language Development Program, Report No. **8**, 1965, 103–37.

Benton, Richard. *Research into the English Language Difficulties of Maori School Children, 1963–1964*. Wellington, Maori Education Foundation, 1964.

Berko, J. 'The child's learning of English morphology.' *Word*, **14**, 1958, 159–77.

Bever, T. 'Associations to stimulus-response theories of language.' In T. R. Dixon and D. R. Horton (eds.), *Verbal Behavior and General Behavior Theory*. Englewood Cliffs, N.J., 1968.

Bever, T., Fodor, J. A. and Garrett, M. 'A formal limitation of associationism.' In T. R. Dixon and D. R. Horton (eds.), 1968.

Bever, T. 'The cognitive basis for linguistic structures.' In J. R. Hayes (ed.), *Cognition and the Development of Language*. New York, 1970.

Bhaskar, A. W. S. 'An Analysis of Common Errors in PUC English.' *Bulletin of the Central Institute of English* (Hyderabad, India), 2, 1962, 47–57.

Bloom, L. *Language Development: Form and Function in Emerging Grammars*. Cambridge, Massachusetts, 1970.

Boaz, Franz. 'On Alternating Sounds.' *American Anthropologist*, 2.1, 1889, 47–53.

Bondarko, L. V. 'The Syllable Structure of Speech and Distinctive Features of Phonemes.' *Phonetica*, 20, 1, 1969, 1–40.

Braine, M. D. S. 'The Acquisition of Language in Infant and Child.' In Carrol E. Reed (ed.), *The Learning of Language*. New York, 1971, 7–95.

Brière, Eugène. *A Psycholinguistic Study of Phonological Interference*. The Hague, 1968.

Brosnahan, L. F. 'Some Historical Cases of Language Imposition.' In Spencer, 1963.

Brown, R. W. 'Linguistic determinism and the part of speech.' *Journal of Abnormal and Social Psychology*, 55, 1957.

Brown, R. W. and Fraser, C. 'The Acquisition of Syntax.' In Ursula Bellugi and Roger Brown (eds.), *The Acquisition of Language*. Monograph of the Society for Research in Child Development, 29, No. 1, 1964.

Brown, R. 'The development of *Wh*-questions in child speech.' *Journal of Verbal Learning and Verbal Behavior*, 7, 1968, 279–90.

Brown, R., Cazden, C. and Bellugi, U. 'The child's grammar from I to III.' In J. P. Hill (ed.), *Minneapolis Symposium on Child Psychology*. Minneapolis, 1968.

Brown, R. 'Stage I: Semantic and grammatical relations; Stage II: Grammatical morphemes and the modulation of meaning.' Harvard University, 1971–72. Two chapters in a projected book, *A First Language*, in preparation.

Brudhiprabha, P. 'Error Analysis: A Psycholinguistic Study of Thai English Compositions.' M.A. Thesis. Montreal: McGill University, 1972.

Burt, M. K. *From Deep to Surface Structure: An Introduction to Transformational Syntax*. New York, 1971.

Burt, M. K. and Kiparsky, C. *The Gooficon: A Repair Manual for English*. Newbury House, Rowley, Massachusetts, 1972.

Carroll, J. B. *The Study of Language*. Cambridge, 1955.

Carroll, J. B. 'Research on Language Learning and Linguistics.' *Report of the Northeast Conference*, Modern Languages Association, Materials Center, New York, 1966.

Carton, Aaron S. 'Inferencing: A Process in Using and Learning Language.' In Paul Pimsleur and Terence Quinn (eds.), *The Psychology of Second Language Learning*. Cambridge, 1971, 45–8.

Cassidy, Frederic G. 'Tracing the Pidgin Element in Jamaican Creole.' In Hymes, 1971.

Cave, George N. 'Some Sociolinguistic Factors in the Production of Standard Language in Guyana and Implications for the Language Teacher.' *Language Learning*, XX, 2, 249–63.

Cazden, C. and Brown, R. 'The early development of the mother tongue.' Draft of article to appear in Lenneberg, Eric and Elizabeth (eds.), *Foundations of Language Development: A Multidisciplinary Approach*. UNESCO, in press.

Ceraso, J. 'Specific interference in retroactive inhibition.' *Journal of Psychology*, **58**, 1968, 65–77.

Ceraso, J. and Tendler, M. 'Pair vs. list interference.' *American Journal of Psychology*, 1968a, 47–52.

Chomsky, Carol. *The Acquisition of Syntax in Children from 5 to 10*. Massachusetts, 1969.

Chomsky, N. 'A review of B. F. Skinner's *Verbal Behavior*.' In J. Katz and J. Fodor. *The Structure of Language*. Englewood Cliffs, N.J., 1964, 547–78.

Chomsky, N. 'Research on Language Learning and Linguistics.' *Report of the Northeast Conference*, 1966.

Chomsky, N. *Language and Mind*. New York, 1968.

Chomsky, N. 'Linguistics and Philosophy,' in *Language and Philosophy* ed. by Sidney Hook. New York, 1969.

Christian, Jane and Christian, Chester. 'Spanish Language and Culture in the Southwest.' In Fishman, 1966.

Close, R. A. 'Concerning the Present Tense.' *English Language Teaching*, **XII**, 1959, 59.

Cook, Vivian. 'The Analogy Between First and Second Language Learning.' *IRAL*, **7**, 1969, 207–16.

Corder, S. P. 'The Significance of Learners' Errors.' *IRAL*, **5**, 1967, 161–70 (reprinted in this volume).

Corder, S. P. 'Describing the Language Learner's Language.' *Interdisciplinary Approaches to Language*, CILT Reports and Papers, **6**, 1971.

Corder, S. P. 'Idiosyncratic dialects and error analysis.' *IRAL*, **9, 2**, 1971 (reprinted in this volume).

Coulter, Kenneth. *Linguistic Error-Analysis of the Spoken English of Two Native Russians*. Unpublished M.A. Thesis, University of Washington, 1968.

Craig, Dennis. 'Linguistic and Sociolinguistic Problems in Relation to Language Education and Policy in the English-Speaking Caribbean.' n.d.

Crothers, Edward and Suppes, Patrick. *Experiments in Second Language Learning*. New York, 1967.

Curtis, J. 'Conceptual Models of Speech Production and the Description of Articulation.' Paper presented at the 1968 ASHA Convention, Denver, Colorado, 1968.

Dakin, J. 'The Teaching of Reading.' In Fraser and O'Donnell (eds.), *Applied Linguistics and the Teaching of English*. London, 1969.

Darnell, Regna. 'The Bilingual Speech Community: A Cree Example.' In Darnell, 1971.

Darnell, Regna. *Linguistic Diversity in Canadian Society*. Edmonton, 1971.

Da Silva, Z. S. *Beginning Spanish, Second Edition*. New York, 1963.

Dato, D. P. *American Children's Acquisition of Spanish Syntax in the Madrid Environment: Preliminary Edition*. U.S. H.E.W., Office of Education, Institute of International Studies, Final Report, Project No. 3036, Contract no. O.E.C. 2–7–002637, May 1970.

De Camp, David. 'The Field of Creole Language Studies.' *Studia Anglica Posnaniensia I,* **1** and **2**, 1968, 30–51.

Delattre, P. C., Liberman, A. M. and Cooper, F. S. 'Formant Transitions and Loci as Acoustic Correlates of Place of Articulation in American Fricatives.' *Studia Linguistica,* **16**, 1962, 101–21.

Dixon, T. R. and Horton, D. R. (eds.). *Verbal Behavior and General Behavior Theory.* Englewood Cliffs, 1968.

Dubin, F. 'The Sociolinguistic Dimension of Dormitory English.' *ERIC* 038637.

Dulay, H. and Burt, M. K. 'Children's strategies in second language learning.' Unpublished proposal submitted to U.S.O.E., Jan. 1972.

Dulay, H. C. and Burt, M. K., 1972. 'You Can't Learn Without Goofing; An Analysis of Children's Second Language Errors.' (This volume.)

Dušková, L. 'On Sources of Errors in Foreign Language Learning.' *IRAL,* 7, 1969, 11–36.

Ervin, Susan M. and Osgood, C. E. 'Second Language Learning and Bilingualism.' *Journal of Abnormal and Social Psychology,* Suppl. **49**, 1954, 139–46.

Ervin, S. M. 'Imitation and Structural Change in Children's Language.' In E. H. Lenneberg (ed.), *New Directions in the Study of Language.* Massachusetts, 1964.

Ervin-Tripp, Susan. 'Comments on "How and When do Persons Become Bilingual".' In L. G. Kelly (ed.), *Description and Measurement of Bilingualism.* Toronto, 1969.

Ervin-Tripp, Susan. 'Structure and Process in Language Acquisition.' In James E. Alatis (ed.), *Monograph Series on Languages and Linguistics.* Washington, 1970, 313–44. 3 13 - 353

Estacia, C. 'English Syntax Problems of Filipinos.' In *Proceedings of the 9th International Congress of Linguists.* The Hague, 1964.

Fawcett, Nancy Fox. *Teaching Bidialectalism in a Second Language: A Strategy for Developing Native English Proficiency in Navajo Students.* Thesis, UCLA, 1969.

Ferguson, Charles A. 'Diglossia.' *Word,* **15**, 1964, 325–40.

Ferguson, Charles A. 'Research on Language Learning; Applied Linguistics.' *Report of the Northeast Conference,* Modern Languages Association, Materials Center, New York, 1966.

Ferguson, Charles A. 'Absence of Copula and the Notion of Simplicity: A Study of Normal Speech, Baby Talk, Foreigner Talk and Pidgin.' In Dell Hymes (ed.), *Pidginization and Creolization of Languages.* Cambridge, 1971.

Ferguson, Charles A. *Language Structure and Language Use.* Stanford, 1971.

Firth, J. R. and Rodgers, B. B. 'The Structure of the Chinese Monosyllable in a Hunanese Dialect (Changsha).' In J. R. Firth, *Papers in Linguistics,* London, 1957.

Fishman, Joshua *et al. Language Loyalty in the United States.* The Hague, 1966.

Fishman, Joshua. 'Bilingualism with and without Diglossia; Diglossia with and without Bilingualism.' *Journal of Social Issues,* **23**, 1967, 29–38.

Fishman, Joshua. *Readings in the Sociology of Language.* The Hague, 1968.

Fishman, Joshua, Ferguson, Charles and Das Gupta, Jyotirindra. *Language Problems of Developing Nations.* New York, 1968.

Fishman, Joshua, Cooper, Robert L., Ma, Roxana *et al. Bilingualism in the Barrio.* Yeshiva University, New York, 1968.

Fodor, J. and Garrett, M. 'Some Reflections on Competence and Performance.' In J. Lyons and R. J. Wales (eds.), *Psycholinguistic Papers.* Chicago, 1966.

Fodor, Jerry A. *Psychological Explanation; An Introduction to the Philosophy of Psychology.* New York, 1968.

French, F. G. *Common Errors in English.* London, 1949.

Fries, C. C. *Teaching and Learning English as a Foreign Language.* Ann Arbor, 1945.

Fries, Charles C. and Pike, Kenneth L. 'Coexistent Phonemic Systems.' *Language,* **25.1**, 1949, 29–50.

Garrett, M. and Fodor, J. 'Psychological theories and linguistic constructs.' In T. R. Dixon and D. R. Horton (eds.), 1968.

Garvey, Catherine and Rocklyn, Eugene H. *Development and Evaluation of a Tactical Mandarin Chinese Language Course.* Washington D.C., 1965.

George, H. V. 'Teaching Simple Past and Past Perfect.' *Bulletin of the Central Institute of English* (Hyderabad, India), **2**, 1962, 18–31.

George, H. V. 'English for Asian Learners: Are we on the right road?' *English Language Teaching,* **XXV**, 1971, 270–77.

George, H. V. *Common Errors in Language Learning.* Rowley, Massachusetts, 1972.

Gilbert, Glenn (ed.). *The German Language in America—A Symposium.* Austin, University of Texas, 1971.

Gradman, Harry L. 'What Methodologists Ignore in Contrastive Teaching.' Paper presented at the Pacific Conference on Contrastive Linguistics and Language Universals, Honolulu, 1971.

Grelier, S. *'Recherche des principales interférences dans les systèmes verbaux de l'anglais du wolof et du français.'* Senegal. Centre de Linguistique Appliquée de Dakar. n.d.

Grimshaw, Allen D. 'Some Social Forces and Some Social Functions of Pidgin and Creole Languages.' In Hymes, 1971.

Gumperz, John and Hymes, Dell. 'The Ethnography of Communication.' *American Anthropologist,* **66**, pt. 2, 1964.

Gumperz, J. and Hernandez, E. 'Bilingualism, bidialectalism and classroom interaction.' In C. B. Cazden, D. Hymes and V. John (eds.), *Functions of Language in the Classroom.* New York, in press.

Haggard, Mark P. 'Models and Data in Speech Perception,' in *Models for the Perception of Speech and Visual Form,* ed. by Weiant Wathen-Dunn. Massachusetts, 1967.

Hall, Robert. *Pidgin and Creole Languages.* Ithaca, 1966.

Halle, M. *The Sound Pattern of Russian.* The Hague, 1959.

Halle, Morris and Keyser, Jay. *English Stress: Its Form, Its Growth and Its Role in Verse.* New York, 1971.

Halliday, M. A. K. 'The Users and Uses of Language.' In Fishman, 1968.

Hammer, John H. and Rice, Frank A. (eds.). *A Bibliography of Contrastive Linguistics.* Washington D.C., 1965.

Hart, J. T. 'Memory and the memory-monitoring process.' *Journal of Verbal Learning and Verbal Behavior,* **6**, 1967, 685–91.

Haugen, Einar. *The Norwegian Language in America*. Philadelphia, 1953.

Hayden, Robert G. 'Some Community Dynamics of Language Maintenance.' In Fishman, 1966.

Hemingway, Ernest. 'A Clean Well-Lighted Place' in id., *The Short Stories of Ernest Hemingway*. New York, 1953.

Hill, L. A. 'Noun-classes and the Practical Teacher' and 'Form-classes and sub-classes' in *Selected Articles on the Teaching of English as a Foreign Language*, 1967.

Hirtle, W. H. *The Simple and Progressive Forms*. Québec, 1967.

Hockett, C. F. 'A Note on Structure.' *Linguistics*, **14**, 1948.

Hoffman, Gerard. 'Puerto Ricans in New York: A language-related ethnographic summary.' In Fishman *et al.*, 1968, 20–76.

Hok, Ruth. 'Contrast: An Effective Teaching Device.' *English Language Teaching*, **XVII**, 1964, 117–22.

Hughes, Everett C. 'The Linguistic Division of Labor in Industrial and Urban Societies.' In Alatis, 1970.

Hunt, Chester. 'Language Choice in Multilingual Society.' *Sociological Enquiry*, **36**, **2**, 1966.

Hymes, Dell (ed.). *Pidginization and Creolization of Languages*. Cambridge, 1971.

Hymes, Dell. 'On Communicative Competence.' In J. Pride and J. Holmes (eds.), *Readings in Sociolinguistics*, Penguin Books, London, 1972.

Jain, Mahavir. 'Error Analysis of an Indian English Corpus.' Unpublished paper, University of Edinburgh, 1969.

James, Carl. 'Foreign Language Learning by Dialect Expansion.' 1970.

Jakobovits, Leon A. 'Second Language Learning and Transfer Theory; a Theoretical Assessment.' *Language Learning*, **19**, 1967, 55–86.

Jakobovits, Leon A. *A Psycholinguistic Analysis of Second-Language Learning and Bilingualism*. Illinois, 1969.

Jakobovits, L. *Foreign Language Learning: A Psycholinguistic Analysis*. Rowley, Massachusetts, 1970.

Jakobson, R. 'Two Aspects of Language and Two Types of Aphasic Disturbance' in R. Jakobson and M. Halle, *Fundamentals of Language*. The Hague, 1956.

Jakobson, R., Gunnar, C., Faut, M. and Halle, N. *Preliminaries to Speech Analysis*, M.I.T. Press, Cambridge, Massachusetts, 1963, 36.

Jespersen, O. *How to Teach a Foreign Language*. London, 1904. (Reprinted 1956.)

Jordan, E. H. *Beginning Japanese*. New Haven, 1971.

Kachru, Braj. 'The Indianness in Indian English.' *Word*, **21**, 1965, 391–410.

Kachru, Braj. 'Indian English: A Study in Contextualization.' In Bazell, 1966.

Kachru, Braj. 'English in South Asia.' In Sebeok, 1969.

Katz, J. J. and Postal, P. M. *An Integrated Theory of Linguistic Description*. Massachusetts, 1964.

Katz, J. J. 'Semi Sentences.' In J. A. Fodor and J. J. Katz (eds.), *The Structure of Language*. New Jersey, 1964.

Kelkar, Ashok R. 'Marathi English: A Study in Foreign Accent.' *Word* **13**, 1957, 268–82.

Kennedy, G. *Children's Comprehension of Natural Language*. Southwest

Regional Laboratory, Los Angeles, 1970.

Kennedy, G. 'Conditions for Language Learning.' In J. W. Oller Jr. and Jack C. Richards (eds.), *Focus on the Language Learner*. Newbury House, Rowley, Massachusetts, 1973.

Kessler, Carolyn. *The Acquisition of Syntax in Bilingual Children*. Georgetown University Press, Washington D.C., 1971.

Kinzel, P. *Lexical and Grammatical Interference in the Speech of a Bilingual Child*. Seattle, 1964.

Kirk-Greene, A. 'The Influence of West African Languages on English.' In Spencer, 1971.

Klima, E. S. and Bellugi, U. 'Syntactic regularities in the speech of children.' In J. Lyons and R. J. Wales (eds.), *Psycholinguistic Papers*. Edinburgh, 1966.

Kline, Helen. 'Research in the Psychology of Second Language Learning.' Unpublished paper, University of Minnesota, 1970.

Kloss, Heinz. 'German-American Language Maintenance Efforts.' In Fishman, 1966.

Labov, William, Cohen, Paul, Robins, Clarence and Lewis, John. 'A Study of the Nonstandard English of Negro and Puerto Rican Speakers in New York City.' *ERIC*: ED. **028 423**, 1968.

Labov, William. 'Contraction, Deletion, and Inherent Variability of the English Copula.' *Language*, **45**, **4**, 1969, 715–62.

Labov, William. 'The Study of Language in Social Context.' *Studium Generale*, **23**, 1970, 30–87.

Labov, William. 'Variation in Language.' In Carroll E. Reed (ed.), *The Learning of Language*. New York, 1971, 187–221.

Labov, William. 'The Notion of System in Creole Languages.' In Hymes, 1971.

Lado, Robert. *Linguistics Across Cultures*. Michigan, 1957.

Lakoff, George. 'On Generative Semantics,' in *Semantics—An Interdisciplinary Reader in Philosophy, Linguistics, Anthropology and Psychology*, ed. Danny Steinberg and Leon Jakobovits. Cambridge University Press, 1971, 232–96.

Lambert, W. E. 'Behavioral Evidence for Contrasting Forms of Bilingualism.' In M. Zarechnak (ed.), *Monograph Series on Languages and Linguistics*, **14**, 1961.

Lambert, W. A. 'Some Observations on First Language Acquisition and Second Language Learning.' (Mimeograph), 1966.

Lance, D. *A Brief Study of Spanish-English Bilingualism*. Final Report, Research Project Orr-Liberal Arts—15504. College Station, Texas, Texas A. and M. University, 1969.

Lane, H. 'Some differences between first and second language learning.' In *Language Learning*, **XII**, **1**, 1962.

Laver, John. 'Assimilation in Educated Nigerian English.' *English Language Teaching*, **XXII**, **2**, 1968, 156–60.

Laver, J. D. M. 'The Production of Speech' in John Lyons (ed.), *New Horizons in Linguistics*. Baltimore, 1970, 53–75.

Lawler, J. and Selinker, L. 'On the nature of paradoxes, rules and research in second language learning.' *Language Learning*, **XXI**, **1**, 1971, 27–43.

Lawton, David. 'Some Problems of Teaching a Creolized Language to Peace Corps Members.' *Language Learning*, **XIV**, 1964, 11–20.

Leachman, D. and Hall, Robert A. 'American Indian Pidgin English: Attestations and Grammatical Peculiarities.' *American Speech*, **30**, 1955, 163–71.

Lee, W. R. 'Thoughts on Contrastive Linguistics in the Context of Language Teaching' in J. E. Alatis (ed.), Monograph Series on Languages and Linguistics, **21**: *Contrastive Linguistics and its Pedagogical Implications,* 1968.

Lehiste, Ilse. 'Temporal Organization of Spoken Language.' In L. L. Hammerich, Roman Jakobson and Eberhard Zwirner (eds.), *Form and Substance* Denmark, 1971.

Leibowitz, Arnold H. 'Educational Policy and Political Acceptance: The Imposition of English as the Language of Instruction in American Schools.' *ERIC*, Washington, 1970.

Lemaire, Herve B. 'The French Language in New England.' In Fishman, 1966.

Lenneberg, E. *Biological Foundations of Language*. New York, 1967.

LePage, R. 'Problems of Description in Multilingual Communities.' *Transactions of the Philological Society*, 1968.

LePage, R. 'Problems to be Faced in the Use of English as the Medium of Education in Four West Indian Territories.' In Fishman *et al.*, 1968.

Lieberman, Philip. 'Towards a Unified Phonetic Theory.' *Linguistic Inquiry*, **1**.3, 1970, 291–306.

Llamzon, T. *Standard Filipino English*. Manila, 1969.

Lotz, John. 'Contrastive Study of the Morphophonemics of Obstruent Clusters in English and Hungarian,' in *Miscellanea di studi dedicati a Emerico Varady*. Modena, 1966.

Lyons, J. *Introduction to Theoretical Linguistics*. London, 1968.

Ma, Roxana and Herasimchuk, Eleanor 'Linguistic Dimensions of a Bilingual Neighbourhood.' In Fishman *et al.*, 1968.

Mackey, W. F. 'The Description of Bilingualism.' *Journal of the Canadian Linguistic Association*, **7**.2, 1962, 51–85.

Macnamara, John. 'Bilingualism and Thought' in James E. Alatis (ed.), *Monograph Series on Languages and Linguistics*, **23**, 1970, 25–40.

Macnamara, J. 'The cognitive strategies of language learning.' Paper presented at the Conference on Child Second Language, ACTFL Annual Convention, Chicago, October 1971.

MacNeilage, Peter R. 'The Serial Ordering of Speech Sounds.' *Project on Linguistic Analysis Reports* (Berkeley: University of California) second series, **8**, 1968, M1–M52.

MacNeilage, Peter R. and DeClerk, J. L. 'On the Motor Control of Coarticulation in CVC Monosyllables.' *Journal of the Acoustical Society of America*, **41**, 1969.

Macris, James. *An Analysis of English Loan Words in New York City Greek*. Ph.D. dissertation, Columbia University, 1955.

Mafeni, Bernard. 'Nigerian Pidgin.' In Spencer, 1971.

Mager, R. F. 'On the Sequencing of Instructional Content.' *Psychological Reports*, 1961, 405–412.

Marchese, M. 'English patterns difficult for native Spanish-speaking students.'

Mimeo. Hartford, Connecticut Board of Education, 1970.

Marckwardt, Albert H. 'Phonemic Structure and Aural Perception.' *American Speech*, **21**, 1946, 106–11.

Melton, A. W. 'Comments on Professor Postman's paper.' In *Verbal Learning and Verbal Behavior*. C. N. Cofer (ed.). New York, 1961.

Melton, A. W. and Irwin, J. 'The influence of degree of interpolated learning on retroactive inhibition and the overt transfer of specific responses.' *American Journal of Psychology*, **53**, 1961, 173–203.

Melton, A. W. 'Repetition and retrieval from memory.' *Science*, **158**, 1967, 532.

Menken, H. L. *The American Language* (4th edition). New York, 1949.

Menyuk, Paula. *Sentences Children Use*. Massachusetts, 1969.

Menyuk, Paula. *The Acquisition and Development of Language*. New Jersey, 1971.

Michigan Oral Language Series. English Guide—Kindergarten. American Council on the Teaching of Foreign Languages, 1970. (Obtainable from: Foreign Language Innovative Curricula Studies, Ann Arbor, Michigan 48108.)

Miller, G. A. 'Language and Psychology.' In E. H. Lenneberg (ed.), *New Directions in the Study of Language*. Boston, 1966.

Miller, G. A. 'The Psycholinguists.' *Encounter*, **23.1**, 1964.

Milon, J. 'A Japanese child learns English.' Paper presented at TESOL Convention, March 1972.

Mintz, Sidney. 'The Socio-Historical Background to Pidginization and Creolization.' In Hymes, 1971.

Nababan, P. W. J. 'A Note on Transfer and Interference in Foreign Language Learning.' *Working Papers in Linguistics*, **3.4**, 1971, 17–23.

Natalicio, D. S. and Natalicio, L. F. S. 'A comparative study of English pluralization by native and non-native English speakers.' In *Child Development*, **42**, 1971, 1302–6.

Neisser, U. *Cognitive Psychology*. New York, 1966.

Nemser, William J. 'Hungarian Phonetic Experiments.' *American Council of Learned Societies, Research and Studies in Uralic and Altaic Languages*, Project No. 32, 1961.

Nemser, William J. and Juhasz, Francis S. 'A Contrastive Analysis of Hungarian and English Phonology.' *American Council of Learned Societies, Research and Studies in Uralic and Altaic Languages*, Project No. 70, 1964.

Nemser, William. 'Approximative Systems of Foreign Language Learners.' *IRAL*, **9.2**, 1971, 115–23 (reprinted in this volume).

Nemser, William. *An Experimental Study of Phonological Interference in the English of Hungarians*. Bloomington, 1971.

Nemser, William. 'Problems and Prospects in Contrastive Linguistics.' Paper presented at International Conference on Modern Linguistics and Language Teaching. Hungary, April 1971.

Nesfield, J. C. 'Idiom, Grammar and Synthesis.' *English Grammar Series Book IV*, 1953, 290–1.

Newmark, Leonard. 'How Not to Interfere With Language Learning.' In Mark Lester (ed.), *Readings in Applied Transformational Grammar*. New York, 1970, 219–27.

Nickel, Gerhard. 'Variables in a Hierarchy of Difficulty.' *Working Papers in Linguistics*, **3.4**, 1971, 185–94.

Ornstein, Jacob. 'Language Varieties along the U.S.-Mexican Border.' In Perren and Trim, 1971.

Palmer, H. E. *The Principles of Language Study.* London, 1922.

Pap, Leo. *Portuguese-American Speech.* New York, 1949.

Park, Robert E. *Introduction to the Science of Sociology.* Chicago, 1930.

Peirce, C. S. 'The logic of abduction.' In V. Tomas (ed.), *Peirce's Essays in the Philosophy of Science.* New York, 1957.

Perren, G. E. and Trim, J. L. M. *Applications of Linguistics.* Cambridge, 1971.

Philips, Susan U. 'Acquisition of Rules for Appropriate Speech Usage.' In Alatis, 1970.

Pimsleur, P. and Quinn, T. (eds.). *The Psychology of Second Language Learning.* Cambridge, 1971.

Plumer, Davenport. 'A Summary of Environmentalist Views and Some Educational Implications.' In Williams, 1970.

Politzer, R. L. 'Toward psycholinguistic models of language instruction.' *TESOL Quarterly*, **2**, **3**, 1967.

Postman, L. 'The present status of interference theory.' In C. N. Cofer and B. S. Musgrave (eds.), *Verbal Learning and Verbal Behavior.* New York, 1961.

Postman, L., Stark, K. and Fraser, J. 'Temporal change in interference.' *Journal of Verbal Learning and Verbal Behavior*, **1**, 1968, 672–94.

Postman, L. and Stark, K. 'Role of response availability in transfer and interference.' *Journal of Experimental Psychology*, **79**, 1969, 68–77.

Prator, Clifford. 'The British Heresy in T.E.S.L.' In Fishman, Ferguson, Das Gupta, 1968.

Price, E. 'Early bilingualism.' In C. J. Dodson, E. Price and L. T. Williams, *Towards Bilingualism.* Cardiff, 1968.

Pride, J. B. *The Social Meaning of Language.* London, 1970.

Ravem, R. 'Language Acquisition in a Second Language Environment.' *IRAL*, **6**, **2**, 1968, 175–85 (reprinted in this volume).

Ravem, R. 'First and Second Language Acquisition.' Paper given to the BAAL Seminar on Error Analysis, Edinburgh, April 1969.

Ravem, R. 'The development of *Wh*-questions in first and second language learners.' In *Occasional Papers*, University of Essex, Language Centre, Colchester, December 1970 (reprinted in this volume).

Reibel, D. A. 'What to do with Recalcitrant Relatives.' Paper given at the meeting of the Linguistics Association, York, 1969.

Reibel, D. A. 'Language Learning Strategies for the Adult.' Paper read at Second International Congress of Applied Linguistics, Cambridge, 1969.

Reinecke, John. *Language and Dialect in Hawaii.* Honolulu, 1969.

Rice, Frank A. (ed.). *Study of the Role of Second Languages in Asia, Africa and Latin America.* Washington, 1962.

Richards, Jack C. 'A Non-Contrastive Approach to Error Analysis.' *English Language Teaching*, **XXV**, June 1971, 204–19 (reprinted in this volume).

Richards, Jack C. 'Error Analysis and Second Language Strategies.' *Language Sciences*, **17**, October 1971, 12–22.

Richards, Jack C. 'Social Factors, Interlanguage, and Language Learning.'

Language Learning, **XXII.2**, 1972, 159–188 (reprinted in this volume).

Richards, Jack C. 'Some Social Aspects of Language Learning.' *TESOL Quarterly*, **6.3**, 1972, 243–254.

Ritchie, William C. 'Some Implications of Generative Grammar.' *Language Learning*, **XVII**, 1967.

Rivers, W. *The Psychologist and the Foreign Language Teacher*. Chicago, 1964.

Rocklyn, Eugene H. *Self-Instructional Tactical Language Course in Russian*. Washington D.C., 1965.

Rosenbaum, P. *The Grammar of English Predicate Complement Constructions*. Cambridge, 1967.

Rudegeair, Robert E. 'The Effect of Contextual Influence on Children's Discrimination of Initial Consonants.' *ERIC*: ed. **047 307**, 1970.

Samarin, William. 'Lingua Francas, with Special Reference to Africa.' In Rice, 1962.

Samarin, William J. 'Salient and Substantive Pidginization.' In Hymes, 1971.

Sampson, Gloria P. 'The Strategies of Cantonese Speakers Learning English.' In Regna Darnell (ed.), *Linguistic Diversity in Canadian Society*. Edmonton, 1971, 175–99.

Sapon, S. M. 'On defining a response: a crucial problem in the analysis of verbal behavior.' In Pimsleur and Quinn (eds.), *The Psychology of Second Language Learning*. Cambridge, 1971.

Saporta, S. 'Applied Linguistics and Generative Grammar.' In A. Valdman (ed.), *Trends in Modern Language Teaching*. New York, 1966.

Sebeok, Thomas (ed.). *Linguistics in South Asia: Current Trends in Linguistics* 5, The Hague, 1969.

Selinker, Larry. 'Language Transfer.' *General Linguistics*, **9**, 1969, 67–92.

Selinker, Larry. 'Interlanguage.' *IRAL*, **X.3**, 1972, 219–231. (Reprinted in this volume.)

Selinker, L. 'The psychologically relevant data of second language learning.' In Pimsleur and Quinn (eds.). *The Psychology of Second Language Learning*. Cambridge, 1971.

Slamecka, N. J. 'An examination of trace storage in free recall.' *Journal of Experimental Psychology*, **76**, 1968, 504–13.

Slamecka, N. J. 'A temporal interpretation of some recall phenomena.' *Psychological Review*, **76**, 1969, 492–503.

Smith, F. and Miller, G. A. (eds.), *The Genesis of Language*. M.I.T. Press, Cambridge, Massachusetts, 1966.

Spencer, John. *Language in Africa*. Cambridge, 1963.

Spencer, John. 'West Africa and the English Language.' In Spencer, 1971, 1–35.

Spencer, John. *The English Language in West Africa*. Longman, London, 1971.

Spolsky, B. 'A Psycholinguistic Critique of Programmed Foreign Language Instruction.' *IRAL*, **4.2**, 1966, 119–29.

Stern, H. H. 'Foreign Language Learning and the New View of First Language Acquisition.' *Child Study*, **30.4**, 1969, 25–36.

Stewart, William. 'Creole Languages in the Caribbean.' In Rice, 1962.

Stewart, William. 'An Outline of Linguistic Typology for Describing Multilingualism.' In Rice, 1962.

Stockwell, R. P., Bowen, J. D. and Martin, J. W. *The Grammatical Structures of English and Spanish*. Chicago, 1965.

Stockwell, R. P. and Bowen, J. D. *The Sounds of English and Spanish*. The Contrastive Structure Series. Chicago, 1965.

Strevens, Peter. 'English Overseas: Choosing a Model of Pronunciation.' *English Language Teaching*, X, **4**, 1956, 123–31.

Strevens, P. 'Two ways of looking at error analysis.' *ERIC*: **037 714**, 1969. *Styles of Learning Among American Indians: An Outline for Research.* Washington, 1968.

Swain, M. 'Bilingualism, monolingualism and code acquisition.' Paper presented at the Child Language Conference, Chicago, November 22–24, 1971.

Sweet, H. *The Practical Study of Languages: A Guide for Teachers and Learners*. London, 1899.

Tarone, Elaine. 'A Suggested Unit for Interlingual Identification in Pronunciation.' *TESOL Quarterly*, **6.4**, 1972, 325 331.

Thompson, R. W. 'A Note on some possible affinities between Creole dialects of the Old World and those of the New.' In LePage, 1961.

Thorne, J. P. 'Stylistics and Generative Grammar.' *Journal of Linguistics*, I, 1965.

Torrey, Jane W. *The Learning of Grammar: An Experimental Study*. NIMH Progress Report on Grant No. 07167, 1966.

Torrey, Jane W. 'Second Language Learning.' In Carroll E. Reed (ed.), *The Learning of Language*. New York, 1971, 223–65.

Trager, G. L. and Smith, H. L. 'An Outline of English Structure.' *Studies in Linguistics*. Occasional Paper 3, 1951.

Treon, Martin. 'Fricative and Plosive Perception-Identification as a Function of Phonetic Context in CVCVC Utterances.' *Language and Speech*, **13.1** 1970, 54–64.

Troike, Rudolph C. 'Receptive Competence, Productive Competence, and Performance.' In James E. Alatis (ed.), *Monograph Series on Languages and Linguistics*, **22**, 1969, 63–9.

Tucker, G. R., Lambert, W. E. and Rigault, A. 'Students' Acquisition of French Gender Distinctions: A Pilot Investigation.' *IRAL*, 7, **1**, 1969, 51–5.

Tulving, E. and Madigan, S. A. 'Memory and verbal learning.' In *Annual Review of Psychology*, **21**, 1970, 437–84.

Upshur, J. A. 'Language Proficiency Testing and the Contrastive Analysis Dilemma.' *Language Learning*, **12**, 1962, 123–7.

Ure, Jean. 'The Mother-Tongue and the Other Tongue.' *Ghana Teachers' Journal*, **60**, 1968, 38–55.

Valette, R. 'Some reflections on second language learning in young children.' *Language Learning*, XIV, **3** and **4**, 1964, 91–8.

Vildomec, V. *Multilingualism*. Leyden, 1963.

Walsh, N. G. 'Distinguishing Types and Varieties of English in Nigeria.' *Journal of the Nigerian English Studies Association*, **2**, 1967, 47–55.

Watkin, K. L. 'Fossilization and its Implications Regarding the Interlanguage Hypothesis.' Unpublished paper, University of Washington, 1970.

Wardaugh, R. 'The Contrastive Analysis Hypothesis.' *TESOL Quarterly*, **4.2**, 1970, 123–30.

Wax, Murray, Wax, Rosalie and Dumont, Robert. 'Formal Education in an American Community.' *Social Problems,* **2**, **4**, 1964.

Weinreich, Uriel. *Languages in Contact.* New York, 1953.

Whinnom, Keith. 'Linguistic Hybridization and the Special Case of Pidgins and Creoles.' In Dell Hymes (ed.), *Pidginization and Creolization of Languages.* Cambridge, 1971.

Wilkins, D. A. Review of A. Valdman, *Trends in Language Teaching. IRAL,* **6**, 1968, 99–107.

Williams, Frederick. *Language and Poverty.* Chicago, 1970.

Williams, G. 'Analysis of Puerto Rican English.' Unpublished report, Language Research Foundation, Cambridge, Massachusetts, 1971.

Wolfe, D. L, 'Some theoretical aspects of language learning and language teaching.' *Language Learning,* **XVII**, **3** and **4**, 1967, 173–88.